Troubled Pasts

JILL A. EDY

Troubled Pasts

*News and the Collective Memory
of Social Unrest*

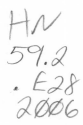
TEMPLE UNIVERSITY PRESS
PHILADELPHIA

For Mom

TEMPLE UNIVERSITY PRESS
1601 North Broad Street
Philadelphia, Pennsylvania, 19122
www.temple.edu/tempress

Published 2006
Printed in the United States of America
2 4 6 8 9 7 5 3 1

Library of Congress Cataloging-in-Publication Data

Edy, Jill A., 1966–
    Troubled pasts: news and collective memory of social unrest / Jill A. Edy.
       p. cm.
    Includes bibliographical references and index.
    ISBN 1–59213–496–3 (cloth: alk. paper) — ISBN 1–59213–497–1 (pbk.: alk. paper)
       1. Social problems—United States. 2. Social change—United States. 3. Social
movements—United States. 4. Social problems in mass media. 5. Democratic National
Convention (1968: Chicago, Ill.) 6. Riots—California—Los Angeles. 7. Watts (Los Angeles,
Calif.)—Social conditions. 8. Long-term memory—United States. 9. United States—Politics
and government. 10. United States—Social conditions. I. Title.
HN59.2.E28 2006
361.10973—dc22   2005056875
                                                                     CIP

∞ The paper used in this publication meets the requirements
of the American National Standard for Information Sciences—Permanence of Paper
for Printed Library Materials, ANSI Z39.48-1992

Contents

Acknowledgments

THIS BOOK IS AN ATTEMPT to better understand the role of the past in our public discourse, how we share it, argue over it, and ultimately use it to make sense of our complex social world. It probably owes at least some of its genesis to my sense of wonder at how the political and social turmoil of the 1960s marked the generation that came before mine—my parents, teachers, and, later, professors. This early curiosity has been sustained by my undergraduates who aren't entirely clear on that whole Cold War thing.

Almost ten years in the making, the book has benefited enormously from the advice and support I have received along the way. The project got its start in my dissertation research, and my adviser, Susan Herbst, has been a wise and supportive guide through every phase of the process. She helped me find the big picture again when I got lost in a sea of details, and she encouraged me to find my voice when I was overwhelmed by the existing scholarship. Swamped with work herself, she nevertheless offered near-instant and always useful comments and advice. She still does. The other members of my dissertation committee, Benjamin Page and James Ettema, asked hard but useful questions and encouraged me to tackle the underlying epistemological and ontological issues raised by the phenomenon of collective memory. Their suggestions formed the basis for much of the revision and expansion of the dissertation research that appears here. Much of my early graduate work was supervised by Robert Entman, and as I look back across these pages, I find a great deal of his influence in them as well.

A summer grant from Middle Tennessee State University helped me make the time to collect additional data and substantially expand and revise the work. At about the same time, a kind invitation from Rod Hart to attend the New Agendas in Political Communication conference at the University of Texas not only gave me access to a willing audience of thoughtful critics, but also helped me to think about how my work fits into contemporary political communication scholarship. Any number of people were kind enough to read and offer comments on manuscripts that stemmed from the project over the years, including Scott Althaus, Dan Hallin, Rod Hart, Regina Lawrence, Lisbeth Lipari, Max McCombs, Tom Patterson, David Ryfe, Bartholomew Sparrow, and anonymous reviewers of the various manuscripts. Michael Pfau was generous in his guidance and support as the manuscript wound its way through the review process.

At Temple University Press, Alex Holzman has been an unfailing supporter of the project and a patient mentor throughout the process of preparing the manuscript.

Family and friends have provided lots of moral support through the ups and downs of working on the project. Special thanks are due to Kriss Rizzolo, Sarah Fairbrother, Makana Chock, Lisa Bell, Amy Pasternack, Dad, and, of course, Mom.

With such good help, any remaining mistakes can only be my own.

CHAPTER 1

Introduction

P EOPLE WHO HAVE LIVED TOGETHER for any length of time have a troubled past. Conflict and controversy are a normal part of social life. The ways that a society deals with such crises tell us a great deal about it, and so does the way it remembers those troubled pasts. On September 11, 2001, it seemed as if the whole world had changed. The brief "Pax Americana" that had followed the end of the Cold War in 1989 was shattered by terrorist attacks in the financial and political heart of the United States. Yet during the first national election held in this apparently new era of global terror in which even a superpower's homeland could not be considered truly safe, an organization calling itself Swift Boat Veterans for Truth resurrected a troubled past from the Cold War era. The group called into question Democratic nominee John Kerry's military record during the Vietnam War and condemned Kerry for his subsequent anti–Vietnam War activism. The Swift Boat Veterans' campaign brought the dormant bad feelings of the Vietnam era back into the public sphere, suggesting that in speaking out against the war, Kerry had been not only hypocritical, but also traitorous. With the Cold War now over, the nature of the treason had subtly changed from sympathizing with communists to betraying American troops in harm's way; yet the accusation had apparently lost none of its potency, for it garnered more than 100 stories in the *New York Times* during the presidential campaign. Moreover, the issue seemed to resonate with then-current debates over the Patriot Act and internal dissent over the war in Iraq. As novelist William Faulkner once observed, "The past isn't dead. It isn't even past."

Even this brief glimpse of the 2004 campaign reveals that memories of social conflict can be a powerful force in political discourse. They can heal rifts, salt wounds, or provoke social transformations. The distinct memories of a social group can be a source of strength in resisting oppression, but where divisive memories are preserved and nurtured, violent social conflict can erupt again. A group's identity is sustained in part by its unique memories, but the possibilities for meaningful engagement regarding long-standing problems are greatly reduced among people who understand their pasts in drastically different ways. Memories can also influence the ways future events are understood and managed, but memory is always an imperfect representation of the past despite the fact that we often treat it as the equivalent of the past itself. Socially shared memories are, in many ways, the tip of the iceberg of political culture. This book tells the story of how collective memories of troubled pasts emerge in public discourse and of the impacts these memories have had on the representation of more recent events.

What is collective memory? All memories are reconstructions of the past, and the essential form of collective memory is narrative. As George Herbert Mead (1929) points out, the past is entirely imaginary. Once a moment is gone, its passing must be reconstructed, as anyone who has ever lost a set of car keys can tell you. Physical traces exist, but in order to reassemble those traces into a coherent whole, we must create stories that connect the various complex elements of the past. In 1932, psychologist Frederick Bartlett theorized that when asked to remember something, people reconstruct, with varying degrees of accuracy, the past they have been asked about. They are affected by the circumstances in which they originally encoded the information and the context in which they are asked to retrieve it. Bartlett's work took the study of psychological memory beyond the realm of "remembering" versus "forgetting" and into the complex interplay between facts and meaning that allow for reconstruction of the past. At about the same time, Maurice Halbwachs (1950/1980)[1] developed the concept of collective memory, or memories shared by social groups. His theory of collective memory, like Bartlett's, posited that the context of both encoding and recalling information was significant, and he went on to argue that as social relationships, geography, and other aspects of social life changed, memories of the past might be altered or lost.

What qualifies memories as collective? For a study of controversial and divisive pasts, this question is a critical one. Halbwachs's work demonstrates that we should not expect—to use Stuart Hall's (1982) term—perfect "closure." That is, we should not expect a story of the past that never changes. Nor should we expect everyone in an entire society to remember the past in exactly the same way. As historian Henry Steele Commager (1965) observed, new members are always arriving who must be taught the shared past. Moreover, far less than perfect agreement about the meaning of a past is required for that story of the past to be powerful. Collective memory has more in common with what Bommes and Wright (1982) and the Popular Memory Group (1982) call dominant memories, which are those that are widely available in the public sphere. Collective memories are the stories that everyone knows about the past, even if not everyone believes the story. Such memories become a kind of common cultural currency—the shared language that one must be able to speak if one wishes to communicate with others about a shared past, even if one's goal is to challenge that shared memory.

Available theories of collective memory offer some guidance for an examination of the ways societies come to remember social conflicts, but they represent an unwieldy collection of tools, and many of their predictions are contradictory. Many place a strong emphasis on presentism, the idea that the form of the past is largely determined by present needs, interests, and concerns (although what, exactly, the past is used to do remains a matter for lively dispute[2]). Gary Alan Fine (2001) points to the identity and power of what he calls "reputational entrepreneurs" in propagating various versions of the past. However, the idea that multiple and competing versions of the past might somehow be pulled together and represented as the collective memory—the story that everyone knows—is generally absent from the literature on collective memory.

Like theories of collective memory, existing theories by scholars of politics and public opinion are of limited usefulness in addressing these questions, mainly because such theories are entirely concerned with the representation of current events. They have nothing to say about how the past is represented in public discourse. Yet some theories of mass political behavior indirectly invoke the idea that political discourse and public attitudes are inflected by collective memories. The theory of issue ownership, for example, posits that some public issues are associated with a particular political party in public thinking because that party has historically handled that social problem "better."[3] Republicans "own" crime; Democrats "own" the environment. Issue ownership is not based upon a party's current handling of the issue, but rather upon its reputation, its past. As yet, the theory does not speak to how such pasts are created and managed.

What is needed is a framework that identifies how collective memories of troubled pasts are negotiated, the characteristics of these collective memory narratives, how those stories influence and are influenced by more recent events, and whose interests they serve. Of course, it is possible that collective memories of social conflicts, divisions, and controversies do not emerge; that divisions remain to the present time. Michael Schudson (1992) argues that two different versions of the Watergate story survive, and work in sociology has described the problems involved in building memorials to controversial events such as the Kent State shootings (Gregory and Lewis 1988) and the Vietnam War (Wagner-Pacifici and Schwartz 1991). However, the original complexity of the past can never be preserved, and the choices about what to remember, what to leave behind, and how to understand it, remain important regardless of the ultimate outcome of the process.

This study develops such a framework through close analysis of two cases of divisive social conflict from the 1960s. The cases might be called textbook examples of controversial events in that they meet anthropologist Victor Turner's (1981) definition of a social breach, the first phase of what he calls a social drama. Social dramas occur within groups that share values and interests and have a common history, whether real or alleged. A breach is defined as a violation of a norm, and is perceived as a sign of a deeper division of interests or loyalties. Breaches may be purposely created to demonstrate differences, or they may "emerge from a scene of heated feelings" (146). Unless the breach is quickly sealed or contained to "a limited area of social interaction, there is a tendency for the breach to widen until it coincides with some dominant cleavage in the widest set of relevant social relations to which the parties in the social conflict belong" (146).

The two breaches examined here, one purposely created and one arising from "heated feelings," exemplified some of the deepest social divisions of the era, divisions that we continue to struggle with today. In 1965, riots broke out in South Central Los Angeles. Sparked by the arrest of an African American man for drunken driving and named for one of the affected neighborhoods, the Watts riots resulted in thirty-four deaths, hundreds of injuries and arrests, and millions of dollars in property damage. In 1968, violence erupted both inside and outside the Chicago Amphitheater during the Democratic National Convention. Unlike the Watts riots, which were often described as unexpected, the Chicago convention violence had been brewing for months. Diverse social movements including poor people's advocates, counterculture Yippies, and antiwar activists had been planning demonstrations while the party's internal divisions over the Vietnam War and the delegate selection process had deepened.

Where might negotiations over the meaning of the past take place? In a modern mass society, it is the mass media that are primarily responsible for disseminating shared stories to a public that is demographically diverse and geographically scattered. The news media have a special responsibility for creating and disseminating stories of "real" events, and in their role as monitors of the social world, they not only tell their own stories but report on the cultural products and stories created by other individuals and institutions that deal in public memory: from the speeches of public officials, to the reminiscences of eyewitnesses, to the content of movies and museums. This study observes the process of negotiating a meaning for the past as it unfolds in the news, exploring how news practices, relationships between actors who make the news, expectations of news audiences, and the impact of current events affect the development of collective memories in a mass society. It also examines the influence of those collective memories on the representation of more recent events. Over time, controversies are resolved, and the key questions for this study are:

- How are they resolved?
- What forms do the resolutions take?

- What impact does the resulting collective memory have on the representation of more recent events?

Available theories of media and politics are used to identify the actors and processes that influence the development of collective memory in the news, but each of these theories must be revised and extended in order to apply it to the past. Collective memory theories point to the social environment as another important influence on public understanding of the past, but these theories disagree about how the present and the past interact.

Theories of news discourse indicate that the main actors influencing the content of the news are journalists and political officials, although the party with the most power in this relationship is sometimes debated. Official sources dominate the news (Sigal 1973), and can limit the range of legitimate perspectives in news (Bennett 1990). Political elites appear to have enormous power to frame stories in ways that suit their policies and purposes.[4] In part, this is because they have extraordinary resources for supplying journalists with information (Gandy 1982). It also occurs because the actions of political elites are defined as "newsworthy," so the work routines of journalism monitor what they do and say (Tuchman 1978; Galtung and Ruge 1965). In contrast, most scholarship shows that average citizens have difficulty gaining access to the news, and the efforts of citizens' groups to raise issues or publicize their perspectives typically fail.

Theorists who emphasize elite power as an explanation for media portrayals of current events recognize social conflict and division as a special case. Social conflicts that erupt in riots, demonstrations, or the like take on many of the characteristics of accidental events, and research has shown that political elites have more difficulty controlling the representation of accidental events than they do controlling more routine kinds of "news" (Molotch and Lester 1974; Lawrence 2000). Riots and demonstrations do not typically enable social movements or citizens' groups to present their points of view, but social conflict can produce divisions between political elites that go beyond the bounds of everyday, ritualized political conflict. This may open the news discourse to a genuine airing of disagreement that no one social actor or group controls (Gitlin 1980; Bennett 1990). For example, during both the Watts riots and the Chicago convention, key conflicts emerged between local and federal officials who promoted different interpretations of events. However, focused as they are on media depictions of current events, theories describing political elites' influence on the news do not directly speak to how officials and elites might influence mediated remembering of social conflict.

Theories of news discourse also reveal that despite their professional norm of objectivity, journalists affect the news they report in a number of ways. Their own professional practices and routines limit both their perceptions of news and their search for information. Recent scholarship has demonstrated that the news has become more interpretive over the last half century (Barnhurst and Mutz 1997; Hallin 1994), suggesting that reporters have more influence on the news than they did at midcentury when they took a more stenographic approach to the coverage of political leaders. American journalism is also a commercial enterprise, and some scholars suggest that this, too, influences the content of news. Scholars adopting a political economy perspective have pointed out that as capitalist businesses, media organizations benefit from the status quo and that news therefore presents audiences with fundamentally conservative points of view that support existing power relationships.[5] Research on the entertainment media's depiction of history would seem to bear out this observation. Scholars have found that fictional presentations of the past focus on the elite elements of society, the rich and powerful (Cohn 1976; Nimmo and Combs 1983). These fictions depict history as the responsibility of individuals rather than social forces (Parenti 1992) and support conservative interpretations of pasts, downplaying revolutionary aspects even of the American Revolution.[6]

While available scholarship on media and politics offers many useful insights about how events are covered as they happen, it says nothing about the impact of time upon the relationships between the major actors as the news of the present becomes the news of the past. Thus, it can offer little insight into how collective memory evolves in news. Yet the passage of time has a profound influence on the relationships between all major actors that produce the news. For journalists, time changes expectations about both the form and content of reporting. Hard news, with its short deadlines and elite focus, is replaced by feature stories with flexible deadlines and an emphasis on human interest. Once an event is past, reporters' dependence on officials for timely information drops sharply, changing the relationships between these actors. Reporters further enhance their authority to interpret past events by privileging meaning over fact in the stories they tell, and they are able to do this in part because the past often appears to play a minor role in the news of current events. For political officials, time reveals the distinctions between individuals and institutions. Political officials' ability to manage the news typically hinges on occupying public office, and once out of office their power to shape the news may end. Subsequent officeholders may or may not have the same goals, especially if a controversial past is or can be connected with an individual leader's reputation rather than with the institution's. At the same time, the increasing rarity—and therefore value—of eyewitness testimony can give citizens new authority to define their past. Thus, over time, the power of reporters and average citizens to narrate the past begins to increase even as the power of individual public officials begins to fade. If the actors involved in creating collective memories in news discourse are familiar to scholars of media and politics, the relationships between them are not.

A great deal of scholarship on media and politics has focused on the phenomenon of "framing" in media discourse. Variously described as an aspect of the text and as a media effect, theories of media framing generally agree that frames function to confer perspective on events, issues, and people; that is, to make them meaningful.[7] Developing collective memory of a troubled past involves a struggle over how to frame something that has many potential and divergent meanings, so the concept of framing is a useful analytical tool. However, collective memory has unique qualities that are not addressed by the burgeoning scholarly literature on framing.

First, examining the framing of controversial events contributes to the literature on event framing by demonstrating that not only can the news media frame similar events in divergent ways,[8] but that media stories can frame the *same* event in various, contradictory ways. However, the presence of multiple competing frames in news discourse raises important issues that current framing theory cannot resolve. Recent experimental studies that have tried to mimic framing as it naturally occurs in media discourse have shown that framing effects cancel each other out when audiences are exposed to contradictory frames for policy issues, as one might expect them to be in an environment of partisan debate (Druckman 2004; Sniderman and Theriault 2004). Applied to the study of collective memory, these findings raise the question of how the public controversies that produced multiple divergent frames are resolved in memory, particularly when the underlying social divisions that fed the controversy are still present in public life.

Of course, one answer may lie in the power relationships that influence how the media represent social reality. Recent research on how issue frames work contains other clues. Several scholars have offered evidence that frames influence what is variously called goal priority (Nelson 2004; Nelson and Oxley 1999) or the weight assigned to various values (Chong 1996). Collective memories of controversial events may, like the issue frames previously studied, preserve contradictory meanings but establish one meaning as predominant. Nelson also argues that frames work by influencing issue categorization, a function that is similar to what other scholars have referred to as "problem definition."[9] Creating collective memory might involve establishing what sort of event occurred and recalling specific events that fit that problem definition. Still, the question remains of how one meaning or problem definition might come to dominate the others as collective memory evolves.

Another part of the answer may lie in a body of theory that while apparently relevant to the framing perspective is rarely used in scholarship on media and politics: the study of narrative. Scholars in a variety of disciplines have described the human impulse to create narrative accounts of real events, an impulse common to both journalists (Fulford 1999) and historians (White 1981, 1987). While various theories of narrative define the concept differently, each contains the idea that narrative imposes order and coherence on real-world experiences (Fulford 1999, Martin 1986; White 1987; Fisher 1985). Walter Fisher's theory of narrative says that audiences judge the quality of narrative based upon expectations of "coherence" and "fidelity," that is, that stories should hang together and ring true, and these audience expectations may influence which stories of the past evolve into collective memories.

Hayden White's (1981, 1987) ideas about narrative are especially useful for thinking about collective memory as it emerges in news. Not only does he consider the role of narrative in historical writing, but his ideas parallel—and in many ways enrich—political scientists' and media scholars' concept of framing. According to White, historians consider narrative the appropriate means of conveying history, and he contrasts the form with alternatives such as annals, which are simple lists of events. Narration and narrativity are "instruments by which the conflicting claims of the imaginary and the real are mediated, arbitrated, or resolved in a discourse" (1987, 4). Because conflicting claims need to be negotiated, there is always more than one way to tell the story, and in fact, the idea that narrators have choices about which elements of reality to include and which to leave out is one of the essential characteristics of narrative. White defines a narrative as a story in which the facts appear to "speak for themselves," but argues that all narrative is essentially moralizing. Although historians (like journalists) argue that their narratives are objective and the events narrativized appear to speak for themselves, the form of narrative is a response to the desire to endow events with moral meaning. Thus, according to White, authority is an essential element in any narrative.

White's theory about how narratives of the past function has many parallels to theories of framing used in the fields of media and politics[10] in their common emphases on authority, on the appearance of transparency and objectivity, on the management of salience, and on moral judgment as essential qualities of stories. However, scholars of media and politics may have been reluctant to embrace this body of theory for at least two reasons. First, narrative theories do not typically address themselves to the effects of narratives on audiences and therefore may not appeal to a field of scholarship that has always been centrally concerned with media effects (Gamson 2001). Second, Fisher's (1985) ideas about stories requiring coherence and fidelity suggest that actual events exert some influence over stories. This kind of limited social constructionism may not have been appealing to early scholars of media and politics who needed to demonstrate to more traditional political scientists that the media did more than hold a mirror up to public affairs, that media effects occurred independently of the objectively "real" circumstances of social life.

Still, available theories of collective memory do not suggest that memory is bound by the circumstances of the actual past but rather than the events and the stories are mutually influential. Because real events never precisely correspond to the requirements of a good story, narrative can affect the content of collective memory in addition to serving as its form. In his work on collective memory, Halbwachs (1950/1980) describes how changes in the social environment can alter memories. In their work on the role of narrative in memory, James Fentress and Chris Wickham describe how narrative can serve as a substitute for these social environments, or what they call external contexts:

> [I]t is convenient to distinguish between an external or social context, which is regularly lost during transmission, and an internal context, which tends to be preserved....Information that is context-dependent...will tend to be lost whenever that context changes....In narrative memory, stories themselves can serve as internal contexts, fixing the memory of images and links in a properly consequential order....In this sense, a plot functions as a complex memory image, and learning a repertoire of plots is equivalent to learning a large scale mnemo-technique that permits the ordering, retention, and subsequent transmission of a vast amount of information. (1992, 72)

Thus, even as the story must fit the facts in order to meet the criteria of a good narrative, the facts must fit the story, and those that don't are likely to be forgotten. Paul Fussell describes the interaction between the past and stories about it as a "simultaneous and reciprocal process by which life feeds materials to literature while literature returns the favor by conferring forms upon life" (1975/2000, ix).

Good stories acquire their own brand of authority, independent of that of their advocates, as Robert Manoff explains in this description of an authoritative journalistic account:

> Narrative fragments...are signs of the eruption of another story through the text of an existing one. They are pieces of a shadow text that force their way into the nominal one, fugitive presences that testify to unresolved tensions between the event reported and the narrative that is doing so. But when event and narrative form coincide, when narrative fit is good, such tension resolves itself in the flow of the story, the news account takes on its particular authority. (1986, 225)

Such stories also enhance the authority of the news more generally because that institution's authority relies largely on a claim of objectivity. Objectivity implies that there is only one story to be told. In an objectively real world of objectively real events, how could it be otherwise? Repeated airing of conflicting narratives casts doubt upon this ultimate truism of news, while narratives that disguise or paper over conflicting elements restore faith in a real world that can be accurately reported.

Stories that attempt to account for social conflict have difficulty acquiring authority both because they contradict each other and because the fit between the story and the event is often poor. The stories lack both coherence and fidelity. Stories that acquire credence, as collective memories should, on the other hand, exhibit better narrative qualities. We might, then, expect the competing news frames of a controversial event to be resolved not only by power struggles between social actors but also by negotiations between reporters and social actors that produce better stories than the initial frames supplied.

Collective memory studies contribute to framing scholarship in at least one more way. Themselves the product of framing dynamics, collective memories can also serve as frames for subsequent events. This study explores how the past is used as a source of meaning for more recent public events. When applied to current events, stories of the past can fulfill all of the functions of a frame described by Robert Entman (1993). They can specify problems, identify responsible agents, establish criteria for moral evaluations, and suggest solutions. Moreover, they do not necessarily require elite sponsorship but can be used by anyone with access to the news discourse, including journalists. In fact, sometimes a connection to the past becomes the credential that gives a speaker access to the news.

The struggle to supply meaning for a controversial past that goes on in the news media takes place before an audience of citizens, and a central concern of scholars of media and politics is whether that public holds any decision-making power of its own. Critical scholars often point out that powerful and determined actors, particularly the state and big businesses, regularly overwhelm the power of citizens to resist their interpretations of present events. One might then argue that powerful social institutions retain the power to unilaterally alter public memory despite the passage of time and the changing relationships between social actors. Yet available research suggests that political leaders are at their most powerful when they are unified, when they are motivated to influence public opinion, or when the public is disinterested—and none of these conditions are met when it comes to collective memory of controversial events. The very existence of controversy suggests substantive disagreement between political leaders (Bennett 1990; Gitlin 1980). Moreover, it is not at all clear that leaders are willing to expend the often-considerable resources needed to overthrow alternative perceptions of reality. Power is a limited resource, and the evidence of this study suggests that political leaders are typically focused on supplying meaning for current events, expending little energy in trying to redefine the past in ways more congenial to their current objectives. Indeed, the development of collective memory can often be a by-product of social actors coping with more immediate concerns. Finally, political officials, reporters, and eyewitnesses who are telling and retelling the stories of a well-known public past are not writing upon a blank slate. Members of the audience will have personal memories of the past being described.

Thus, public acceptance of stories about the past is likely to have an influence on the development of collective memory. Schudson (1992) argues that personal memories are an important check against wholesale historical revisionism by political and social elites, and studies of individual memories of public events show that people with personal memories of those events have stronger and more diverse attitudes about those pasts than people who cannot remember living through the event (Lang and Lang 1989; Johnson 1995).

There are several possible mechanisms by which the living memories of audiences can affect the ways collective memories develop in news. Journalists' authority is in part dependent on "the integrity of their relationship with their audience" (Hallin 1994, 32). Stories and values cannot simply be imposed on an audience that actively resists them, and personal memories of social conflict create favorable conditions for such resistance. Even narratives with powerful advocates may not prevail if audiences reject them as implausible or too divergent from their own memories of the event. Because journalists must maintain their credibility with audiences as well as their relationships with political officials, collective memories of social conflict are more likely negotiated than imposed.

Of course, many would point out that it is rare indeed to see audiences rise up to reject the news media's representations of public events. However, both E. E. Schattschneider's (1975) and V. O. Key's

(1961) theories of the role of the public in public affairs demonstrate that they don't have to. They explain that political actors anticipate audience responses and incorporate those projections into their own strategies. Even if the audience never actually responds to media coverage, its anticipated reaction becomes a part of the process that creates media messages and public policy.[11] Schattschneider also considers the role of organized groups in political discourse. He argues that political debate is structured and restructured in ways that either encourage or discourage the expansion of political conflict to bystander groups (and audiences). Political actors on the losing side of a struggle seek to expand the conflict to new groups that might aid their cause, while those on the winning side seek to contain the conflict and preserve their advantage. Applying the model to collective memory, we might expect that those who wish to lay a social conflict to rest will craft stories designed not to raise the ire of groups with a stake in the way that past is remembered. Those who reject the legitimacy of the story that is told, on the other hand, would step into the fray and offer alternative accounts of the past, expanding the conflict over how to remember. Thus, elite actors' expectations about audience reaction may shape the development of stories about the past in a variety of ways.

These interactions between various social actors and journalists in the forum of the news media before an audience of citizens occur in a constantly evolving social context that also gives shape to collective memory. Collective memory scholarship defines this changing social context as "presentism," the idea that memory is influenced by current events and circumstances. While scholars agree that the present always has some impact on what is remembered, the size and nature of that impact is debated in the field. At one extreme is what Schudson (1992) refers to as "radical social construction," the idea that what past we believe we have is invented in the present. In the realm of fiction, the ultimate radical social constructionist is George Orwell. In *Nineteen eighty-four,* he describes a nightmarish society in which the past is a complete fabrication managed by a large government bureaucracy. The power of this bureaucracy over the collective memory is so complete that people have little or no faith in their individual memories. In the realm of scholarship, Eric Hobsbawm and Terence Ranger (1983) demonstrate that a variety of social traditions observed around the world are pure inventions, their basis in the past wholly unsubstantiated.

Less extreme is what Schudson (1992) refers to as "cultural theory." Here, the past can be remade, but only within the limits of existing social symbols and relationships. The past is somewhat harder to change because these social symbols and relationships are mutually reinforcing. Schudson represents this perspective with the work of Barry Schwartz. For example, Schwartz, Zerubavel, and Barnett (1986) attempt to explain the reasons for the recovery of the Masada story by Palestinian Jews in the 1920s. Rejecting pragmatism, which would suggest that a remembered past always serves some social good, Schwartz and his colleagues argue that the Masada story resonated because it "fit." The Palestinian Jews of that era felt that their plight was congruent with that of the Jews at Masada. Although they were aware of the unhappy ending of the Masada story, they chose it above other possible memories to symbolize their situation because it expressed their concerns.[12]

Schudson (1992) himself rejects both of these formulations, arguing that they deny historicity by claiming that people are unconstrained by the past. Because the past constitutes people, it cannot be completely constituted by them, and he offers nine impediments to reconstructing the past at will. Among the most important for our purposes are living memory and the presence of multiple versions of the past. He also notes that in some cases, the past is a "scar": "When the past is visibly, viscerally, or palpably alive in the present, it cannot be reorganized at will" (218). He contends that, "An all-powerful monolithic version of the past will not triumph in a pluralistic society where conflicting views have a good chance of emerging, finding an audience and surviving" (208). This tendency is enhanced by another item on Schudson's list, the "ambiguity of stories."

Ultimately, then, the collective memories that emerge in news are the product of political leaders at multiple levels of government, journalists, and citizens who interact under the influence of time and several key environmental constraints. In general, both the power and the desire of elites to control the story of a public event wanes over time, while the power of journalists and average citizens to narrate the past grows. Yet the framework laid out here suggests that no one social actor can control the development of stories about the past. Some stories will exhibit better narrative fidelity and coherence than others, and the perceived degree of fidelity and coherence may be influenced by current events. Citizens with personal memories may be unwilling to accept stories that do not jibe with those memories, and citizens who have long been exposed to one story of the past may be loathe to embrace an alternative version. The collective memories that result are the product of these tensions and bear the marks of the pressures that created them. However, the pasts we create also become the resources we use to make sense of current events, so though their form is governed by evolutionary processes that are not entirely intentional, they are stories with tangible consequences.

The Study

The Watts riots and the 1968 Democratic National Convention were selected for study not merely because this nation still struggles with questions of racial equality, democratic practice, and the efficacy and morality of Third World military interventions. These events both occurred recently enough that much of the process of developing collective memories of them can be effectively observed. Prior to 1970, the *New York Times* was the only American daily news outlet that was indexed in any way, and prior to 1980, full-text, keyword-searchable databases of news content, which are essential for tracing the development of stories about the past, were unavailable. At the same time, each of these events is a little over a generation old, a time frame that is considered important by many scholars working in the tradition of Manheim's "theory of generations." By now, a substantial proportion of Americans (including the author) has no personal memory of the events and relies instead upon the collective memory that has developed. Finally, each of these events was invoked as a thinking tool for understanding more recent events approximately a quarter century after they occurred. In 1992, riots again broke out in South Central Los Angeles following the trial of four Los Angeles police officers for assaulting an African American motorist. Named for the victim of the beating, the Rodney King riots were more destructive than those of twenty-seven years earlier, but both political leaders and journalists perceived the Watts riots as a relevant past. In 1996, the Democrats returned to Chicago to nominate Bill Clinton for a second term, breaking the longest dry spell in convention hosting in the city's history. Both Democrats and reporters saw this as event as a chance to "put the past behind them." These more recent events offer an opportunity for a focused examination of the form collective memories of the Watts riots and the Chicago convention had taken, the stability (or instability) of that form, and the impact of these memories on the representation of recent events.

The study first examines contemporary news coverage of these two events and then traces retrospective coverage of them for the quarter century after they occurred in order to identify the processes involved in the development of collective memory. Contemporary newspaper coverage of both the Watts riots and the Chicago convention was voluminous and has been well documented in previous research. Rather than cover this ground again, the study turns to newsmagazine coverage to get a feel for how these events were covered in their own times. In the 1960s, newsmagazines like *Time* and *Newsweek* offered roundups of the week's events based not on original reporting but rather upon the coverage of prestige papers, particularly the *New York Times*. Their value to readers thus lay in their tight summaries, their writing style, and their interpretation of events. *Time*, in particular, is well known for its consistent prose style and its authoritative, if selective, presentation of the facts (Nourie and Nourie 1990). Thus, in the context of this study, newsmagazine coverage offers summaries of the daily papers' content and clearer insight into the interpretive strategies used by journalists and officials to make sense of these events as they occurred. Existing scholarly research on newspaper coverage of the events and an examination of the detailed index of the *New York Times* both show that newspapers and newsmagazines used roughly the same narratives to structure their accounts of events.

To explore retrospective coverage of the Watts riots and the 1968 Democratic National Convention, the study turns to newspaper coverage. Although television is no doubt an essential element of citizens' personal memories of these events and probably has some impact on the evolution of collective memories, it is not adequately archived to be useful in this study. Although contemporary news coverage of the Chicago convention is stored in the Vanderbilt news archives, the Vanderbilt *Indexes and Abstracts* does not catalog content in sufficient detail to illuminate how either the 1968 convention or the Watts riots have been subsequently remembered in national television news. At the time of the Watts riots, nightly television news was not archived.

Instead, for each case, the development of collective memories is traced in a local paper in the affected area (the *Los Angeles Times* and the *Chicago Tribune*, respectively) and the national paper of record, the *New York Times*. Newspapers are chosen both because they provide the most data for analysis and because at every point in time, they are the best archived and catalogued news resources. Looking at both the local and the national newspapers allows for the possibility that local and national memories of these events may not match. It also recognizes that the editorial philosophy of the newspaper may make a difference (the *New York Times* is considered a liberal paper, while both the local papers are described as conservative). Further, it makes it possible to discern whether processes of memory development work differently in local and national contexts.

Newspaper indexes are used to locate coverage during the 1960s and '70s. The *New York Times* was indexed throughout this period. Indexes for the *Los Angeles Times* and the *Chicago Tribune* first appeared in 1972. Indexes provide a very limited picture of the process of collective memory development because stories indexed under likely keywords (such as "Watts" or "Democratic National Convention, 1968") tend to be commemorations of the events, and controversial events are unlikely subjects of commemoration. Better data become available when the content of these newspapers was made available in a keyword-searchable database. The *New York Times* was available on Nexis beginning June 1, 1980. The *Los Angeles Times* and the *Tribune* became available on January 1, 1985. Keyword searches offer a much richer picture of how the past gives shape to the present, in addition to the ways it is remembered. The searches reveal that both of these pasts play an active role in the cities where they occurred and in the nation as a whole. The *Chicago Tribune* referred to the 1968 convention about three times per month between 1985 and 1995, and the *New York Times* mentioned it about half as often between 1981 and 1995. The *Los Angeles Times*, too, referred to the Watts riots about three times per month on average between 1985 and 1991. The keyword searches also reveal that the negotiation of collective memories of these events was still ongoing in the early and middle 1980s.

The 1996 Democratic National Convention and the 1992 Los Angeles riots serve as an end point for the study. However, in order to ascertain whether and how stories about the past diffuse through the news media, the study includes a brief look at more recently published stories about these two events that appeared in regional newspapers throughout the country.

Some who read this analysis may find themselves objecting, "But that's not how I remember it"; particularly those with personal memories of the 1960s. As a student of collective memory, I approach these cases with the advantage (or disadvantage) of having no personal memory of the events I am studying. Indeed, William Parker, chief of the Los Angeles Police Department during the Watts riots, died the day I was born. It is difficult, then, for me to appreciate the gap between personal memory and public memory that those who remember these events may perceive. However, I may be better qualified to describe how future generations are likely to recall the Watts riots and the Chicago convention than I would be if I myself remembered them.

Plan of the Book

Chapter 2 examines the raw materials of which collective memory is made. It uses elements of framing theory to identify the story components that were used to construct meanings for these events when they occurred. Many stories that attempted to make sense of these social conflicts are so incompatible that they shun all efforts to integrate aspects of the events. News stories profiling the 1968 Democratic nominees for president and vice president appear next to reports of running battles in the streets but don't refer to them. Stories describing looting and arson during the Watts riots often do not describe the poverty of the neighborhoods involved. There are major and minor story threads, but in general, a kind of narrative chaos prevails. Yet the elements of these disparate tales form the foundation for stories that do integrate aspects of the events into a meaningful whole and the ontological "facts" for which later, integrative stories would have to account.

Chapter 3 considers the ongoing role of political elites in shaping collective memories of social conflict and controversy. The first part of the chapter describes political elites' efforts to supply meaning for events through practices Victor Turner (1981) calls "redressive rituals," such as investigations, trials, and policy responses. The latter part of the chapter considers what happens when leadership of political institutions changes and when former leaders pass away and are no longer present to defend their reputations. It also considers the changing roles of various other social actors as news sources in stories about the past.

After describing when and where the news remembers the past, Chapter 4 explores the concrete processes by which "passions cool" and people "move on." A variety of reporting practices serve to downplay remaining controversies, creating pasts that are safer for public discussion and paving the way for the evolution of shared, rather than competing, stories. Some, like the fragmentary quality of news reporting, are normal journalistic practices. Others, like avoiding descriptions of the events themselves and managing salience through the creation of lists, may be peculiar to collective memory processes.

Chapter 5 describes the ways various stories are integrated and the forms those shared stories take. A theory that explains how individuals simplify and integrate complex images to create memorable stories offers a methodological wedge to examine wider social processes that affect how news stories about the past come together. The ability of relevant social groups to protest their portrayal also drives the search for a narrative acceptable to all parties. Meanwhile, changing social circumstances can transform stories to match current political dogma, even when political elites play no direct role. These stories can be passed between newspapers via a variety of mechanisms and acquire local coloration as they are used to think about local events.

In Chapter 6, the role of collective memory in more recent events is explored. These applications of collective memory illustrate some of the pitfalls of thinking with the past: most fundamentally, of treating the story of the past as if it were the past itself. Where collective memory of the Watts riots was used to think about the 1992 civil unrest in Los Angeles, it may have interfered with effective government response to the unrest by encouraging reporters and officials to fixate on economic issues rather than police malpractice. The relevance of the 1968 Democratic National Convention to our current public life, meanwhile, was dismissed because by the time the Democrats returned to Chicago in 1996, the convention demonstrations were consistently associated with the Vietnam War, which was by now safely over. The broader critique of democracy contained in the demonstrations, despite its modern-day relevance, had been lost over the years.

Chapter 7 consolidates the findings of the case studies and returns to the original questions posed: Does collective memory emerge from our troubled past? What influences its form and content? Whose interests does it serve? It also considers the implications of the case study findings for the development of collective memory of the terrorist attacks of September 11.

CHAPTER 2

Real-Time News

*Covering the Watts Riots and
the Chicago Convention*

T O UNDERSTAND HOW COLLECTIVE MEMORY of social conflict evolves, one must begin with the ways that the event was represented in its own time. Contemporary media coverage of events fuels memories in at least two ways. First of all, in most cases, we experience major national events through media coverage of them. Most of us experienced the events of September 11 through televised reports, for example. Thus, in some ways, the content of personal memories of the past can be recaptured when one looks back at the media coverage of an event. However, in one key respect, that moment can never be recaptured. Modern observers know how the story turns out, while for those who live through an event, particularly a traumatic or divisive one, uncertainty is an important part of the experience. On September 11, no one knew how many had died, how many more attacks might come, or what other targets might be. Observers looking back at news coverage of that day will no doubt detect that uncertainty but will never be able to completely embrace it themselves. A second way that contemporary news coverage fuels collective memory is by providing its raw materials. As collective memories of the Watts riots and the Chicago convention evolve, they combine, recombine, and eliminate aspects of the original stories that were told. Virtually all of the material used to create collective memory existed in the earliest coverage of these events, and it is rare to see novel interpretations.

In this chapter, the historical contexts of the Watts riots and the 1968 convention are sketched, and contemporary print media coverage of the two events is outlined. Although television news was an important source of information and images for audiences, at the time of the Watts riots, television news was not archived, so contemporary televised reports of the Watts riots have not been systematically preserved. News archiving at the Vanderbilt television archives began with the 1968 Democratic National Convention, but the live, continuous coverage is so extensive that it is difficult to distill it into key moments after the fact. Newspaper coverage of these events is likewise too voluminous to be easily distilled into major narrative threads and key events and accounts, and has also been extensively studied by other scholars.[1]

To condense contemporary coverage so that it can be manageably presented, most of the examples here come from the three major newsmagazines, *Time*, *Newsweek*, and *U.S. News and World Report*, and from an "instant book" on the Watts riots created by *Los Angeles Times* reporters Jerry Cohen and William Murphy (1966), which draws its material from the coverage carried in local Los Angeles newspapers. The central purpose of newsmagazines during this era was to provide a brief summary of the week's major events, and both *Time* and *Newsweek* frequently relied on the reporting of the *New York Times* for their factual information. Similarly, Cohen and Murphy's book offers a summary and a bit of perspective on local print coverage of the Watts riots. These resources, then, suit the purposes of this chapter: to identify the major narratives and iconic incidents and events that emerged at the time the Watts riots and the Chicago convention occurred. Comparisons of the newsmagazine and "instant book" coverage to both the content of the newspapers' indexes during the same time and previous research on newspaper coverage of these events are made throughout the chapter. They show that while the emphases of individual news organizations were often distinctive, the newsmagazines include the key events and narrative elements that were also present in the daily press.

Searching for Story Threads

From a storytelling perspective, the problem facing reporters and their sources at the moment social conflict erupts is that the events evoke too much meaning. Victor Turner (1981) notes that social dramas are defined in their early phases by indeterminacy, but notes, "Indeterminacy should not be regarded as the absence of social being; it is not negation, emptiness, privation. Rather, it is potentiality, the possibility of becoming" (154). The same event can support a variety of narratives. Still, the desire to render the chaos in Chicago and Los Angeles comprehensible by means of narrative is apparent even in the earliest reporting. Hayden White (1987) argues that we take comfort in assigning to real events the coherence of a story. Faced with a welter of facts and events and a nagging sense of uncertainty, White argues, we seek both meaning and a moral. In doing so we selectively remember both the past and its significance. A variety of narrative theorists have observed this "narrative impulse" at work in a variety of settings including journalism (Fulford 1999). At its heart is the desire to order experience in meaningful ways.

In truth, any event can produce surplus meaning. As White notes, one of the essential qualities of a narrative is that it is one of several possible stories. Critical scholars point out that surplus meaning is typically edited out of the news product through the interactions between journalists and political elites such that social reality as represented in news attains meaning without key elements of struggle ever being apparent to audiences. The result is that the meaning and significance of events seems to have been discovered rather than made. This is not the case, however, with social dramas. In the breach and crisis phases elites lose control over events and their meaning either because the pace of events outstrips their abilities to supply meaning or because groups of elites clash over meaning. Under these conditions, the struggle for meaning is not settled behind the scenes but actually breaks through into news coverage. Because of this, the raw materials for collective memory, the competing narratives and the conflicting facts and accounts, are preserved and publicly available.

Robert Entman's (1993) definition of a frame offers a useful tool for identifying the elements of competing narratives. Unlike second-level, or aspect, agenda setting,[2] which considers frames thematically,

Entman uses a functional perspective that describes elements of a text in terms of how they "work" in the broader context of the story. In doing so, his conceptualization preserves a sense of narrative that alternative definitions do not. Although he himself does not cite the literature on narrative theory, similarly functional approaches to narrative sequence are used by some of these theories as they seek to define the essence of "plot" (Martin 1986). Such theories, which suggest that all literature is a series of variations on a small number of archetypical stories, have ultimately been rejected by a more recent generation of literary scholars (Martin, 1986), but the idea that news reporters draw upon a small collection of story archetypes has persisted.[3] Entman's definition of a frame simplifies stories into four elements. They

> define problems—determine what a causal agent is doing with what costs and benefits, usually measured in terms of common cultural values; diagnose causes—identify the forces creating the problem; make moral judgments—evaluate causal agents and their effects; and suggest remedies—offer and justify treatments for the problems and predict their likely effects. (52)

The idea that moral evaluation is involved is also a key link between narrative theory and Entman's conceptualization of framing: White (1987) notes that narratives have morals and that without a moral there is no story.

There is one other reason that Entman's approach to framing is a better fit for sorting through contemporary coverage than aspect agenda setting. Aspect agenda setting focuses on the presence or absence of various themes that either make up or have bearing on an issue. Framing, as Entman conceives it, opens up the possibility that the same information can perform different functions depending upon the story in which it is embedded. In the early coverage of the Watts riots and the Chicago convention, one finds competing stories that attempt to make meaningful the same body of information. Such stories do sometimes omit information, but they also incorporate the same information into multiple unique, irreconcilable story structures. The same phenomenon also occurs as the stories pass from contemporary coverage into popular history. Rival stories account differently for the same facts.

Using Entman's conceptualization, the following analysis involves a close reading of newsmagazine texts looking not only at facts or themes, but also at how various story elements function within the texts. In many cases, the same facts function quite differently depending upon how the narrative is shaped. For example, some stories of the Chicago violence identify the protesters as the agents responsible for the problem whereas others identify the police. Oftentimes, especially in early coverage, framing is inconsistent within a story, or stories with conflicting frames are placed side by side in order to maintain narrative coherence in the face of insurmountable contradiction.

Evidence of Indeterminacy

Throughout the chapter, "real-time" news coverage of the two events is organized according to the major narrative frameworks that were used at the time, which to some degree masks the indeterminacy of the original text. Yet reporters' uncertainty emerges everywhere. Their reports are unfailingly professional, but it is clear that normal news routines have broken down.[4] It might be argued that of course coverage was chaotic. Reporters were working under hazardous conditions as well as under deadline. However, even reporters working on newsmagazines— writing from the safety of their news rooms for deadlines over a week after the worst crises were past—demonstrate the confusion these social breaches wrought.

During the Watts riots, journalists were uncertain about which sources to treat as authoritative. For example, Ann Kathleen Johnson (1994) points out: "[L]ooking at the *New York Times* edition of the fourteenth [of August], it was not clear who was in charge, the Lieutenant Governor, the Chief of Police, or the commander of the California National Guard General Roderic Hill" (8). As a result, key differences appear in the construction of "true"—as opposed to contested—information in each magazine. Consider two reports of the "last shots fired" in the riots, when Los Angeles police raided a Black Muslim mosque. *Time* reported it this way: "Fifty police rushed to the Black Muslim mosque in Watts on a tip that arms were being laid in there, arrested 59 Negroes after a half-hour gunfight" (The loneliest road 1965, 9). Here is *Newsweek*'s report of the same raid:

Gunfire rang out earlier Wednesday, this time at the Black Muslim Mosque on South Broadway at 56th Street. Police charged the building, shattered its windows and arrested 59 Negroes in the area. They said they had raided the mosque to check reports that the Muslims were carrying rifles into the building. And police also claimed the Muslims had returned fire, but witnesses disputed the story. When a search produced no weapons, cops suggested that guns had been sneaked out the back way and hidden. (Mopping up 1965, 15)

Under normal circumstances, given the reputation of the Black Muslim organization, sometimes referred to as a "cult" by journalists, the *Time* version would probably be accepted without question. But in the wake of this social breach, news organizations were careful to assume little about what was going on. Thus, in the above excerpt, *Newsweek* reports the claims of the police *as claims* rather than as an authoritative account of what happened. Many news organizations both produced and gave credence to multiple versions of events. However, one common understanding existed virtually from the beginning: the Watts riots were represented as a story about race.

No such agreement over the basic cleavage expressed in Chicago appears in the contemporary coverage of the 1968 Democratic National Convention and the demonstrations that occurred during convention week. Indeterminacy in this case can be found in the changing portrayals of important actors in the drama and in the lack of detail regarding these actors' motivations.[5] Protestors began convention week as instigators and ended the week as victims, while reporters went from bystanders to unwilling participants in the news. These complex characterizations and the lack of apparent reason for the actors' behavior would provide a great deal of interpretive latitude for later tellers of the tale. The crisis of authority was undoubtedly as great or greater in Chicago than it had been in Los Angeles, but it is less apparent in contemporary reporting, in part because contemporary coverage devotes the bulk of attention to the "normal" news event, the convention, despite the chaos in the streets.

The Watts Riots

It may seem a bit strange to begin a study of collective memory by contemplating the history of Los Angeles. After all, the city seems quintessentially American—a new city in the new world, constantly growing and changing, with its eye on the future and little heed for the past. But in 1965, an event occurred that would remain part of the memory of both the city and the nation. The southeastern sections of the city experienced what were then the most deadly riots of the century, named for a community that remained untouched until the third day of violence: Watts. Although urban unrest was not unheard of, the Watts riots generated a mad scramble for meaning in both the city and the nation. Citizens sought explanations and government officials (federal, state, and local), reporters, the police, the National Guard, civil rights groups, and fellow citizens struggled to supply them.

In order to understand how people tried to make sense of the violence in Los Angeles, we must consider the broader environment of events in which it occurred. Prior to the riots in 1965, there had been a great deal of national focus on civil rights. Earlier that year, the abortive first Selma to Montgomery march by nonviolent demonstrators had taken place. Americans had been shocked at the conduct of local police in Selma who beat back the marchers with billy clubs (Garrow 1978). National Guardsmen, on the other hand, had overseen the integration of several schools in the South, and their image was more ambiguous. In the spring of that year, President Lyndon B. Johnson had signed the Voting Rights Act of 1965, a follow-up to the 1964 Civil Rights Act. Nonviolent civil rights campaigns were still more prominent, but urban unrest in African American neighborhoods like the 1964 Harlem riots was clearly on the minds of those writing about the disturbances in Los Angeles the following year. By this time, the Black Muslim movement had gained some attention from the national press, most of it negative. Black Muslims spoke out against the war in Vietnam, among other things. Black Muslim leader Malcolm X was assassinated in 1965 prior to the Watts riots. Finally, 1966 would bring midterm elections. Los Angeles would elect a mayor and California a governor barely a year after the riots were over.

Four major narrative threads appear in contemporary coverage of the riots: the riots as lawless behavior, the riots as an insurrection, the riots as a protest against police brutality, and the riots as a protest against economic and social conditions in the ghetto.

Lawlessness

The most prominent of the early narratives attempting to make sense of the violence in Watts attributed these events to wanton lawlessness on a massive scale. There are a variety of ways to account for the popularity of this story in early coverage. Stuart Hall and associates[6] argue that the crime story is the most basic narrative genre in news. Todd Gitlin (1980) also observes that demonstrations are often covered as crime stories. Further, this sort of frame was very available to journalists since the dynamic of the riots from the beginning was a confrontation between police and members of the community. The Watts riots began following the drunken driving arrest of an African American man and the subsequent arrest of his brother and mother. Marquette Frye, most accounts now concur, resisted arrest. Whether the police used undue force to subdue him is less clear. Soon after nightfall, however, inner-city neighborhoods in Los Angeles were in flames. The eight days and nights that followed provided journalists with dozens of stories of shootings, looting, arson, and arrest. In the months that followed, regular news-gathering routines would provide stories about arraignments and trials of those accused of crimes during the riots and inquests into the shooting deaths that mostly involved officers of the law, all of whom were absolved of wrongdoing. All of this would support a crime narrative. The lawlessness story could embrace most of the visual evidence that seemed to pour forth from the neighborhood in news photos filled with smoke and National Guardsmen. Moreover, local officials usually told the story in these terms.

U.S. News and World Report used a crime frame almost exclusively, beginning with the headline for its main story about events in Los Angeles: "Race Friction—Now a Crime Problem?" The title was also the headline on its cover for that week, August 30, 1965. The magazine selected President Johnson's most condemnatory statements about the rioters, which called them "lawbreakers" and compared them to Klansmen. U.S. News bolstered its assessment of the Watts riots as crime by explicitly separating them from the ongoing struggle for civil rights. The magazine denied the legitimacy of charges of police brutality by putting the phrase in quotes[7] and by asserting that this riot, like others, began with "Negroes reacting against routine police actions" (Race friction 1965, 24). While the crime frame is the central interpretive tool in *U.S. News*'s reporting, it appears to some extent in all three newsmagazines. All of the magazines reported the number of arrests made and the amount of property damage that occurred. All described incidents of looting and arson, using these terms. These are the sorts of facts Gitlin describes as essential elements of a crime frame.

Perhaps unsurprisingly, it is in the work of Cohen and Murphy (1966) (two Los Angeles journalists creating a summary of their work and that of their colleagues at the *Los Angeles Times* and other local papers) that the lawlessness narrative finds its most varied expression. Especially noticeable to modern eyes is their extensive use of animal metaphors to describe the actions of those involved in the violence:

- "The mob not only had not dispersed of its own accord, but was growing and reacting like a wounded animal" (62).
- "[M]otorists moving along Imperial and unaware of what had developed, drove into the teeth of a yowling beast" (73).
- "Looters swarmed through supermarkets like ants over rotting fruit" (120).
- "Meanwhile, another fire crew was set upon by a flock of Negroes of all ages" (140).

That they used these expressions is all the more interesting because at the time, Police Chief William Parker had stirred controversy for comparing the rioters to "monkeys in a zoo," a phrase that most media outlets, and Cohen and Murphy elsewhere in their book, recognized as demeaning to African Americans. Describing the rioters as animals renders them incapable of rational action by definition. Cohen and Murphy describe a kind of carnival atmosphere emerging, especially on Friday, August 13: the single most destructive day of the riots. Those in the streets are described as drunk or even crazed as they seem to celebrate the destruction. Here, they quote a colleague at the *Los Angeles Herald-Examiner*, James P. Bennett: "Looters moved in and removed hoses from the [fire] trucks and did a snake dance with them as they chanted and raved down the streets" (142). The implication seems to be that a kind of mass insanity had settled over the inner city. Wanton lawlessness had replaced rational action. Johnson (1994) finds similar references to a carnival or festive atmosphere in the *New York Times*.

The newsmagazines include many claims that support a lawlessness interpretation, though they often offer this information without explicitly tying it to an interpretive framework. One supportive contention was that most of those arrested had some kind of criminal record. Evidence regarding this was quite sketchy at first since hundreds of people were arrested during the disturbances. However, even after evidence was available, its meaning remained contested. Those who supported the lawlessness narrative argued that since so many arrested during the riots had police records the violence could be attributed to the "criminal element" within the community, a view popular with Mayor Sam Yorty. Others argued that the proportion arrested who already had records was not that great, or that it was hard to be a Negro living in South Central Los Angeles and not have a criminal record.[8]

A second argument pointed out that many African Americans had come to Los Angeles from the South. These recently arrived migrants, it was argued, came with chips on their shoulders because of the treatment they had received in the South, especially at the hands of the police. The argument was troublesome in that it opened up the possibility for comparison as well as contrast between local law enforcement. However, it did have the advantage of distinguishing many residents of the riot zone from "real" members of the Los Angeles community without overtly expressing racism.

A third argument used to support the lawlessness narrative was the apparent senselessness of destroying one's own community. This argument was used to defend the lawlessness interpretation from those who might argue that the violence was some sort of protest. Arson was the act that best supported this story, and the fires of Los Angeles are some of the most indelible images of that time. Another aspect of the neighborhood destruction as lawlessness interpretation appeared almost immediately after the riots and became the most lasting contribution of this frame to the collective memory of the violence. Contravening the hopes of those who imagined that the government would be forced to build back the ravaged community, reporters told stories of businesses that would not or could not rebuild in the area and of middle class residents who feared the violence and fled the neighborhood. Many stories of neighborhood decay in central Los Angeles would trace the decline to the aftermath of the Watts riots.

The most difficult crime to explain away in this context was looting. In the lawlessness narrative, looting is an act of greed, and these stories focus on the looters who emptied liquor stores and who took from shops far more items than they could possibly find useful. Cohen and Murphy (1966) sometimes used the word "plunder" to describe the activities of looters. The idea that people were behaving irrationally was also a key element of the crime story. However, looting grocery stores— especially in the later days of the violence when stores were closed and transportation unavailable—was harder to explain.

The riots were perceived as unprecedented, which was an idea used by several officials to insist that the violence should be interpreted as crime rather than as protest. Governor Edmund G. (Pat) Brown insisted: "Here in California, we have a wonderful working relationship between whites and Negroes. We got along fine until this happened" (quoted in Cohen and Murphy 1966, 261). These riots were often compared to those that had occurred in Harlem the previous summer, and the contrast between the tall urban jungle of New York City and the expansive urban savanna of Los Angeles was much remarked. Los Angeles did not look like the cities where racial unrest had previously occurred, a perception that contributed to the sense that the Watts riots were an unprecedented event.

Insurrection/Conspiracy

Integral to interpreting the unrest as an insurrection is the reputation and involvement of the Black Muslims. In 1965, the Black Muslims' agenda was very different from what was by then the more mainstream approach of other civil rights groups. Unlike the NAACP or the Southern Christian Leadership Conference, which through the courts or nonviolent demonstration sought to integrate society, the Black Muslims advocated a separatist agenda of African American self-reliance. Cohen and Murphy (1966) argued that they preached a "fanatic hatred of the white race" (268). They further reported that the Muslims had circulated inflammatory literature during the riots. Rumors apparently circulated at the time that the Muslims were coordinating riot activity. Such allegations were also made about other groups, such as gangs.

Other, more nebulous organizations were also suspected of conspiracy. Mayor Yorty blamed the charges of police brutality on a "worldwide subversive campaign" orchestrated by communists (quoted in Johnson 1994, 14). Cohen and Murphy also entertained the argument that the violence was coordinated more informally by people in the neighborhood who happened to meet in local gathering places and discuss their plans for the evening. This element of conspiracy or coordination was critical to move the story from a lawlessness narrative to an insurrection narrative. However, coordinated activity also raised the possibility of meaningful political action. Thus, the conspirators were always delegitimated groups.

A second aspect of the riots that could be used to support an insurrection narrative was the directed nature of some of the violence. Reporters explained that African American businessmen wrote "Blood," "Blood brother," or a similar designation on their businesses to protect them from looting and arson. The signs were not always effective, but the implication was that riot violence was purposefully aimed at whites, and in some cases more specifically at Jewish business owners in the riot area. This aspect of the violence was further enhanced by media focus on white victims and black rioters. Johnson (1994) reports that the only riot victims to have their pictures printed on the front page of the *Los Angeles Times* were white.

Interestingly, rumors of conspiracy did not seem to fade with the appearance of the government report on the riots (Governor's Commission on the Los Angeles Riots 1965). The McCone Commission Report specifically rejects the notion that the riots constituted a coordinated insurrection against the government. The rumors, however, remained, and to this day one finds terms such as "revolt" or "rebellion" replacing "riots" in some commentaries on the event.

Both the lawlessness story and the insurrection story are supported by a descriptive motif that probably owes much of its existence and power to the salience of the Vietnam War to contemporary audiences. Both *Time* and *Newsweek* describe events in Los Angeles in military terms and draw direct analogies to the war in Vietnam, especially after the arrival of National Guardsmen in South Central Los Angeles. Johnson (1994) reports similar applications of war metaphors in the daily press. *Newsweek* described the strategic situations as similar: there was no well-defined combat zone in Vietnam or in Los Angeles.

Cohen and Murphy (1966) regularly describe police and firemen being "bombarded" with rocks and bottles, which are in turn often referred to as "missiles." Police are described as "fighting a guerilla war." Firefighters are "besieged." These references add to the sense of urgency about what was happening in Los Angeles.

Police Brutality

The most dangerous narrative about the Watts riots, from the perspective of the Establishment, was also perhaps the most obvious. It said that the black community in Los Angeles had long endured brutal treatment from the Los Angeles Police Department and other law enforcement agencies. The arrest of Marquette Frye—in which he suffered a baton blow to the head from a California Highway Patrol officer and appeared to many in the gathered crowd to be kicked and have his feet slammed in a car door—was the straw that broke the camel's back. The people rose up in protest of their ill treatment at the hands of the white Establishment.

If the reason for the riot was police brutality, the blame for the riots rested on the shoulders of the powers that be. Allegations of police brutality, if true, meant that the police in northern cities were no better than Selma Sheriff Jim Clark whose men had beaten unarmed protestors earlier that same year. They would mean that conditions in the North were no better for blacks than they were in the South, a new and terrible idea that would destroy existing conceptualizations of "us" and "them" on several levels.

The police brutality narrative is actively contested during and immediately after the riots. In some ways, it is the equal opposite of the lawlessness narrative. All of the newsmagazines address the possibilities of police misconduct, but *Newsweek* offers few conclusions about whether the police acted appropriately. For *Newsweek*, there are no white hats in Watts. The magazine condemns the violence, but also paints an extremely unflattering portrait of the mayor, the police chief, and individual officers involved in quelling the violence. It describes police/community relations in dire terms:

> For all their celebrated professionalism, Chief Parker and his men are as despised by Watts Negroes as Sheriff Jim Clark and his

beefy minions are hated by Selma black folk. There is ample evidence to suggest why....Among some LA cops, a billy club is familiarly known as a "nigger knocker".... (The reasons why 1965, 18)

African Americans in Los Angeles were described as having a "naked hatred" of the police chief. Black participants in the riots are typically described as tragic, angry, and misguided. However, the power of this narrative is not completely realized even in *Newsweek's* coverage. The animosity between police and residents is presented as a backdrop for the riots. In its search for causes, *Newsweek* turns to the economic conditions in Watts.

Time's writers appear convinced that police did act appropriately, and the contrast with *Newsweek* this produces is well demonstrated in the reporting on the raid of the mosque described above. The magazine does describe the poisonous atmosphere between police and African Americans, but it attributes this to the recent migration of many of these black citizens from the South. *Time* quoted a "Negro" Los Angeles judge who said, "What they know about sheriffs and police is Bull Conner and Jim Clark....The people distrust the police and the police distrust the people. They move in a constant atmosphere of hate" (Trigger of hate, 13). *U.S. News*, reinforcing its theme of criminal violence met with appropriate police action, did not report the specific allegations of police brutality that touched off the violence and frequently enclosed the term "police brutality" in quotes. All three magazines appear to applaud the conduct of the National Guard.

Debate over police brutality begins with the reporting of Marquette Frye's arrest. *Newsweek* reports that angry words were exchanged between police and the gathered crowd and "suddenly, the rocks flew" (Los Angeles 1965, 16). *Time's* report adopts a "he said, she said" narrative style, quoting the officer's contention that the man resisted arrest and the onlookers' reports that the police beat and kicked him into the squad car (Trigger of hate 1965, 16). Cohen and Murphy (1966) describe the whole incident as a terrible misunderstanding that flew on wings of rumor through the community, provoking its misguided rage.

Another site at which the police brutality narrative was contested was in the reporting of Los Angeles Police Chief William H. Parker's comments on the violence. Parker got a lot of ink in all three magazines, but the contrast between *U.S. News and World Report* and *Newsweek* is the most extreme. *U.S. News* reprinted verbatim the questions and answers from an interview Parker granted the magazine and declined to print some of his more inflammatory remarks that circulated widely in other media. This transcript occupied one full page in the four page main story on events in Los Angeles (Back of riots 1965).

Newsweek also devoted a box to statements by Parker, two thirds of a page in an eight-and-one-third-page story (though two pages are devoted to pictures). However, *Newsweek* exercised its journalistic authority to edit and contextualize Parker's remarks. The chief's views are still plain: he argues that the riots were in large part the work of experienced criminals, that the good living and civil rights conditions of Negroes in Los Angeles mean that this is not a demonstration by any stretch, and that a lack of respect for police and the rule of law is producing a disintegration of the social order. However, *Newsweek* also published in its box Parker's most inflammatory comment: "One person threw a rock...then, like monkeys in a zoo, others started throwing rocks..." (ellipses in original, The tough cop of L.A. 1965, 17). A picture caption calls Parker a "Cop under fire," and Parker himself is quoted as saying, "I may go down in history as the only chief they sacked a whole city to get rid of."

In general, Cohen and Murphy (1966) support the conduct of the police. They note that all of the inquests into officer-involved riot deaths absolved the officers. The chief is described as "tough, dedicated Bill Parker" (63). He is said to be the only person to offer competent leadership in the city's hour of need when Governor Brown vacationed in Greece, Lt. Governor Anderson took six hours to respond to a request to call out the National Guard and Mayor Yorty left the city to attend speaking engagements in San Diego and San Francisco. Parker is said to be "outspoken," and his "monkeys in a zoo" comment is dismissed as "undoubtedly an innocent remark" (250). The authors point to the rising crime rate in Los Angeles and also argue that some charges of police brutality stem not from alleged physical harm but from a feeling that officers have not treated the community with respect. The overall contention seems to be that police do no more than is necessary to preserve public safety. Johnson (1994) finds that this kind of support for the action of police is far more prominent in the *Los Angeles Times* than it is in the *New York Times* and in the *Washington Post*.

The accusations of police brutality and stories of police professionalism coexist uncomfortably in Cohen and Murphy's book (1966). They
interview and profile several people who claim to have been mistreated
by police. Frequently they try—perhaps unconsciously—to resolve this
difference by locating brutality narratives and professionalism narratives in different chapters. The experiences of those who claim police
brutality seem to have no relation to the actions of the heroic officers
struggling against long odds to contain and end the violence. Where
such stories cannot be separated, as in the case of police shooting
bystanders, the narrative genre is usually that of an unavoidable tragedy
blamed on the general climate of lawlessness rather than poor judgment or lack of compassion on the part of police. However, the writers
cannot seem to dismiss the claims of local residents to such an extent
that they fail to relate them at all. Even this small opening for a police
brutality interpretation probably seemed threatening to many.

Economic Deprivation

Even very early coverage of the Watts riots entertains the idea that the
riots were in protest of the economic privations of ghetto life. Early
postriot coverage blames both the white Establishment, which squabbled
over poverty funds and neglected the inner city, and rioters, who took
the law into their own hands. *Time* and *Newsweek* each develop this
narrative slightly differently, while *U.S. News and World Report*
acknowledges the narrative by rejecting it. Both *Time* and *Newsweek*
describe the anger of South Central Los Angeles residents. They report
the high level of crime and unemployment, the overcrowding, the decay-
ing housing, and the de facto segregation and isolation of the neighborhood. In addition to these substantive criticisms of life in the inner city,
they report a more procedural tiff involving the failure of the city to
release federal antipoverty funds due to a dispute between federal and
city officials. These facts support an understanding of the riots as a reaction to economic conditions and at the same time imply a need for
financial solutions to remedy the ostensible causes of the riot. This
interpretation was also supported by federal authorities.

While both magazines contain elements of a narrative of economic
deprivation, *Newsweek* develops this idea the furthest. Its first report
about the riot rejected Chief Parker's reported assessment that the riots

had been caused by civil rights militants in favor of the "men on the dole, the kids out of school and out of work, the broken families and blighted hopes, the smoldering resentment of the cops born long before the black nationalists turned up with their predictable 'police brutality' leaflets." (Los Angeles 1965, 17) Note that this statement captures the hopelessness that was reportedly present in Watts but nevertheless rejects charges of police brutality.

The following week, the magazine further developed its theme that a political/economic approach to the unrest in Los Angeles was the appropriate response. It observed that while force was a necessary first response, it "was not the final answer to the conditions that make riots" (After the blood bath 1965, 14). While it reported Lyndon Johnson's speech comparing the rioters to Klansmen, it surrounded this with reports of two other speeches, which it claimed balanced the need for law and order with the need to attack the "causes" of the violence. It was the attack on these causes, *Newsweek* claimed, which were the "real meaning of Los Angeles." However, the magazine stops short of arguing that the cause of the riots was social injustice.

Time also began by describing the poor social conditions in Watts and the failure of city and federal officials to ameliorate those conditions. It reported that federal programs had prevented riots in cities where there had been violence in the summer of 1964, a claim that was probably contestable but reported as fact.

U.S. News and World Report examined and rejected economic privation as a cause of the riots, continuing to emphasize individual responsibility:

> The Watts area, where the riots centered is densely populated, almost entirely by Negroes, many of whom are jobless and more than half of whom get some form of government assistance. But its housing is a far cry from the tenement slums of New York's Harlem. The crime rate in Watts is high. More than 500 of its youngsters are parolees. (Race friction 1965, 23–24)

The implication is that conditions are not so bad and the government has responded adequately.

The economic deprivation narrative adopts the language of human dignity that had long been a part of mainstream civil rights, but adds demands for economic opportunity to existing demands for equal treat-ment for African Americans. This changes the concept of civil rights in many ways. Placing the riots in a larger narrative about the civil rights movement—whether because of economic conditions in the inner city or because of police malpractice in the community—represented a great risk to the movement. In 1965, most of the major civil rights advances were recent, and it seems reasonable that movement leaders and those who supported their cause feared rollbacks in the wake of urban unrest. Therefore, resistance to a civil rights narrative appears not only in lawlessness and conspiracy stories, but also with civil rights leaders distancing themselves and being distanced from the violence.

The best example of this is *Time* and *Newsweek*'s reporting of Martin Luther King Jr.'s visit to Watts after the unrest. King was appar-ently poorly received by the neighbors of Watts. *Time* quoted a resi-dent's view: "The Negroes of Watts were less polished but no less forceful in condemning their leadership. 'We've got enough big nigger preachers here doing nothing but taking our money and talking for the white man...'" (The loneliest road, 10). Both magazines made a point of discussing the mainstream civil rights movement organizations' failure to organize in the inner cities of the North. They quoted Robert Kennedy's statement that "the army of the resentful and desperate in the North is an army without generals, without captains, almost without sergeants"[9] (The negro after Watts 1965, 17). *Time* published a sidebar reporting the reactions of civil rights leaders to the disturbances and emphasized the lack of organization in the inner city. Civil rights lead-ers did not dismiss the Watts riots as meaningless, criminal acts. However, the riots seemed to make it apparent that the mainstream civil rights leaders did not speak for the residents of the inner cities. This distanced the Watts riots from the mainstream civil rights move-ment and its leaders and interfered with the interpretation of the riots as meaningful political activity rejecting police brutality or the living conditions in the neighborhoods of the curfew zone.

Another way of separating the civil rights movement from the Watts riots was through the mechanism of social class. Sometimes this ele-ment of class discriminated between middle-class blacks and poor, inner-city blacks. At other times, the class factor was used to group middle-class blacks with their white counterparts in opposition to the poor. A good example of the former is *Time*'s editorial analysis "The

Negro After Watts," which appeared on August 27. In its first week's coverage, *Time*'s reporters soundly affirmed the actions of the police and the National Guard but acknowledged that the poor and isolated conditions in the inner city were a social problem that needed to be addressed. However, the following week *Time*'s writers argued that the riots were poorly timed because recently enacted policies would improve the lot of African Americans given time to work. The writers further argued that the real problem was that African Americans who had attained middle-class and even upper-class status were not reaching out a hand to help their brethren who still lived in the slums of the cities or mired in rural poverty, implying that the white community has done all it can or needs to and that remaining problems are the responsibility of the black community. There are several potential interpretations of this charge to African Americans to take care of their own. It is certainly an attempt to absolve the white majority of responsibility for what happened in Los Angeles. It may also be an attempt to carefully separate "good" (or middle-class) blacks from "bad" (or poor) blacks.

However, *Time* also contains material suggesting that class, not race, is the true social division implicated in the riots:

> [M]ost Negro leaders interpreted it as a class explosion in which The Man—the white cop and shopkeeper, the social worker and politician—was attacked more because he was a symbol of the Negro's deprivation than because his skin was white…. In fact, the rioters' resentment was aimed at the successful, assimilated Negro as well as the white man. (The loneliest road, 10)

Many scholars have pointed out the lack of true class consciousness in American society, and the prominence of these ideas in the Watts riots coverage should not be overestimated. However, the fact that such an interpretation is made available at all suggests the variety of narratives which appear as storytellers scramble to make sense of social crises. Like other forms of distancing, discussions of class could be used to undermine a vision of the riots as meaningful protest. However, the class issue was a complex one. Many elements of classism were supportive of an economic interpretation of the rioting.

Narratives of the riots as an act of protest invoked the single most powerful visual image to emerge from the Watts riots: fire. Hundreds of buildings—whole city blocks—burned to the ground. Smoke billowed up toward news helicopters, and most of the rioting occurred at night, making the fires even more visible. The catchphrase used by rioters, coined by a local disc jockey describing a hot record, was "Burn, baby, burn!" The weather during the days of violence was hot and humid, and the expression "long, hot summer" was used in connection with these riots, though it originated earlier. Although the chaos fed into narratives of meaningless violence, these symbols of heat were easily connected with an emotional state of rage. The adjectives "anger" and "frustration" appear throughout the reporting on the violence. The whole situation seemed to coalesce into a single loud expression of fury. To identify those on the street as enraged raised a very obvious question: what were they so angry about? The question itself makes an important assumption—the violence is *about* something. It is meaningful human action. Recognizing the rioters as angry gave credence to narratives that could offer explanations for their anger and discredited narratives that could not.

Struggling for a Frame

The Watts riots produced genuine indeterminacy. To appreciate the level of narrative chaos that emerged from the riots, consider that the major narrative threads diverge on all of the framing dimensions identified by Entman (1993). The lawlessness story defines the problem as wanton criminal behavior and the rioters (and more generally, residents of South Central Los Angeles) as responsible. This frame is highly individualistic: even in their description of people in groups, journalists show a tendency to write in individualistic terms. This is best seen in the odd grammar of Cohen and Murphy (1966), who describe police talking to a "mob" and telling "it" to go home. The solution to the problem seems obvious: more law and order in the form of larger police forces with more power. Indeed, several candidates for election in 1966 would run successfully proposing just such solutions. Such a solution could probably be considered successful if there were no more riots, although it is easy to see this solution as a kind of slippery slope where later violence is interpreted as evidence that the existing solution does not go far enough.

The insurrection/conspiracy story defines the problem as a civil war, a "race war," by inner-city African Americans against the

Establishment. The story does not really offer a motivation for an insurrection in its earliest forms, dismissing the anger in the community as a kind of false consciousness based on rumors and false propaganda and suggesting that the insurrection is misguided. Organizations that "preach hate" and spread false information, such as the Black Muslims, are responsible. The solution to this problem is not immediately evident but appears soon afterward. The appeal of black militancy and its associated Black Nationalism must be countered. Evidence that the problem of insurgency is solved is the decline of black militant and nationalist organizations. How far the government would go to achieve these goals would not be apparent until the 1970s.

The police brutality narrative was the most dangerous to the Establishment. It implied that the problem was racism, and it defined the structures of authority as responsible for the problem. Solutions to the problems offered at the time included citizen review boards and better training in community relations for officers. Cohen (1967) suggested more liberal guidelines for expunging arrest records, which seems a bit like closing the barn door late. A group of residents in the curfew area took matters into their own hands. They established squads that trailed police officers entering African American neighborhoods and photographed arrest procedures. The police and many city officials strenuously resisted all of these proposals. Most were never instituted. Those that were do not seem to have survived for long.

The economic deprivation narrative defined the problem as a lack of economic opportunity and social services for inner-city residents. Initially, the blame for inner city privation was placed on social-structural characteristics of the inner city and neglect by the white community, but the potential for spreading the guilt was always present. The solution to this problem was a galaxy of large-scale social programs providing services such as health care, transportation, education tailored to the needs of poor urban children, job training for the unskilled, and jobs for everyone who needed one. If the poor were lifted out of poverty and joined the middle class, then these programs were a success. Strangely, this solution also has a connection to the insurrection/conspiracy narrative, since such programs might also decrease the popularity of black militancy.

These stories are very different on all of the framing dimensions. Although they do not necessarily contradict each other at every point, they also do not suggest that people agreed on what caused the riots or how to deal with them. Almost immediately, however, the steps taken to deal with the aftermath of the unrest began to affect the stories told about the Watts riots. Some stories were reinforced. Others began to fade.

The 1968 Democratic National Convention

Chicago has long been famous for its politics. For decades, the democratic party reigned supreme in the city through a tradition of "machine" politics, notoriously corrupt but stunningly effective. Chicago has also been a frequent host to national political nominating conventions. Indeed, the city holds the record for hosting the largest number of major-party nominating conventions. Beginning with the Republicans, who nominated Lincoln in Chicago in 1860 at a convention site known as the "Wigwam," major parties have come to the city to nominate their candidates twenty-five times. But the twenty-fourth was almost the last.

In 1968, at a time of world-wide strife and uncertainty, the Democrats came to Chicago to select a successor to Lyndon B. Johnson. Hosted by Richard J. Daley, one of the last of the old party-machine city "bosses," the convention that nominated Hubert H. Humphrey for president would come to be described as "infamous." Although it lasted only four days, the mark it left on the reputation of the city might rival that left by Al Capone. Of the all the conventions hosted by the city, the one held in 1968 became "the Chicago convention."

To understand the evolution of collective memory of the Chicago convention, a broader look at its historical and political context is required.

From A Mile Away

In contrast to the 1965 Watts riots, which startled both media and city officials, everyone seems to have known that the 1968 Democratic National Convention in Chicago was going to be a site of discord. The year was a remarkable political watershed throughout the world, and by convention time, reporters, city officials, and citizens could see trouble coming from a mile away.[10] As Democrats and Republicans wound their way through the prenomination months, events around the world and in the U.S. detonated all around them. Overseas, the Tet offensive in the spring of that year was a military defeat for the Vietcong but a political victory of enormous importance as American public opinion hardened against the Vietnam War. War policies involving de-escalation of various degrees and kinds became legitimate subjects of debate. Also in that year, Soviet tanks entered Prague, Czechoslovakia, to undo the reforms enacted by a more moderate Czech government during what was known as the Prague Spring. In May, students in Paris held mass demonstration against the French government and English students marched on the American embassy in London to protest American involvement in the war in Vietnam.

Domestic strife had reached remarkable levels. In previous years, rioting had occurred in most major American cities, including the 1967 Detroit riots, the most violent of the century. Many outbreaks of urban violence were linked to the struggle for civil rights. Two major assassinations occurred in 1968. Martin Luther King Jr. was assassinated in Memphis, Tennessee, in April, and his death provoked nights of rioting in many major American cities including Chicago. Robert F. Kennedy was shot on June 5 after winning the California primary and died the following day. Fears of assassination or riot would have been very plausible for delegates converging on Chicago in August.

Groups opposing the war and often questioning the American system of government had drawn support on many college and university campuses throughout the nation. They espoused some views that might be termed "traditionally political," but their group identity also involved a number of lifestyle choices seen as strange, to say the least, by many people of their time. Some groups questioned the sexual, political, and language mores of "mainstream" culture in addition to rejecting the Vietnam War. Their critique of American culture was often based on their belief that the war in Vietnam was immoral, but their rejection of traditional American culture was, for many, more broadly based and included critiques of the electoral system, the status of minorities and women in society, and other perceived deficiencies (Farber 1988). Catchall terms such as "hippies," "counterculture," or "youth movement" blurred the differences between these groups.

The use of catchall categories also obscured the variety of political activities younger opponents of the war or the "system" engaged in to express their dissent. Some groups, often labeled by the media as "radical," had disrupted university campuses by holding teach-ins or student strikes. Others had occupied buildings—especially administration buildings—on college campuses. In 1968, several buildings at Columbia University were occupied by students. Some young people, however, took their political activism in very traditional directions and worked on political campaigns. The campaigns of Robert Kennedy and Eugene McCarthy were known for their youthful staffs.

In Democratic politics, major changes were clearly afoot. Early in the year, Eugene McCarthy entered the Democratic primary in New Hampshire and "beat" incumbent president Lyndon Johnson by becoming the focus of protest votes against the war in Vietnam. Although most primaries were at that point mere "beauty contests" rather than the basis for awarding convention delegates to candidates, on March 31 the president announced that he would not run for re-election. An incumbent president who was eligible to run again and did not was virtually unprecedented. Humphrey, Johnson's vice president, soon became the favorite for the nomination, but his bid was challenged by McCarthy and Robert Kennedy, who also opposed the war in Vietnam. McCarthy and Kennedy both won several primaries and were awarded delegates for the coming convention, but their campaign organizations were unable to successfully traverse the pitfalls of party rules about delegate selection—including the unit rule that required all the delegates from a state to vote for a single candidate. Although Humphrey avoided the primaries, he seemed to have the nomination sewn up prior to the convention.

Not only did campaign workers for McCarthy and Kennedy feel shut out of the nomination process, so did African Americans. Democratic Party rules had been changed in 1964 to deny convention credentials to state delegations selected through discriminatory practices, but many southern delegations at the 1968 convention were chosen by party regulars and contained few or no African Americans. Many women were similarly shut out of the process.

In early August, the Republicans nominated Richard M. Nixon in Miami in what the media described as a stultifyingly dull convention. It was just to the Republicans' taste after their raucous 1964 convention in San Francisco in which newsman John Chancellor had been dragged off the convention floor by security and the party had nominated Barry Goldwater who was crushed by Johnson in November. Nixon selected Spiro Agnew as a running mate, and Republicans sat back to watch the Democrats' meet, which was held August 25 through 29 at the International Amphitheater, next to the Stockyards on the South Side of Chicago.

If the events of the year and the looming schisms in the party did not tell the Democrats that they were in for a bad time of it, events in Chicago surely should have. Threats of protest at the convention came from civil rights and antiwar groups even before the election year began. In March, the *New York Times* reported that the National Mobilization Committee to End the War in Vietnam was holding an organizing meeting to develop plans with New Left, Black Power, and other groups to disrupt the convention. In that same month, the Youth International Party, christened the "Yippies," announced plans to hold a "festival of life" in a large city park during the convention. During the riots following King's assassination in April, Mayor Daley sought to restore order in his metropolis by commanding the police department, "Shoot to kill arsonists....Shoot to maim looters." His directive was widely quoted in the media. By August, city officials said they were expecting more than 100,000 demonstrators to descend on Chicago. To discourage them, the city denied parade permits to dissenting groups and refused applications allowing people to sleep in city parks.

Security at the convention was to be tighter than it had been for any previous convention. Manhole covers around the Amphitheater were sealed. Reporters were warned not to shoot pictures through upper-floor windows lest they be mistaken for snipers. Merchants along some major routes to and around the convention site were told to keep their windows closed, a tall order in the dog days of August. Several of these streets were closed to all traffic except buses. Security men watched the airports and train stations for the arrival of "troublemakers." Electronically marked credentials were required to gain access to the convention hall, and security agents monitored the convention floor from catwalks above it.

While security arrangements moved on apace and became more dramatic as threats against the convention multiplied, other important preparations ground to a halt. In June, Chicago telecommunications

workers went on strike and telephone installations at the convention
hall and in the major convention hotels ceased. This was a nightmare
not only for state delegations and candidates but for media who wanted
to bring the nation live coverage of the convention itself and of any
accompanying disturbances. The phone strike could limit coverage by
delaying or even preventing the installation of needed equipment, and
several network executives and McCarthy accused Daley of purposely
limiting coverage to the convention hall because of anticipated disturbances. Bolstering their claim, the Chicago police department refused
to allow news vans to park in front of convention hotels.

With all of the talk of trouble to come, several party leaders lobbied
to move the convention from Chicago. Miami, where Republicans had
just met and infrastructure was in place, seemed a reasonable choice.
But Daley's political clout and the lateness of the hour kept the convention in Chicago. With just nine days to go before the convention opened,
cab drivers went on strike. But the decision was made; the demonstrators and the delegates and the candidates were coming. The police
department and the National Guard were waiting to receive them. As
one city official put it as the convention was about to begin, "Anything
could happen....The only thing that would surprise me is if nothing
happens" (Daley city under siege 1968, 19).

A War on Two Fronts

In media coverage of the Watts riots, multiple narratives of the riots
typically vied with each other for prominence in a single news story. In
contrast, coverage of the 1968 Democratic Convention is fragmented
along two dimensions—space and time—which separate different narrative threads into different stories. First, events occurring at the convention and events occurring in the streets are separately reported.
Despite the extreme circumstances, coverage of the convention itself is
quite ordinary. Stock campaign stories like candidate profiles appear
next to pictures of clashes between police and demonstrators but don't
actually mention the street battles. Second, coverage of the relationship
between the demonstrators and the police changes considerably over
the course of convention week.

At least some of this fragmentation may be attributable to the
nature of the beat system. Reporters on the campaign trail or listening

to the Washington rumor mill discerned cleavages in the Democratic Party that were likely to erupt at the convention. Reporters sent to Chicago to cover the city's preparations for hosting and providing security, and perhaps to make preparations of their own for covering the convention, filed reports focused on the security preparations and officials' expectations about the course of events. Both types of stories were printed, sometimes side by side, as media tried to provide comprehensive coverage at the convention. Until very late in convention week, reporters assigned to the convention floor did not see the violence in the streets—though they undoubtedly heard or read about it—while reporters who covered the demonstrations did not necessarily have the latest information from the convention hall.

The longer lead times of the newsmagazines made integration more possible—at least after the convention—than it would have been for the daily papers, yet the fragmentation remains. Therefore, some other mechanism is probably at work. Gitlin's (1980) analysis of media coverage of the New Left suggests that one reason for the split is the media's continuing efforts to delegitimate social protest. Disconnecting the violence in the streets from the legitimated political activity of nominating a candidate would have furthered that end.

The bifurcated coverage obscured the fact that in many ways the struggles anticipated inside the hall were also struggles that, in a more radical form, might be expressed in the streets. Within the Amphitheater, debate over the Vietnam plank of the party platform was expected to be the most contentious of the convention. The National Mobilization Committee to End the War in Vietnam wanted what its name suggested, and its leaders were active in the early planning stages of the Chicago demonstrations. Other antiwar organizations were present in Chicago as well. At the convention hall, a record number of credentials challenges affecting nearly 20 percent of the delegates dominated the news from inside the hall during the week before the convention opened. The Coalition for an Open Convention objected to the delegate selection rules. Many of its members were McCarthy supporters who resented the party maneuvering that seemed to deny their candidate the nomination. The Youth International Party (Yippies) rejected the political system even more completely, as did several other organizations preparing to demonstrate in the streets.

At the International Amphitheater

To say that the Democratic National Convention in 1968 was contentious is a gross understatement. Bitter seems to come closer to the mark. However, news coverage of events inside the hall is remarkably traditional. Media scholars would be unsurprised to discover that events were reported in terms of strategy rather than substance, despite the extraordinary policy issues facing the party and the nation. This emphasis on strategy linked disparate aspects of the convention into one larger narrative which might be characterized as "How Hubert H. Humphrey Was Nominated." In Entman's (1993) terms, the "problem" is how he attained the nomination, and the agents responsible are the clashing party activists maneuvering to achieve or prevent Humphrey's victory. Stories about credentials challenges, the Vietnam War platform plank, and so on, represented these debates as smaller battles in the larger war for the nomination. What is interesting for our purposes is the way in which this focus on strategy would affect the developing memory of events inside the convention hall. Though prominent in contemporary coverage, strategy frames quickly became dated. On the other hand, the sublimated substance of the convention—the struggles over delegate selection and the Vietnam War—would find new salience in collective memories of the convention.

The first major convention issue was seating the state delegations. There were so many credentials challenges that the credentials committee began meeting several days before the convention opened in order to complete its work. Several southern delegations were challenged because they had been appointed by state party regulars. A rebel Mississippi delegation, the remains of that state's Freedom Party, was seated instead of the regular delegation since the regular delegation contained no people of color. The Georgia delegation, hand-picked by Governor Lester Maddox, was challenged by a rival delegation led by a young man named Julian Bond. The conventional wisdom is that Bond's speech to the credentials committee was so eloquent that the power brokers at the convention could not send him away empty handed. In a strange compromise, they seated half of the regular Georgia delegation and half of the insurgents. Later, Bond's name would be place in nomination for the vice presidency even though had he been selected he would have been too young to serve. While

Humphrey's forces were able to seat Governor Connally's Texas delegation, they were not able to save the unit rule as Connally wished. It was shouted down on the first night of the convention. Individual delegates could now cast their votes as they chose. After settling these issues, the convention gavel closed the first day's session at 3:00 A.M.

Major newsmagazines covered this aspect of the convention not in terms of race or democratic principles, but in terms of campaign strategy. The floor fight waged over the unit rule and seating the Texas delegation was considered by reporters at *Time* and *Newsweek* to be a major test of strength between McCarthy and Humphrey (The winner 1968; The man who would recapture youth 1968). *Newsweek* speculated that the Georgia delegation challenge was issued by McCarthy forces more because the delegation was packed with Humphrey supporters than because it was selected by a segregationist governor (The winner 1968).

The next major struggle was over the Vietnam War plank in the party platform. After losing their fight to schedule the debate on the war for the wee hours of the morning, Platform Committee Chair Hale Boggs and Convention Chair Carl Albert issued a majority report and debate began. The difference between the majority and minority planks was the difference between leaving Vietnam sooner or later, but they defined essential differences between the candidates. Ultimately, the majority plank won, prompting several delegations led by New York to begin singing choruses of "We Shall Overcome" from the floor, even as the convention band had the questionable taste to strike up with "Happy Days Are Here Again."

Contemporary media praised the thoughtfulness of the two-hour debate, but only *Newsweek* describes its substance (Vietnam 1968). *Time* describes the stratagems employed in the fight over the plank but has little to say about its content (The man who would recapture youth 1968). Further, the newsmagazines devote considerable attention to the ways this key platform debate affected the candidacies of the major contenders. In this era before party nominees were determined by the primary system, McCarthy and late entry George McGovern could hope to gain the nomination even at the convention itself by wooing delegates. The Vietnam plank was an important element in this attempt, as well as being a critical element of policy for whichever candidate was ultimately nominated. Thus, the identity of the nominee and the content of the plank were bound together. Events became even more complex as a movement to draft Edward Kennedy as the nominee got underway and seemed to pick up steam. Concerned about the content of the plank, Lyndon Johnson had called several key conventioneers back to the White House for briefings and consultations, increasing speculations about his handiwork at the convention. The machinations of the moment are captured, but the substance of this remarkable policy debate is essentially lost.

Chaos in the streets had now reached a fever pitch and began to invade the convention hall via television, even though Chicago police had confined demonstrators to locations miles away. Delegates began to view the taped coverage, and many were outraged by what they saw. Connecticut Senator Abraham Ribicoff stood up to nominate McGovern for president but diverted his speech to condemn what he called the "Gestapo" tactics of the police in the streets. Mayor Daley, famous for his temper, shot out of his seat and began yelling at Ribicoff from the floor. A family newsmagazine politely interpreted one of his comments as "You fink!" (The winner 1968, 36). The Wisconsin delegation repeatedly moved to fold the convention, postpone it, and move it to another location. But the roll call of states went on, and in the late hours of August 28, Humphrey won what must have seemed a hollow victory.

Although they lead with the violence in the streets, convention wrap-ups in the newsmagazines are otherwise typical. They contain profiles of Humphrey and his vice presidential choice Edmund Muskie. They profile McCarthy and describe the strategic elements of the movement to draft Kennedy. Describing the continuing discord in the party, the magazines note McCarthy's refusal to endorse Humphrey. The most remarkable aspect of the contemporary print media coverage, then, is that it reports the incredible as normal. While half or more of the photographs published in the magazines depict events occurring outside the convention hall, those events receive relatively little space in the accompanying text. Where they are discussed, they are frequently segregated into separate articles. This presentation is quite different from that of the television news media, which, for example, interspersed recorded footage of a violent police-demonstrator encounter in front of the main convention hotel with live footage of

Humphrey's acceptance speech. Indeed, several of the newsmagazines criticized their television counterparts for this sort of portrayal.

Street Demonstrations: Preconvention Coverage

Images of the police and the demonstrators change dramatically as convention week progresses. Early coverage of convention preparations in the news media emphasized the potential for clash between officers and demonstrators, typically from a lawlessness perspective. Demonstrators were usually portrayed as unkempt, unwashed, foul-mouthed, unruly young people who had no respect for the social order, yet they were also described as powerful in a strange sort of way. *Time* asserted that it was their threats of disruption that made stringent security necessary in the first place: "[The convention] is, physically at any rate, the tightest in U.S. history—a kind of Stalag '68. Already the demonstrators have achieved the feat of forcing a major party to pick a candidate for President behind barbed wire, in a charged atmosphere reminiscent of a 'police state.'"[11] *Newsweek* similarly portrayed the demonstrators and the police as equal opposites, neither of which was particularly palatable:

> For even as the mostly youthful non-delegates arrived, by bus, airplane, train, car and motorcycle ("Where's the action?" growled a bushy-haired advance man for the Racine, Wis., Motorcycle Club, "I got 50 bikes coming in."), weapons carriers full of National Guard troops rumbled into Chicago, too. Their stated mission: to maintain "law and order...in connection with threatened mob disorders that may occur." Their instructions: "Shoot to kill" as a last resort in cases of looting or arson. (Hippies, Yippies, and mace 1968, 25, ellipses in original)

Neither magazine connected the elaborate preparations with the assassinations that had occurred that spring and summer, though perhaps each felt such reminders were unnecessary.

Encouraging the impression of demonstrators and police as equal opposites with regard to their power to disrupt and maintain order, most media reported on the demonstrators' preparations to face the police as well as officers' preparations to deal with demonstrators. Time reported,

"One contingent [of demonstrators] was trained in Lincoln Park to control crowds, administer first aid and break through police lines" (Daley city under siege 1968, 18). The upshot of this early coverage was that while security measures at the convention were bound to be extremely inconvenient for delegates, they still might not be enough to control the expected protests. *Time* offered advice about what the well-equipped delegate would need to navigate the convention:

> Goggles (to protect the eyes from tear gas and Mace), cyclist's crash helmet (from billy clubs, bricks, etc.), flak jacket (from snipers), Vaseline (from Mace), Mace (from rioters), washcloth (from teargas)...wire cutters (in case delegate is trapped inside the amphitheater, or outside because of pickpocketed credentials), all-purpose bail-bond credit card (if arrested)....chrysanthemums (for flower power if cornered by militant hippies), first aid kit, gross of aspirin.... (The compleat delegate 1968, 19)

As demonstrators arrived in town for the convention, the biggest worry of convention planners, according to the journalists, was unrest in the African American neighborhoods that experienced rioting only four months before, following King's assassination. Police and "hippies" clashed even before the convention opened. On August 22, police shot and killed a young man they said was dressed as a hippie and in town for the convention.

Dissenters are initially lumped into one large group, and as Gitlin (1980) would predict, their most outrageous actions are the ones the media seize upon. Seven Yippies were arrested just before the convention began, and their symbolic presidential candidate, a pig named Pigasus, sent to the humane society according to *Time* (Daley city under siege 1968). The Yippies' threat to lace the Chicago water supply with LSD was widely reported. Expected protest groups were the "usual suspects" of demonstrators of that era.

The Chicago police were not associated with their chief as the Los Angeles police were during the Watts riots. Like all other city services in Chicago, they were associated with Mayor Daley. His prominence on welcoming banners, even on stickers under telephone receivers at the convention hotels, and media portrayals of him suggested that this was as much his convention as the Democrats'. He is portrayed as commanding the police force with his "shoot to kill" order in April. *Newsweek* refers to officers as "the mayor's cops" (Hippies, Yippies, and Mace 1968, 26), and after the disorders, *Time* embellished this description to "Mayor Richard Daley's heavy-handed cops" (Survival at the stockyards 1968, 14). Daley also personifies the city in some reports, so he connects the actions of officers in the streets with the reputation of the city itself. *Time* describes "Daley City Under Siege" one week before the convention opened (Daley city under siege 1968). Authority in Chicago began and ended with Richard J. Daley, and as conditions deteriorated, media evaluations of his handling of the situation would have impacts on the image of his city and his police force, as well as on his own political legacy.

Street Demonstrations: Convention Week

Demonstrators came to Chicago in large numbers, but not nearly so large as had been predicted by organizers and city officials. Of the 100,000 anticipated, contemporary reports estimated that only about 10,000 had shown up. Police clashed with demonstrators every night of the convention as officers moved through city parks to clear them of demonstrators who were there after closing without permits. On the first three nights of the convention, the main clashes between police and demonstrators occurred in Lincoln Park, where the Yippie festival of life was being held. Reporters were often caught up in these clashes in which demonstrators were Maced, tear-gassed and beaten. Some journalists were also casualties.[12] Many protestors, for their part, provoked the police, perhaps in an effort to demonstrate the repressive nature of the state. On the third night of the convention, after being cleared from Lincoln Park, the demonstrators marched to Grant Park. Across the street was the main convention hotel, the Conrad Hilton, which housed the Humphrey and McCarthy campaigns as well as many delegates and members of the press. The next day, Humphrey would become the nominee. The "ghetto riots"—so anticipated and feared—never materialized.

In the media, the images of both demonstrators and police were transformed following these clashes. The exception to this pattern was *U.S. News and World Report*, which remained staunchly convinced that Chicago police had done what was necessary to preserve order. The demonstrators' image became very complex. While the old image remained, a new image of the protestors developed, in part due to an important link between events inside the Amphitheater and in Grant Park: the campaign of Eugene McCarthy. During the most violent clashes between authorities and dissenters in Grant Park, McCarthy and his staff created a makeshift emergency ward in his campaign headquarters in the Hilton. Reporters in his suites to cover nomination night events photographed his campaign staffers tending the wounded and transfixed by television images of the violence occurring outside their windows. Victims and campaign staff looked very much the same. Later, McCarthy would address some of the demonstrators. In the early morning hours of August 30, Chicago police officers raided McCarthy's convention headquarters.

Another factor promoting a new image of the demonstrators was that reporters themselves were sometimes clubbed, gassed, or both, even—according to reports—after they flashed press credentials. Some reporters claimed that they were targeted by police, especially if they had cameras. This may have made them more likely to be sympathetic to the plight of demonstrators. The results were descriptions like these:

> Pushed up against a wall by a phalanx of cops, a pretty blonde begged for mercy. No one listened. Instead, a group of police prodded her in the stomach with their clubs, sending her to her knees, her face in her hands, screaming: "Please God, help me. Please help me." When a neatly dressed young man tried to help, the police beat him over the head—leaving boy and girl, blood-drenched and whimpering, wrapped in each others' arms. (The battle of Chicago 1968, 24)

> [E]leven policemen swarmed up to the McCarthy headquarters. They claimed that the volunteers had tossed smoked fish, ashtrays and beer cans at the helmeted cops below. With neither evidence nor a search warrant, they clubbed McCarthy campaign workers. One cop actually broke his billy club on a volunteer's skull. (Dementia in the second city 1968, 24)

The image of the police took nearly as bad a beating as the demonstrators had. *Time* and *Newsweek* both interpreted the chaos in Chicago as the product of a collapse of police discipline:

> With billy clubs, tear gas and Mace, the blue-shirted, blue-helmeted cops violated the civil rights of countless innocent citizens and contravened every accepted code of professional police practice. No one could accuse the Chicago cops of discrimination. They savagely attacked hippies, yippies, New Leftists, revolutionaries, dissident Democrats, newsmen, photographers, passers-by, clergymen and at least one cripple. (Dementia in the second city 1968, 21)

> Miraculously, no one was killed by Chicago Mayor Richard Daley's beefy cops, who went on a sustained rampage unprecedented outside the most unreconstructed boondocks of Dixie. "Kill 'em! Kill 'em!" they shouted as they charged the harumscarum mobs of hippies, yippies, peace demonstrators and innocent onlookers in the parks and on the streets outside the convention headquarters hotel....Time and again, the police singled out reporters and photographers for clubbing—attacking more than a score. (The battle of Chicago 1968, 24)

Nevertheless, the preconvention image of demonstrators as troublemakers survived. *Time* and *Newsweek* extended their sympathy to the wounded and the bystanders but noted that some of the demonstrators attacked police and "clearly had come to Chicago to raise hell" (The battle of Chicago 1968, 24). The result was mixed presentations like this: "In some of the wilder fighting, the demonstrators hurled bricks, bottles, and nail-studded golf balls at the police lines. During the first three days, the cops generally reacted only with tear gas and occasional beatings" (Dementia in the second city 1968, 22).

These mixed presentations may account for the public opinion poll results of the time. Despite media reports that police officers had savagely beaten both demonstrators and bystanders, polls consistently found that the majority of the public supported the authorities' actions. Poll results reported in the *New York Times* on August 31, 1968, showed that nearly 57 percent of a national sample did not feel that authorities had used excessive force in containing demonstrations. Opinion remained relatively stable, for a Gallup poll reported in the *Times* on September 18 showed that 56 percent of those surveyed supported the police.[13] However, the fact that the question of police wrongdoing was raised at all may have represented an important step. Even though the idea was rejected, it was now at least considered and dismissed rather than ignored entirely.

Because of the narrative barricades created between events outside the hall and those inside the hall, the protests and the convention are typically reported as if they were entirely separate events. This, of course, was not how the demonstrators saw things at all (Farber 1988), and such constructions failed to point out the similarity of the issues raised in the hall to those of the demonstrations outside it. While the National Guard took part in subduing demonstrators during convention week, security arrangements were associated with the city rather than with the nation. This, too, did not suit the demonstrators since it contained their wider critique of the system within the province of a single city (Farber 1988). The actions of the National Guard during the convention are largely ignored in the media or are lumped in with the actions of the Chicago police, and it is the actions of the latter that are highlighted.

Frames and Blame

While strategy was emphasized over substance inside the convention hall, outside the hall substance was ignored altogether. Actions were detailed; motivations were largely ignored before the convention began and completely ignored as chaos broke out in Chicago. Since media paid little attention to motivations, the struggle to assign meaning to what had happened outside the convention hall became a struggle over images, and the struggle for reputation in Chicago began as the convention ended: Were the Chicago police the heroes or the villains? Were the demonstrators aggressors or victims? Certainly in the aftermath of the convention, there were no unsullied reputations, though some were perceived as more directly culpable than others.

One frame says that violent mobs of demonstrators intent on disrupting the convention descended on Chicago in large numbers. The Chicago police and National Guard took the necessary steps to protect citizens and the convention. A variant on this says that media presence encouraged the demonstrators and/or that media coverage misrepresented the efforts of the police to contain the unrest. Here, the problem is lawlessness, demonstrators are to blame, and the media may be accomplices. Contemporary public opinion polls suggest that this is the version of the story that most Americans accepted in 1968.

An alternative version says that the city conspired to prevent demonstrators from coming to Chicago and that when the demonstrators came, the Chicago police used unnecessary force and arbitrarily enforced laws in order to prevent the demonstrators from expressing their concerns to assembled delegates. To avoid publicizing this violation of citizens' rights, the police also attacked journalists. In this narrative, the problem is police brutality, and police and city officials are to blame.

In the convention hall, a strategy frame so dominated the contemporary coverage that the narrative seems self-contained, finished—a part of the past as soon as the final gavel fell. Speculation about how the violence in the streets would affect the Democrats' chances in November began soon after, but stories of how Humphrey was nominated seemed dated. Nevertheless, memories would eventually emerge of the convention's substance and its effect on the future of American politics. For now, we might simply note that like the narratives associated with the Watts riots, each of the stories told about the Chicago convention had unique framing dimensions.

How do more unified and coherent stories emerge in media? The chapters that follow highlight some of the processes important to the development of collective memories as they appear in the news and then trace the impact of these processes on the memories of the Watts riots and the 1968 Democratic National Convention.

CHAPTER 3

Political Officials
and the Public Past

T HE EVENTS THEMSELVES WERE OVER. The fires were put
out, the last hot spots doused. The Democrats and the demonstrators went home. Humphrey lost the election; the war in
Vietnam went on. But the stories were far from finished. Narratively,
anyway, the chaos would continue for years to come.

Early on, public officials were the most important and prominent
sponsors of stories to account for events in Chicago and Los Angeles.
They had been unable to control the news media's stories about the
Watts riots and the 1968 convention as they occurred—partly because
the breaking news stories overwhelmed their ability to supply meaning
for events, but partly because they disagreed with one another over how
to frame events. They also dominated public discourse immediately
after the events. Both the Watts riots and the Chicago convention
inspired government investigations, public trials, and policy changes.
However, once these official responses to the events had played themselves out, officials' ability to manage the evolution of collective memory began to ebb. This chapter explores how political leaders attempted
to authorize stories of the Watts riots and the Chicago convention
through the actions they took in response to them and how their power
to influence the stories of these event faded over time.

When official action is taken in response to a social breach, Turner (1981) calls it a redressive ritual. These rituals, he says, are attempts to seal the breach before it widens further and to reintegrate parties to the conflict. Redressive rituals are not about restoring order, for most of them take place weeks or months after the original breach occurs. They are instead about assigning meaning to what has happened. Such rituals occupy a space somewhere between the events themselves and memories of those events. They are memorial in the sense that they are retrospective—they look back across what has happened and attempt to give events context and meaning. They can also provide yet more raw material for collective memory in that these redressive rituals in some cases become part of the collective memory that evolves. Many of the redressive rituals undertaken in response to the Watts riots and the Chicago convention were purely symbolic, having the sole purpose of determining "what happened." However, a few rituals involved substantive policy changes that were justified by a particular framing of the events. None of the government responses proved authoritative in establishing the "truth" about what had happened.

Other than these redressive rituals, government officials did not sponsor commemorations of these events. Instead, reporters took their cues from other sources when they turned their attention back to the Watts riots and the convention. Yet this is only one reason that the power of officials to manage memories declined over time. The complex interplay of individuals, institutions, and reputations changed public officials' ability to gain access to the media and their motivations for sponsoring a particular version of events. As research in media and politics has shown, the matrix of sources reporters use to produce stories is crucial to the content of the stories themselves.[1]

Political Rituals of Redress

In the wake of each of these social breaches, government officials enacted a variety of redressive rituals that involved assigning meaning to the events. Some rituals were symbolic. The government-sponsored investigations into each event, for example, produced reports that were intended to be authoritative accounts of what happened. Other rituals had both symbolic and substantive components. The trials held in the wake of the Watts riots and the Chicago convention were attempts to hold individuals accountable for those events, and thus they had the potential substantive effect of punishing people for their behavior. They also supplied meaning for the event, for the trial discourse would supply all the elements of a frame: it would define a problem, identify the agents responsible, evaluate the moral situation, and propose a solution. Finally, the policy changes enacted following both the Chicago convention and the Watts riots were primarily substantive in their intent, but they also supplied meaning for the events. They were presented as solutions to problems, and they directly or indirectly invoked the other elements of a frame as well.

During all of these redressive rituals, the struggle over meaning continued. While the government that sponsors a redressive ritual may have the strongest influence on its content, in most cases it cannot maintain complete control because the reaction of other key stakeholders and the public at large to the ritual is critical to its effectiveness in establishing an accepted version of events. To put it in E. E. Schattschneider's (1975) terms, the government cannot control the scope of the conflict. Following both the Watts riots and the Chicago convention, there were many social actors who had adherents, sympathizers, and access to the media, all of which made them capable of resisting meanings the government might attempt to impose on the events through redressive rituals. Indeed, in both of these cases it is an overstatement to use the term "government" in a monolithic sense. After the Watts riots, the local, state, and federal governments each had their own distinctive take on the meaning of the event, and following the Democratic National Convention, divisions within the Party and between Party leaders and city officials meant that the struggle over meaning continued. None of these rituals proved authoritative in establishing a coherent narrative of the past, but each was influential in its way, and several supplied further raw materials for the collective memories that would later emerge.

Investigation as a Redressive Ritual

In both 1965 and 1968, the government took steps to heal the social breaches by producing a report on the incident. The McCone Commission report (Governor's Commission 1965) was issued in

December, 1965—five months after the Watts riots in August. The Walker report (Walker 1968) appeared in November of 1968, three months after the Democratic National Convention violence, though its publication was delayed when the Congressional Printing Office refused to print the obscenities of demonstrators and police quoted in the report and Walker refused to excise them. The reports took contrasting approaches in their work to establish "what happened," and the results suggest that early attempts to create a definitive story may backfire.

The McCone Commission report consistently built bridges between warring factions, and its authoritative quality was enhanced by the fact that it seems to have been the only official report issued. John McCone was a former head of the CIA and well-known conservative, appointed by the liberal governor of California, Edmund G. ("Pat") Brown. Although the eight-member commission did not include representatives of people who lived in the riot zone, the bipartisan auspices of the report may have helped defuse political cleavages produced by the Watts riots.

Rather than endorsing a single perspective on the divisions represented by the breach, the McCone Commission report considered a variety of factors contributing to the unrest. It gave a nod to the lawlessness perspective but found that the group of rioters was fairly small, alienated from the wider African American community, and mostly from the South. Thus, it cleared the African American community as a whole of wrongdoing. It also more or less cleared the police of wrongdoing but made some recommendations about how to improve policing of the community. However, most of the commission's recommendations addressed economic conditions in South Central Los Angeles—making its views more similar to that of the federal government, which was in the process of implementing massive antipoverty programs, than to those of the state and local officials who had imposed "law and order" to end the violence. The report warned of a rift between black America and white America that, if not addressed, could make Watts a small taste of the civil disturbances to come.

The McCone Commission report can be evaluated as an effective redressive ritual in the sense that it did not contribute to the crisis phase of the social drama. It didn't make things worse, and in listening to "all" sides of the story, it may have helped to reduce tensions. Rather than imposing a perspective on the riots, it performed the literal function of a "hearing:" all of the parties to the dispute had their points of view included in the final report. While the federal government's voice is loudest, no voice is silenced in the McCone Commission report. Further, the report itself represents a coming together. A conservative commissioner appointed by a liberal state official produced a report in which the perspective of the federal government emerges as dominant. Yet the McCone Commission report achieves this success largely by *not* assigning a definitive meaning to the Watts riots. The report reads much as a synopsis of contemporary media coverage might; it preserves the incompatible narratives of its time.

The Walker Report, on the other hand, resolved nothing and in some ways hardened the breach it might have helped to heal. The report was controversial from the first, and not just for containing obscenities. Although Walker's report, like McCone's, embraced many of the available stories about what had happened in Chicago, where McCone's commission had exonerated various social actors, Walker's apportioned blame. It accused both demonstrators and police of misconduct, arguing that while demonstrators had provoked officers, the officers' reaction constituted "a police riot." The report did suggest, though, that it was only a minority of police officers and demonstrators who sought and were responsible for the violent confrontations. The report also criticized city and federal authorities for not accommodating peaceful demonstrations. But the provocative words "police riot" became the most frequently quoted—and perhaps the most memorable—of the Walker report. Even today, the term is almost invariably placed in quotation marks whenever it appears in the media, suggesting that the legitimacy of this conclusion remains in question.[2]

Moreover, where the McCone Commission and its report could be perceived as building bridges between various political actors and institutions—and thus gained authority as a ritual for redressing the breach—the Walker Report could be perceived as a political document rather than an authoritative summary. The National Commission on the Causes and Prevention of Violence (NCCPV), which appointed Walker, was headed by former Illinois governor Otto Kerner. Walker himself had political aspirations, and in 1973 was elected governor of Illinois.

Further undermining the authority of the Walker Report were the wide variety of reports on the Chicago convention violence issued at about the same time. Mayor Richard J. Daley's office issued a report on the violence, which, of course, exonerated the Chicago Police Department. The NCCPV issued a number of reports in 1968 and 1969 that assessed broader aspects of civil unrest, but the timing of their release implied that, in large measure, they spoke to the events in Chicago. The Commission released Walker's report without evaluation, which the *New York Times* suggested might mean that Commission members were divided over the content of the report. Thus, there was a great deal of competition among various government authorities to assign meaning to what had happened, and the media reported the release of these narratives, adding commentary of their own.

Neither of these reports, then, was effective at establishing a meaning for the social breach. The McCone Commission Report did not attempt to construct a coherent narrative of the Watts riots. Instead, it preserved the discrepant stories that had emerged during the riots themselves. The Walker Report did attempt to assign meaning to the Chicago convention violence, but in doing so, it blamed important social actors involved in the breach. The controversy provoked by Walker's report, along with the variety of other reports that also claimed to tell the true story of what had happened in Chicago, only added to the narrative confusion that was already present in contemporary press accounts.

Trials as Redressive Rituals

A trial is a classic form of redressive ritual, responding to the breach by holding some parties accountable and absolving others of guilt. Trials serve some of the functions of hearings. However, they must ultimately adjudicate between the narratives they entertain, and in establishing responsibility for the breach, they also supply meaning for the event. Trials were held in the wake of both the Watts riots and the 1968 convention, but the outcomes in each case were remarkably different. The trials in Los Angeles were more substantive than symbolic. Although they punished individual rioters for crimes, they did not link those crimes to the larger social context in which they occurred. The trial in Chicago was almost entirely symbolic: it tried not those who threw rocks and bottles and resisted arrest, but rather leaders of the major social movements of the 1960s in order to make examples of them.

Hundreds of people were arrested for everything from curfew violations to murder during the Watts riots. Many were subsequently tried, and the courts held special sessions to process the influx. However, these trials never became politically symbolic, nor did they play an important role in supplying meaning to the riots. In general, the brute facts of people's behavior, rather than the social context in which they acted, were at issue in the trials. They were not prominently reported in the news, and their defendants were primarily African American men who lived in South Central Los Angeles, 75 percent of whom already had arrest records (Cohen 1967). It may be that little significance was attached to these trials because the defendants were "typical" targets of law enforcement charged with "typical" crimes, regardless of the extraordinary circumstances that surrounded them.

The trials held in the wake of the Chicago convention, on the other hand, were political trials whose symbolic content was at least as important as their substantive impact (Dee 1990; Scheutz and Snedaker 1988). On March 21, 1969, the *New York Times* reported that a federal grand jury had indicted eight Chicago convention demonstrators for conspiracy to incite riot and eight Chicago police officers: seven for assault and one for perjury. From the beginning, news coverage of the demonstrators' trial was more prominent than that of the police officers, though the potential had always existed for the reverse to occur. For example, on the day that the indictments were handed down, U.S. Attorney Thomas Foran denied that the Justice Department had balanced them "so [the] grand jury will not seem to be blaming police for violence during conv[ention] w[ee]k" (*New York Times Index* 1970, 1340). But on March 22, indicted demonstrator Rennie Davis told the *Times* that he planned to use his trial as a forum to discuss political issues. Seven of the eight police officers were tried and acquitted without incident and went unremembered. Charges against the eighth officer were dropped and forgotten. The Chicago Sixteen had become the Chicago Eight, and they willingly cooperated as the media made them celebrities. They would become the Chicago Seven after Black Panther Bobby Seale's case was severed from that of the others.

Rather than bringing resolution to the events of convention week, the indictment of the Chicago Eight likely expanded the crisis. Contemporary and later commentators recognized the Chicago Eight as representatives of the major social movements of the late 1960s, including groups that had not actually participated in the demonstrations in Chicago. Juliet Dee (1990) notes, "The defendants in the....Chicago Seven trial included representatives of the major antiwar groups, the youth counterculture, the campus protest movement, and the Black Panther party, making the trial a microcosm of the politics of protest against the Vietnam War." While Dee misses the larger scope of the Chicago protests, she captures the idea that the indictments broadened the scope of the crisis by expanding the number of parties involved. It is apparent in both media coverage and later scholarly analysis that these young men became icons representing more groups and incidents than actually occurred in Chicago. To borrow Barbie Zelizer's (1992) terminology, the trial of the Chicago Eight became a synecdoche for the issues of the 1960s.

The indicted eight were tied together also by the crime of which they were accused. They were charged under two separate provisions of the federal antiriot law passed earlier in the year: crossing state lines with the intent to incite riot and conspiracy to cross state lines to incite riot. The conspiracy charge suggested that they were all in it together, despite the fact that Seale had never met the other defendants until the trial (Dee 1990; Ely 1994).

Although the city made a federal case out of the demonstrators' behavior during convention week, the trial was perceived as a local production in many ways. The judge who convened and charged the grand jury was a good friend of Mayor Daley's, and the attorney who prosecuted the case owed his appointment to Daley.

That the trial was to be a pitched battle was indicated early as well. On the opening day of the trial, Judge Julius Hoffman issued bench warrants for the arrest of four defense attorneys who had been involved in pretrial legal work but had sent wires withdrawing from the case. Hoffman declined to recognize their telegraphed notices. Outside the federal building, a thousand demonstrators gathered, and three police officers were injured and four demonstrators arrested in a scuffle. The trial lasted four and a half months, from September 1969 until February 1970. On November 5, 1969, Seale's case was severed after Judge Hoffman declared a mistrial in his case. Seale had been bound and gagged in the courtroom since October 29, at Hoffman's order, for disrupting the proceedings. It is somewhat surprising that he was singled out.

Many analyses of the trial are interesting in the way that they contextualize it. The authors clearly think of the trial as discourse about the political and lifestyle issues of the 1960s rather than about the events in Chicago.[3] In some ways, this is a tribute to the defense team's efforts. Throughout the trial, the defendants and their attorneys tried to raise the issues that had concerned the protestors in Chicago: the Vietnam War, the failings of the political system (including the court system), and the validity of alternative lifestyles (Dee 1990). These issues were broader than the events of convention week, so the trial has come to be analyzed as a microcosm of a much larger series of events. As Janice Schuetz and Kathryn Snedaker (1988) point out, the "crime story" of what happened in Chicago "became less and less relevant as the trial progressed, and the courtroom drama became increasingly significant to the outcome of the case" (223). The broad mandate of this trial was thus unlikely to resolve "what happened" in Chicago.

Dee (1990) finds dramatic differences in the ways that various print media reported the trial. For the mainstream media, two issues were central: the defendants' courtroom behavior and whether the new federal antiriot statute was constitutional. Right-leaning media, such as the *Chicago Tribune*, condemned the demonstrators' behavior in the courtroom. Middle-of-the-road media, such as the *New York Times*, disparaged the behavior of both the judge and the defendants. The defendants were disrespectful, and the judge favored the prosecution. Liberal media, including the *Washington Post*, argued that the judge and prosecutors lacked a sense of humor and were more likely to focus on the Vietnam War, the possibility of a police riot, and other issues raised by the defense. The principle of selective exposure, Dee points out, suggests that audiences would gravitate to media that supported the point of view they already held. The expanding crisis that was playing itself out in the courtroom was spreading through the society via media representations of it.

The verdict in the trial was no help either. The jury, sequestered for five months, deliberated for four days. The judge refused to accept two notices saying they could not reach a verdict. In a compromise verdict, the jury acquitted all the defendants of conspiracy and convicted five of the seven for crossing state lines with the intent to incite riot. The judge toted up the numerous contempt citations against all eight defendants and their attorneys and handed out sentences long enough to stun both the media and the legal community. Both the verdict and the contempt sentences were appealed. In 1972, an appellate court reversed the contempt convictions. Later in the same year, the convictions for violation of the antiriot statute were also reversed. The government decided not to pursue retrial on the substantive violations but did retry the defendants and their attorneys for contempt. In 1973, a judge agreed that the eight and their lawyers were guilty of contempt, but he declined to sentence them to jail terms.[4] The mixed verdict and long appeals process that followed did not establish a narrative for the events of convention week since various courts embraced various stories in the course of reaching their contrasting verdicts. Instead, the variety of verdicts may have continued the spread of blame and division.

The trial of the Chicago Eight failed both as a redressive ritual and as a means of consolidating a narrative of the Chicago convention. In many ways, it expanded and deepened the crisis following the breach that occurred during convention week in Chicago. There may be many reasons for this, but one seems especially important. Trials create winners and losers. The jury, as Scheutz and Snedaker (1988) point out, is asked to choose the most plausible story offered to account for the events. A verdict means that one story has won out over another. The opportunity to blend stories—to create a tale that contains something for everyone—is limited. To compound this problem, the effectiveness of a trial for redressing a social breach or for supplying meaning for one depends in part upon the legitimacy of the institution sponsoring the trial. Yet a serious social breach can call the legitimacy of such institutions into question, and when it does, the inability of elites to control the scope of the conflict (Schattschneider 1975) becomes apparent. When a court's authority can be effectively disputed, its judgment is no judgment at all, and one has to wonder whether any verdict in the Chicago Eight trial would have been accepted by all parties capable of meaningful resistance. Given the state of social crisis, the trial could not supply a definitive narrative of the Chicago convention.

Policy as a Redressive Ritual

At first glance, policy making and meaning making may seem like separate processes, but the literature on the construction of social problems illustrates that they are, in fact, intimately linked. Malcom

Spector and John Kitsuse (2001) observed that social problems are not discovered "in nature," as it were, but are instead created through discursive processes that define the scope and features of the problem and, crucially, make the case that the problem is created by or can be affected by human action. Because policies respond to "social problems," they contain implied narratives that retrospectively define the problem and identify the agents responsible for it. Narrative theory describes a related phenomenon, "retrodiction" (Martin 1986). In contrast to making predictions about where a story might go, readers of narrative use later elements of the narrative to make sense of earlier events. The way a story turns out tells the reader how to interpret elements he or she encountered along the way.

If we imagine people, including reporters, assigning to real events the coherence of a story, the power of outcomes to influence meaning becomes apparent. Both the Watts riots and the Chicago convention were followed by policy changes that seemed connected to the events that had occurred and thus had the potential to endow those events with meaning, even though this almost certainly was not the primary intent of those who promulgated the policies. For policy makers, the events justified the policies, instead of the policies giving meaning to the events.

Federal antipoverty programs were in place before the Watts riots began, but almost immediately after the Watts riots, the torrent of social programs that came to be known as the Great Society, or the War on Poverty, was activated. These programs were not really a response to the Watts riots, since they had been planned and approved before the riots began. They became intimately linked with the riots by temporal proximity and narrative connections. The Watts riots seemed to demonstrate the necessity of the Great Society programs, and the Great Society programs seemed to be a constructive response to the riots. The programs fostered the economic deprivation narrative of the Watts riots, suggesting that the ultimate source of the problem was urban poverty and that by eliminating the poverty, one would eliminate "the conditions that make riots" (After the blood bath 1965, 14).

Los Angeles became part of the Model Cities Program, and all sorts of social programs were initiated in the neighborhoods where the riots had occurred. Construction began on a local hospital, for residents of Watts had to travel for hours to obtain medical care. Jobs programs began. A factory opened, making baseball bats called "Watts Wallopers." More substantially, Lockheed opened a plant in South Central Los Angeles and hired locally. Arts programs began as well— writing workshops and theaters were funded.

Like the trial of the Chicago Seven, these programs had the potential to expand rather than narrow the breach. Even as the trial of Chicago Seven created defendants who stood in for the national discord of the time, the Great Society programs might have indirectly elevated the Watts riots to symbolic status, deepening the crisis as the divisions it represented spread. The Great Society turned government and public attention from the struggle for legal equality that had dominated the civil rights agenda in the South to the economic disparities between races. The programs constructed urban poverty, and urban minority poverty, as a national problem. That such problems still haunt our society is one indicator of the divisive potential of the social breach in Los Angeles. However, media coverage suggests that the Watts riots remained localized. In the *Los Angeles Times*, national parallels do not interrupt the story of revitalization in Watts. The story is handled as local. In the *New York Times*, the national story of the Great Society is the focus of the tale, and the Watts revitalization is an example in a broader story. To call it an icon (Bennett and Lawrence 1995) would be to overemphasize its centrality in these tales.

The power of the policy as a framing device becomes apparent once the Great Society had been declared a failure. In 1975, the *Los Angeles Times* produced a special anniversary section on the Watts riots that was more a critique of the Great Society than a commemoration of the riots. The *Times* concluded that the War on Poverty had generally been a flop and that there was considerable evidence that given the weaker economy in 1975, conditions in Watts were actually worse than they had been when the riots broke out (Kendall 1975). Although questions were raised about whether perceived failure was due to unreasonable expectations, a point made in some of the letters to the editor responding to the special section,[5] no one suggested a different approach altogether (such as a focus on police reform). Questions were raised about the best solution to the "problem" in Watts, but the definition of the problem (economic and social deprivation) was undoubted (Kendall 1975; Jones 1975).

The economic deprivation story fared well in the development of collective memory of the Watts riots for a variety of reasons, but the impact of the Great Society programs on the story of the Watts riots suggests that the government can have considerable power to frame an event over the long term through the actions it takes in response to it. Most studies of framing have examined the government's attempt to frame an event as it happens or in its immediate aftermath.[6] Alternatively, they have explored the government's ability to manage media coverage of an issue of long standing[7] or how government attempts to define social problems in ways that warrant its desired policies [8] The limited abilities of government investigations such as the McCone Commission Report and the Walker Report to establish meanings for controversial events suggests that the active attempts at framing described in these studies do not work well in the wake of social unrest. Policy, on the other hand, works indirectly: the solution defines the problem. The response to the violence in Watts was social welfare programs, so the cause of the Watts riots must have been poor social and economic conditions. By taking action, the government supplied meaning for the event, and the meaning survived even after the actions were perceived as failures. That the framing power of the War on Poverty programs outlasted the programs themselves suggest that frames are hierarchical in nature, with problem definition forming a relatively unassailable foundation.

In the wake of the Chicago convention, it was not the federal government but the Democratic Party that implemented policy changes in response to the event. In April 1970, the McGovern Commission issued its report advising an overhaul of the Party's delegate selection system. Although this may seem a somewhat off-point response to anti-war protests, in fact, it captures much of the protesters' broader critique. The Vietnam War was a major political issue in 1968, but the presidential race offered voters no real choice on the issue. Both Nixon and Humphrey were considered hawks. Dove Democratic candidates who had earned significant public backing running in primaries were in the end defeated by a candidate who had run in none. Supporters of one of those candidates, Eugene McCarthy, had become involved in the demonstrations in Chicago, and McCarthy's campaign headquarters provided refuge to demonstrators as the violence escalated.

Unlike the investigative reports issued by Walker and McCone, the McGovern Commission report contained concrete reform proposals that, according to McGovern, were mandatory for state party organizations. State Democratic organizations complied. Critics of the modern primary system have virtually nothing kind to say about the McGovern Commission reforms, and in many ways the changes failed to achieve their aims. Still, the specific goals the commission laid out were responsive to the perceived causes of the disorder in the convention hall if not to the protests in the streets. The commission sought to build a delegate selection system that would enhance the roles of women, minorities, and young people at the convention. Further, the commission sought to create procedures more responsive to average citizens, letting their concerns, as well as the Party's, emerge in the nominating process.

The long-term problems of the McGovern Commission reforms were not apparent in 1970, but the report was unsuccessful in supplying meaning for the 1968 convention for another reason. Issued almost two years after the breach and not fully implemented until 1972, like the Chicago Seven trial, it came too late to have much influence on a spreading crisis. Another reason for the failure of the McGovern Commission report is the way that politics are reported in the U.S. media. As numerous scholars have pointed out,[9] media reporting on the political system focuses on strategy rather than substance. Rather than considering the democratic potential (or lack thereof) of the McGovern Commission reforms, the media tended to ignore the report (it was, after all, issued in the "off-season"). When they at last reported on the changes, journalists evaluated the reforms in terms of their potential strategic advantages and disadvantages for various candidates.

The unrest at the Chicago convention seemed to be something no one actually did anything about. The war continued, the election went off despite the lack of meaningful choice, the Chicago Seven were acquitted, and Mayor Daley was re-elected. The narrative potential of the McGovern Commission reforms, regardless of whether they were a meaningful response to the true causes of the breach, were never a real factor in assigning meaning to the breach and crisis in Chicago.

Officials, News, and Memory

Redressive rituals are officially sponsored events, and as such, they draw media coverage that political officials can manage, if not control. However, once the official redressive rituals are over, the news media's remembrance of these social conflicts is not typically cued by official events. This reduces the power of political officials to manage public remembering for several reasons. First, once there are no more "events" to cover, reporters' practices for gathering news change. Events, like the Watts riots and the Chicago convention, are typically covered as "hard news." Hard news stories focus on what happened, taking their most classic form in the coverage of "spot news," specific events relayed in the absence of much context. These are the stories that relate the who, what, when, where, and why. The Watts riots qualified as "breaking news" in their own time. "Breaking news" involves telling stories about "unexpected" events, though often these events are anticipated by news routines such as monitoring police scanners. While the events inside the convention hall had some "breaking news" qualities, many aspects of the convention could be covered as a "media event," a pre-arranged event that is staged for the news media in order to generate coverage. The street demonstrations in Chicago have a similarly mixed quality in that they were intended in part to garner media attention but also took unexpected turns.

Although political leaders' abilities to control the representation of breaking news, or unexpected events, is more limited than their ability to manage routine news (Molotch and Lester 1974; Lawrence 2000), hard news stories are often dominated by elite voices for a variety of reasons. First, the surveillance routines that turn up spot or breaking news are often centered around official activities, such as police patrols (Tuchman 1972). Second, because the news media are oriented to monitoring official activities, elite-sponsored media events are more likely to be covered. Third, officials and other elites often have more resources to subsidize information for reporters (Gandy 1982). Subsidizing hard news coverage can include hosting media events, having dedicated professionals available to answer reporters' questions about spot or breaking news, and gathering information about events reporters were unable to witness for themselves. Fourth, hard news is valued to the extent that it is timely. Deadline pressures make it difficult for reporters to seek alternative voices and perspectives to counter those of officials. Early news reports of the Watts riots and the Chicago convention are indeed dominated by official voices.

Eventually, however, the news moves on. No longer a "breaking story" or the target of official actions, the past may fade from the hard news pages and make its way to the back pages and sections of the newspaper, where a different storytelling paradigm prevails. The chief alternative to "hard news" is "soft news" or "features." Most news—indeed, most media content—revolves around the lives and activities of the social elite, but for a variety of reasons, political leaders have more limited influence on feature news than they do on hard news. Feature stories are not typically driven by events (although they are sometimes planned to coincide with significant dates such as the release of a film or the anniversary of an event), so they are less tied to the activities of officials. Moreover, reporters producing features do not face the kinds of deadline pressures that hard-news reporters face. They have time to contact unofficial, sometimes hard-to-find, sources about issues that officials have no particular interest in managing. All of this means that feature stories can be less influenced by official perspectives than hard news typically is and that alternative voices may influence the development of stories about the past.

A second reason that officials begin to lose control over the ways the past is represented has to do with the dynamics of their identities. Typical studies of the relationship between reporters and officials equate those officials with the positions they hold because they analyze reporting on events as they happen. When time is introduced as a variable, complex relationships emerge between the office and the individual who holds it. Reporters turn to officials as sources for a variety of reasons, but with the passage of time, the reasons for using an official as a source change.

Frequently, reporters are not direct witnesses to events. Since one of the traditional functions of news is surveillance of the social world, this is an important problem that reporters often solve by using official accounts of events. During the Watts riots, white reporters could not get into the riot zone without incurring great personal risk, and many relied on police and fire department reports. Eyewitness accounts from nonofficial sources are harder to acquire as an event is occurring. Nonofficial eyewitnesses can be more difficult to locate than officials are, and their accounts do not synthesize events as official reports and briefings do, so the information they offer is more difficult to process on a tight deadline. As that deadline pressure eases, interviewing citizen eyewitnesses becomes more feasible. Moreover, institutional eyewitnesses who provided "authoritative" information lose the institutional positions that gave them their authority. Retired officers may not have any more authoritative status (or be any easier for reporters to find) than community residents.

Even where reporters are direct witnesses to events, they often turn to experts, officials, and fellow eyewitnesses in their reporting. The Chicago convention offered more opportunities for reporters to witness events for themselves than the Watts riots did, but the traditions of political reporting, crime reporting, and, later, court reporting still ensured that official voices were prominent in the initial coverage of the convention melee. Robert Entman and Benjamin Page (1994) argue that reporters covering a developing story are drawn to sources who have the power to affect the outcome of those events. Political soothsayers who could predict the impact of the convention on Humphrey's chances in the fall and police officials who could explain how the city would handle the growing unrest in the streets would be attractive during convention week, but such sources would lose their allure once the events themselves were over.

Finally, as time passes, distinctions emerge between political institutions and political office holders. In some cases, people retain their status as authorities in the media even after they leave the institutional positions that gave them official authority. In other cases, access to the media is dependent on holding an office. When the office is lost, the access is lost. Moreover, in some cases, the reputation of the officeholder is tied to an event. In others, it is the reputation of the institution itself that is implicated, giving any person who leads the institution both access to the news and a motive for attempting to shape collective memory of the event. In some instances, part of the struggle over collective memory involves wrangling over whether the institution or the individual was the key to how the past played itself out.

These distinctions between individuals and institutions and between having and losing access to media matter because stories with sponsors tend to survive in the collective memory process while those that lose sponsorship disappear relatively quickly. However one looks at it, reporters need sources for their stories. From the perspective of objectivity, it is unseemly for reporters to intrude in the stories they report. The "mirror metaphor" of reporting may have been long since debunked and many reporters, especially television reporters, may now be recognizable celebrities, but the idea that "reporting" the news is different from "making" the news remains. Even interpretive journalism, which has reduced the voices of sources to short sound bites, continues to rely on those abbreviated comments as a starting point for the interpretations that surround it. Journalists still turn to sources for raw material.

Collective memories of the Watts riots and the Chicago convention evolve quite differently in large part because the sources used by journalists to construct narratives of the past were quite different. The Watts riots was linked to the leadership of individuals rather than the conduct of institutions, while the 1968 convention became caught up in institutional reputations and the dynastic local politics of Chicago.

The Watts Riots

In the years immediately following the Watts riots, officials of the city of Los Angeles retained a vested interest in how the event was remembered. In 1966, Los Angeles Mayor Sam Yorty ran for re-election with a law-and-order campaign and won. Ronald Reagan was elected governor of California using similar campaign rhetoric. By 1973, however, things had changed. Tom Bradley, an African American, was elected mayor by a coalition that included African Americans and Jews. As most mayors do, he replaced most city officials who had served during the Watts riots with his own staff. The new mayor's office had little to gain from promoting a law-and-order story of the Watts riots since they could not take credit for restoring order. With Chief Parker gone as well, everyone who had a direct stake in promoting a lawlessness interpretation of the Watts riots was gone from public office, their access to the media reduced or cut off altogether. The lawlessness story disappeared just as quickly: by 1975, almost no trace of it remained.

Rather than linking the LAPD's institutional culture to the riots, the Department made Police Chief William Parker a symbol of its conduct prior to and during the Watts riots. Parker retired almost immediately after the riots and died a year later, and so had no further opportunities to defend his reputation. By 1975, Parker was described as "a focal point of black criticism" (Kendall 1975, 8). His "monkeys in a zoo" comment had become emblematic of his handling of the riots, and in the retrospective published in the *Los Angeles Times* that year, at least one expert attributed positive changes in police-community relations to the former chief's passing (Kendall 1975). Obviously, this association of Chief Parker with the Watts riots did not completely destroy his reputation—the police headquarters building in Los Angeles is named for him. Still, linking the riots to Parker's leadership rather than to the department itself helped the LAPD to associate the riots with the "bad old days" that, by 1975, were over. Several passages in the 1975 *Los Angeles Times* retrospective on the Watts riots illustrate the way the past was demarcated from the present:

> I see an interest and courtesy on the surface by officers. I see a degree of empathy probably for the first time in my 19 years....But at least they're demonstrating a commitment to the citizen and that's the first real commitment I've seen in 19 years between the citizen and the policeman.[10]

> We've tried to change the image of the policeman in the community and I would say that even despite this there are a lot of things still going on.[11]

This acknowledgment that the department had once been troubled and was now on the mend was a far cry from the heroic language of Cohen and Murphy in 1966. Yet the idea that the problems were safely in the past was crucial to the LAPD's willingness to admit them. Had the riots been associated with current leadership or current institutional practices, it is most unlikely that the department would have sanctioned such comments by its officers.

The LAPD's success in appearing to put its past behind it made it less important for the department to deny the police brutality story of the Watts riots. Indeed, the quotes above indirectly acknowledge a connection between poor police-community relations and the Watts riots, elicited as they are in the context of a retrospective on the riots. In scapegoating Parker, the LAPD had put its past behind it.

As time passed, eyewitnesses to the Watts riots became more valued sources, acquiring an authority by virtue of having "been there"[12] that rivaled that of academic experts and historians. Often, too, their authority rivals that of former officials, perhaps because the officials no longer have the power to determine the outcome of the event,[13] perhaps because the officials were now nearly as difficult to locate as the eyewitnesses.

Witnessing the Watts riots served as a credential mainly for those who had no other claim to legitimacy as a source of information. For example, Los Angeles Police Chief Darryl Gates was an officer in the city during the Watts riots and Mayor Tom Bradley instituted many of the key rebuilding programs that followed them, but neither man is very prominent in the stories mentioning the Watts riots. Where they do appear, it is their status as city officials rather than their status as eyewitnesses to the Watts riots that gives them authority to speak in the news. The exception to this general tendency was Warren M. Christopher, a Deputy Attorney General during the Johnson administration who had also headed a commission that investigated the Rodney King beating. His 1960s credentials were frequently mentioned in the stories that touched on the Watts riots.

While the Watts riots thus served as a vehicle to give nontraditional speakers access to the debate over events in Los Angeles, these speakers tended to be recognized only briefly. They did not become regular commentators. Nevertheless, they did have some power as commentators. Michael Frisch (1986) observes that the types of sources that journalists employ are not as important as what those sources are allowed to comment on. For example, he notes that reporters interviewed combat veterans to produce a documentary about the Vietnam War, but the veterans were only quoted about their personal experiences in Vietnam. Academic experts and government officials were the sources of interpretation about the "meaning" of the war in terms of American and world politics and of American culture. For the Watts riots, a different pattern emerges. Local residents build upon their personal experiences to explain what the riots were about. Alice Harris ("Sweet Alice") was a long time community activist who also looted stores during the 1965 riots. She explains that they did not think of it as stealing: "'We weren't criminals. We were just family folk. We knew it was going to burn anyway, so why not get what we could?'" "She was a looter, but that was less like stealing and more like reclaiming what was hers," the reporter explains, going on to quote Harris's views on how people in Watts were taken advantage of (Banks 1985, 1). In this excerpt, Harris is given the power to interpret her own experiences and, in doing so, she supports an economic deprivation story of the Watts riots. Of course, the reporter structures the questions to which Harris responds and chooses which parts of her interview with Harris will appear in the story, but she does not limit Harris's voice to simple description of what she experienced during the 1965 civil unrest. The reporter also validates Harris's perspective with her own authorial voice.

Being an eyewitness to the Watts riots could also credential speakers to comment on the more recent urban unrest in 1992. A *New York Times* story, for example, chronicled a community organizer's struggle to rebuild after the 1992 civil disturbances. The story was headed "Watts Organizer Feels Weight of Riots, and History," and in it, organizer Ted Watkins and his daughter trace the history of the community after the Watts riots for the reporter and her readers. The reporter also quotes Watkins's analysis of the 1992 unrest: "'This riot was much deeper, and more dangerous....More ethnic groups were involved'" (Rimer 1992, A12).

In general, then, because the Watts riots were associated with individuals rather than institutions, the power of public officials to influence the emerging collective memory declined rather rapidly. Officials who had an interest in shaping memory disappeared from public life, while those who replaced them had little or no interest in managing memories at all. Meanwhile, the relative authority of eyewitnesses to the event grew substantially. These transformations had their greatest effect on the lawlessness story. Though it dominated media coverage at the time of the riots, it did not survive for long because those who sponsored it did not.

The Chicago Convention

Unlike Los Angeles Mayor Sam Yorty, who left public life eight years after the Watts riots, Chicago Mayor Richard J. Daley continued to be re-elected mayor of Chicago until he died in office in 1976. His reputation continued to be associated with the 1968 convention in a variety of ways. For example, his "shoot to kill" order following the King assassination continued to be widely quoted in stories referring to the convention. In 1989, his son, Richard M. Daley became mayor of Chicago. The younger Daley had attended the 1968 convention with his father and in 1996 would host the Democrats' return to Chicago, the first major party convention to be held in the city in twenty-eight years.

The dynastic local politics of Chicago were only one reason that the mayor's influence persisted in collective memories of the 1968 convention. The reputation of the city also became bound up with the 1968 convention. A travelogue published in the *New York Times*, for example, informed readers: "Chicago politics came into searing national focus as television cameras transmitted the violent confrontation that took place..." (Kennedy 1985, 16). *Chicago Tribune* columnist Mike Royko put it on a list of "municipal tragedies:" "To hear them tell it, as a municipal tragedy, the Cubs' losses eclipse the Chicago Fire, the Capone era and the 1968 Democratic Convention" (Royko 1994, 3). The second mayor Daley had an interest in preserving the reputation of his father and restoring the reputation of his city, and he had continuing access to the media to advocate for his preferred version of events or to resist the narratives sponsored by others. Although not directly sponsored by the Daley administration, stories that describe the protestors as instigating the 1968 convention disturbances and the police as restoring order survive for much longer in the *Chicago Tribune* than they do elsewhere. At the same time, stories that Daley sponsored in an attempt to integrate convention memories would be looked on with suspicion because of his vested interest in how the event was remembered.

Not only were the reputations of the mayor's office and the city of Chicago implicated by the convention, but evidence also shows that over the long term, the convention became associated with the reputation of the Democratic Party as well. Conventional wisdom says that over the short term, the 1968 convention debacle was damaging to Humphrey's reputation and to his campaign, but the damage seemed to continue. Indeed, for a time in the early 1980s, it began to appear that the 1968 convention would be constructed as emblematic of all Democratic conventions. During the primary seasons of 1980 and 1984, reporters regularly referred to the convention as the ultimate expression of Democratic disunity that was being repeated during the current election cycle. Further, while the McGovern commission reforms were never described as responsive to the issues raised at the convention, they were linked to the convention by temporal proximity, as in this headline: "Democratic Party 'reforms' since 1968;" (Wicker 1992, 34). When the new system produced losing Democratic candidates, the current loss could be connected to their loss in 1968 as if no time had passed at all.

Because the Party itself was implicated in stories of the 1968 convention, changes in the leadership of the Party made no difference to its interest in the story. As political elites, Party representatives had access to the news, and could resist (or potentially resist) stories that had pleasing narrative qualities but did further damage to the Party's reputation. Most importantly, the Party could resist stories that linked the strife inside the convention hall to the violence outside it. The usual form of such a story was that the discord within the party was expressed and amplified in the streets. For example, the *Chicago Tribune* referred to "a party torn to pieces by the Vietnam War and a convention that mutated into a street riot" (Madigan 1988, 1). Such a story is plausible, given the similarity of the issues discussed in the Amphitheater and protested in the parks and streets of Chicago. It offers an image—aesthetically appealing from a narrative point of view—of an island of (largely) symbolic conflict surrounded by a sea of physical violence, and it unites the disparate stories of events inside and outside the hall. But for obvious reasons, even those Party leaders who rose to positions of authority long after the 1968 convention had an interest in resisting the connection. Democratic Party officials themselves did not often weigh in on the 1968 convention in the years prior to their 1996 return to Chicago, but when they did during the 1996 meeting, they were united behind a story that had less aesthetic appeal but presented fewer image problems for them.

While political leaders typically acquire access to the news as a result of their institutional authority, social movement members typically gain access for a different reason. Todd Gitlin (1980) described some of the people selected by reporters as spokesmen for the political activists of the late 1960s as leaders without followers because they were chosen for their media savvy rather than because they represented their groups. In other words, they were celebrities, and their status as celebrities did not fade when the organizations they supposedly led deteriorated. The doings of the Chicago Eight remained "newsworthy" more than twenty-five years after their first trial ended.

Over the years, the media reported the apparent taming of the Chicago Eight. In 1974, the *New York Times* reported that John Froines had become the Director of Occupational Health for the state of Vermont. The appointment became an issue in the state's gubernatorial race, for many conservative citizens and officials objected to it. In 1978, Froine's appointment as director of the Office of Toxic Substances was reported. In 1977, the *Times* reported that Rennie Davis now sold insurance in Denver. In 1983, Bobby Seale made headlines with the publication of a barbecue cookbook. Abbie Hoffman, on the other hand, went underground, was arrested on drug charges, and hosted a radio show, among other things. His association with the Chicago Eight was regularly revived in the stories of these events. It was also a key element in his obituary, as it was in Jerry Rubin's. These men were newsworthy because of their association with the 1968 convention, so their activities were news pegs that prompted recollections of their trial.

Tom Hayden's story is a bit different. He ran for and won a seat in the California State Assembly and married Jane Fonda. Like most of the other members of the Chicago Eight, he appeared to have "mellowed" over the years, but he also lived down his activist celebrity in ways that the others did not. Hayden's media coverage did not necessarily entail remembrances of the Chicago Eight. One way to document this is by examining the *New York Times Index*. Unlike his codefendants, Hayden would come to have his own subject heading while the others continued to have reports of their activities filed under standard headings for the convention or for the trial. His newsworthiness derived from his institutional position (and his wife's celebrity) in addition to his celebrity as a 1960s activist.

Although the Chicago Eight's continuing exploits offered opportunities to revisit the past, none but Hayden was ever permitted to narrate that past. Their later activities were rather an opportunity for journalists to retell the story of Chicago '68. It is hard to say how their contributions might have affected developing memories. Perhaps, as they mellowed, they would have searched for stories that both preserved their perspective and at the same time were accepted by other groups who had participated in convention week. Perhaps they would have ignited continuing controversy as they sought to preserve their legacy, their celebrity, or both. Yet their continuing presence in the news also had the potential to keep alive the narratives of convention week they represented.

While eyewitnesses also testify to what they saw in Chicago during convention week, they almost always have some other authoritative credential that subsumes their eyewitness status: Eugene McCarthy, Tom Hayden, Richard M. Daley, and a variety of reporters all describe what they remember, but none is dependent solely on their eyewitness status. Further, the presence of so many journalists in Chicago during the convention expands the scope of eyewitnesses, making them much easier to find a quarter century later, unlike the Watts eyewitnesses whose value was likely increased by their rarity.

Unlike Los Angeles, where representatives of alternative points of view faded from the public scene, in Chicago, important political actors with a stake in how convention week was remembered retained their access to media and their divergent points of view. Given this state of affairs, it is unsurprising that a shared memory of the 1968 convention is much slower to develop and even a generation later was much more uneasy and unstable than the collective memory of the Watts riots.

Conclusion

The power of the government to give meaning to events continues even after order has been restored. Investigations, trials, and policy initiatives can all influence the developing meaning of the past. Although in both of these cases, the power of the government to impose a meaning on the past proved to be quite limited, it may be possible to say something about the characteristics of effective and ineffective redressive rituals when it comes to generating a meaning for the past.

Authority would appear to be key. The Walker Report was just one more in a litany of reports that offered a variety of reasons and solutions for urban unrest, whereas the McCone Commission Report could claim to be the "official" story of the Watts riots. The Chicago Seven trial depended on the legitimacy of the judicial system in the person of Judge Hoffman, but that legitimacy was undermined by both the judge's conduct of the trial and the perception that the men on trial were scapegoats. Without authority, redressive rituals may be able to generate meanings, but they cannot establish meaning. However, the McCone

Commission Report maintains its authority in part by entertaining a variety of narratives, so the relationship between authority and the ability to invest events with meaning is complex.

Timeliness also seems important. The Great Society programs appeared as a swift response to the Watts riots, so even though they were not created because of the riots, they became narratively entangled with the event in ways that promoted the economic deprivation story of the riots. In contrast, the McGovern Commission reforms took effect so long after the convention that they seemed not to be connected to it at all. The long appeals process and complex verdicts in the Chicago Seven trial meant that there was no resolution to the ritual until five years after the convention. Rather than establishing a story of the Chicago demonstrations, in many ways, it had the effect of muddying the meaning of the event.

Further, there are instructive differences between the Chicago Seven trial and the War on Poverty, and to a lesser extent between the McCone Commission Report and the Walker report, in terms of their orientation to the past. The War on Poverty is a forward-looking redressive ritual. Its practical and rhetorical energies are expended on preventing future outbreaks of urban violence in Los Angeles and elsewhere. Whether or not it would or could achieve this goal is a separate issue from its intent. The trial of the Chicago Seven, on the other hand, is a backward-looking redressive ritual. Its energies are expended on exacting retribution for past crimes. Similarly, the McCone Commission Report speaks of ameliorating "the conditions that make riots" while the Walker Report works to apportion blame fairly. The fact that the War on Poverty proved to be the more effective ritual may be somewhat counterintuitive, since its forward-looking orientation appears to imply that the crisis is likely to continue. The Chicago Seven trial, on the other hand, looks like an attempt to supply closure to an event that has already occurred. However, in these cases, the focus on prevention gave the parties to the breach a reason to come together, while the focus on blame emphasized the wedge between parties and actually fed the crisis.

The War on Poverty and the Chicago Seven trial also differed in the types of synecdoches they constructed. Zelizer (1992) has described the role of synecdoches in the creation of collective memory. She analyzes how specific elements of John F. Kennedy's assassination in 1963 have come to stand in for the whole of the event. Other scholars, too, have described simplification as an important part of the process of both social and individual remembering.[14] The Chicago Seven trial created a synecdoche in which the part stands in for the whole. The men on trial were held accountable not only for the events in Chicago but for broader social trends that many found disturbing. Indeed, the specific events of the Chicago convention were almost entirely ignored by the defendants and the media. In the short term, this served to expand the scope of the conflict (Schattschneider 1975) and the crisis (Turner 1981). The War on Poverty created a synecdoche in which the whole stands in for the parts. Specific incidents of urban unrest were subsumed by the wider crusade to end poverty. The evidence both in this section and in later chapters of this study suggests that synecdoches in which specific actions, events, and grievances are subsumed by a more generalized story tend to lend themselves to collective memories.

These redressive rituals, regardless of their effectiveness, are a kind of last hurrah of official power to define the past. Over time, the ability of government to dominate the process of collective memory development wanes. As the relative power of the government declines—in part because its information subsidies become less critical to telling the story and in part because officials lose interest in promoting a particular narrative—other groups become more powerful. In the end, it is the sheer endurance of long-time local residents that provides them with some narrative authority to tell their own stories of the past. Their credentials as eyewitnesses to the past become more persuasive over time as they become rarer.

A complicating factor enters this relatively neat explanation of the relationship of sources to stories in the connections that exist between individuals and institutions. Some commentators on current events draw their authority from their social location. The chief of police is an expert commentator because he is the chief of police. The mayor's office confers authority on the person who occupies it. Other commentators' authority is based upon their personal identity—that is, their celebrity or reputation. Henry Kissinger continues to be perceived as an expert on foreign affairs though he is no longer secretary of state.

In Los Angeles, the relationships between individuals and institutions conspire to encourage the demise of certain stories about the past. To the extent that the riots are associated with particular individuals rather than with the reputations of institutions, the turnover in city government contributes to the perceived irrelevance of some stories. The reputation of the city is not at stake, so the lawlessness story fades with the end of the Yorty regime and the arrival of Tom Bradley. The police brutality story becomes strongly linked not with the Los Angeles Police Department as a whole but with the reputation of Chief William Parker through the repetition of the "monkeys in a zoo" comment. Parker's retirement and death served to cool some of the passions that surrounded the police brutality story. The LAPD could claim that it was now a "new" force, acknowledging and defusing the police brutality story.

In Chicago, on the other hand, the relationship between people and organizations conspired to preserve animosities. It was not the people but the institutions that were implicated in many of the stories that were told. The reputation of Richard Daley and that of his city were powerfully linked in the stories that were told; the connection was perpetuated with the election of his son as mayor. It is critical to note here that the perception of a connection between the Daleys and the expectation that the son would wish to protect his father's reputation was as important as any action on Richard M. Daley's part to shore up his father's legacy. The Chicago Eight, for their part, were celebrities whose activities continued to be reported along with their "Chicago connections." Since the sponsoring sources remained prominent, the stories with which the were associated were likely to remain prominent as well, though reports on the activities of the Chicago Eight continued to neglect their interpretation of what had happened during the convention.

At the same time that these sources sought to tell their stories of the past and the practices of reporters chained their stories into news, other narrative and cultural forces affected the developing collective memory.

CHAPTER 4

Defusing Controversy and Paving the Way for Collective Memory

I T MAY SEEM COUNTERINTUITIVE TO think of a meaning for the
past evolving in journalistic media, since news is supposed to
answer the question, "What's new?" However, recent research has
reveled that news media increasingly turned to the past over the course
of the last century (Barnhurst and Mutz 1997). Where late nineteenth-
and early twentieth-century news reports tended to be bare-bones
descriptions of events (Barnhurst and Mutz), modern news reporting
has taken a more interpretive turn (Schudson 1978; Hallin 1992;
Patterson 1993) and tends to place events in the context of larger issues
and previous events (Barnhurst and Mutz). But how often does a specific past come up in news reports? In the two cases examined in this
study, the answer turns out to be very often indeed.

Tables 4.1 and 4.2 show the results of a keyword search of the *New
York Times* and the relevant regional daily newspaper for each of the
social breaches examined in this study. The most remarkable feature of
these tables is the sheer number of references to each of these events
made in the papers. The *Chicago Tribune* mentions the infamous convention an average of more than three times per month, even if we
delete the year that the Democrats returned to Chicago to renominate
Bill Clinton. The *New York Times* refers to the convention about three

Table 4.1: Number of Stories Referring to the Watts Riots by Year

Search term: "Watts" within 50 words of "1965"

New York Times (N=86)

YEAR	NO. OF STORIES
1980	4
1981	5
1982	6
1983	0
1984	8
1985	3
1986	3
1987	2
1988	2
1989	5
1990	3
1991	5
1992	40*

*2 pre-riot references

Los Angeles Times (N=431)

YEAR	NO. OF STORIES
1985	25
Jan–Mar	7
Apr–Jun	8
Jul–Sept	8
Oct–Dec	6
1986	16
Jan–Mar	3
Apr–Jun	5
Jul–Sept	4
Oct–Dec	4
1987	26
Jan–Mar	3

Los Angeles Times (N=431)	YEAR	NO. OF STORIES
	Apr–Jun	6
	Jul–Sept	11
	Oct–Dec	6
	1988	29
	Jan–Mar	4
	Apr–Jun	8
	Jul–Sept	10
	Oct–Dec	7
	1989	25
	Jan–Mar	5
	Apr–Jun	8
	Jul–Sept	7
	Oct–Dec	5
	1990	54
	Jan–Mar	9
	Apr–Jun	14
	Jul–Sept	24
	Oct–Dec	7
	1991	47
	Jan–Mar	11
	Apr–Jun	7
	Jul–Sept	16
	Oct–Dec	13
	1992	205
	Jan–Mar	7
	Apr–Jun	137**
	Jul–Sept	35
	Oct–Dec	26

**4 pre-riot references

Table 4.2: Number of Stories Referring to the 1968 Democratic Convention by Year

Search term: "Convention" and variations of "Democrat" within 50 words of "1968"

New York Times (N=373)	YEAR	NO. OF STORIES
	1980	31
	1981	14
	1982	16
	1983	19
	1984	30
	1985	12
	1986	16
	1987	25
	1988	36
	1989	17
	1990	8
	1991	15
	1992	28
	1993	16
	1994	22
	1995	16
	1996	51

Chicago Tribune (N=666)	YEAR	NO. OF STORIES
	1985	30
	1986	31
	1987	40
	1988	69
	Jan–Mar	3
	Apr–Jun	15
	Jul–Sept	41
	Oct–Dec	10

Chicago Tribune (N=666)	YEAR	NO. OF STORIES
	1989	44
	Jan–Mar	8
	Apr–Jun	19
	Jul–Sept	10
	Oct–Dec	7
	1990	32
	1991	26
	1992	36
	1993	39
	Jan–Mar	8
	Apr–Jun	9
	Jul–Sept	12
	Oct–Dec	10
	1994	56
	Jan–Mar	11
	Apr–Jun	10
	Jul–Sept	25
	Oct–Dec	10
	1995	50
	Jan–Mar	9
	Apr–Jun	6
	Jul–Sept	23
	Oct–Dec	12
	1996	211
	Jan–Mar	17
	Apr–Jun	47
	Jul–Sept 1	127

times every two months in the years between 1981 and 1995. The *Los Angeles Times* refers to the riots a little less than three times per month, excluding the year in which violence again broke out in South Central Los Angeles. Indeed, the estimated number of references to the 1968 convention in Table 4.2 may be low. There are a variety of terms which refer to the events in Chicago that summer including iconic references to "the Chicago convention" and allusions to the "Chicago Seven" (or Eight), the men who were tried for fomenting the street disturbances during convention week. The search term used was developed from the paper indexes of the *New York Times*, which classified the Chicago Seven/Eight trial, as well as that of the Seattle Seven, under the general heading of the Democratic National Convention of 1968. While the search yields an extremely varied discourse about the convention, it probably does not capture every reference to it.

Some interesting differences between these pasts also emerge in the number of times they are mentioned in the media. Although both events were covered by the national media at the time they occurred, it is clear from the tables that the Watts riots developed as a local memory, while the Chicago convention was both a local and a national past. The difference in number of references to the convention between the *New York Times*, a newspaper with a national audience, and the Chicago *Tribune*, a regional newspaper, is not nearly as great as that of the *New York Times* and the *Los Angeles Times* referring to the Watts riots.

It is also clear that remembrances of the Chicago convention follow a cyclical pattern, while references to the Watts riots do not. This is in part because the Chicago convention is often recalled in connection with a regularly occurring phenomenon, the election of a president, while the Watts riots are recalled in connection with a variety of community events that do not follow a pattern. Although the Watts riots were commemorated in a number of ways, even major anniversaries of the event often do not produce a noticeable change in the number of references to the riots.

The relatively stable pattern of references suggests that the many changes that occurred in the news industry during the period under study have not significantly affected when and how journalists refer to these particular pasts. For example, the growth of feature sections in the newspaper (Cose 1989) and the advent of computerized databases that provide easy reference to newspaper morgues do not seem to result in larger numbers of references to the past. Nor does the increased contextualization described by Barnhurst and Mutz (1997).[1] But how and when does the past come up?

In earlier work, I described the occasions for journalistic remembering: commemorations, analogies and contexts (Edy 1999). First, the news sometimes commemorates the past. Anniversaries—of the births or deaths of major public figures or of important events—can be moments that news organizations choose to mark with commemorative coverage. In the summer of 2004, for example, the news media commemorated the seventieth anniversary of D-Day. Some of these commemorations will be linked to official events that mark the anniversary. In other cases, the news commemorates the past without official sponsorship. It is also possible for unexpected or unplanned events to provoke commemorative journalism. Over the same weekend that the D-Day anniversary was observed, former President Ronald Reagan passed away, and reporters took the opportunity to recall his life and presidency.

A second way in which news refers to the past is through the use of historical analogies. Reporters (or their sources) claim that present circumstances are similar to some past event or circumstance. The fact that reporters construct historical analogies without relying on sources to initiate the connection between present and past suggests that reporters perceive the past as an objective commentator on events. However, these analogies can have powerful interpretive effects. For example, the past can be used to predict the future, as when a contemplated military engagement is described as "another Vietnam." In drawing these analogies, reporters and sources imply that there are "lessons of history" to be gleaned from the past to which they refer. The catch, of course, is that the conflicting narratives associated with controversial pasts make such lessons quite uncertain.

It is perhaps surprising to learn that a disputable past is can be used effectively as a source of historical analogy. Yet the Chicago convention in particular is the source of a wide variety of historical analogies. For example, a reporter writing in the *New York Times* used an analogy to the Chicago Seven trial in the context of a gang trial in one year (Schmidt 1987), while a different reporter writing for the paper in the following year drew a connection between the conduct of the Chicago police in 1968 and the New York City police in a more recent incident

(Pitt 1988). The first analogy drew upon a narrative of the demonstrators as troublemakers to make the analogy while the second drew upon a contradictory narrative of the Chicago police as unnecessarily brutal to make its connection. The fragmented nature of journalistic storytelling, discussed in more detail below, allows contradictory "lessons of the past" to coexist unnoticed. In 1989, comparisons between the 1968 convention demonstrators and the prodemocracy protestors in Tiananmen Square sparked some objections about likening the troublemakers in Chicago to the brave young men and women in China, but this is the exception, not the rule.

A third way in which reporters use the past is as a historical context. While this may seem similar to a historical analogy in many ways, contexts differ in that they describe the series of events that lead up to the present moment. Profiles of presidential candidates, for example, may describe their personal biographies as part of the story of their run for the White House. This is, of course, quite distinct from describing a candidate as a similar to a famous political figure of the past. Contexts, like analogies, can be constructed by journalists without violating the norms of objectivity despite having powerful interpretive potential. As Janet Abu-Lughod (1989) has pointed out, one's perception of the past is largely a matter of punctuation. For example, to date white residents' departure from inner city Los Angeles with the Watts riots places the event in a very different context than dating it from the repeal of restrictive covenants that had preserved residential segregation in those neighborhoods. Like historical analogies, historical contexts are capable of preserving and using several contradictory narratives of a past. However, historical contexts also have an implicit quality that makes them difficult to locate even with keyword searches, for contexts can appear as unspoken common ground.[2] References to the past that do turn up in keyword searches also contain hints of this implicit quality. Time is marked in South Central Los Angeles "since the Watts riots." Why the Watts riots would be a relevant benchmark is not made explicit. Obituaries note that the deceased was a delegate to the 1968 Democratic National Convention as if it were just another convention.

In my earlier work, I noted that commemorative journalism offers the only real opportunity to reexamine the past in news (Edy 1999). When reporters draw historical analogies or employ historical contexts, the focus is on the present. The past is represented as a known fact rather than as a contestable construction, as indeed it must be for analogies or contexts to function. Thus, commemoration is very important to the process of building collective memories. Commemorative stories pull together scattered references to the past to encourage both reexaminiation and integration. In the absence of commemoration, contradictions can pass unnoticed and the process of integrating the narrative threads associated with a controversial event may slow. The fact that the Watts riots are regularly commemorated through the mechanism of anniversary journalism helps to constrain, and sometimes to consolidate, the meaning of the past. In contrast, the Chicago convention never sparks anniversary coverage and is only reconsidered at length in the news following the Democrats' decision to return to Chicago for their 1996 convention.

Although commemorative stories are an important part of the collective memory process, they also represent a risk to those trying to contain and resolve the social drama, for they can reinvigorate the social crisis they recall. Indeed, the retrospective reporting of a social breach, like official redressive rituals, has the potential both to ameliorate the crisis and to add fuel to the fire. That is, they have the potential to blend or subsume competing narratives or to point up the disharmony and narrative chaos in these competing stories. This chapter considers reporting practices that serve to pave the way for collective memories to develop, not by advocating for or blending tales but by distracting from the narrative chaos and crisis that dominates contemporary reporting of controversial events. The news stories found in the keyword searches were read to discover how the narrative threads present in the contemporary coverage reemerged in later news stories that referenced the Watts riots and the Chicago convention. Stories were grouped first according to whether the past was being commemorated, used as an analogy, or used as a context. Then, specific techniques for avoiding the contradictions between competing narratives were identified. Some of these techniques flow from the way the past is used; others are the product of storytelling practices. As the results reveal, some reporting practices that serve to gloss the conflicts are easily recognized by media scholars and do relatively little to shape any collective memory that may evolve. Others, however, are uniquely related to representations of the past and illuminate both how reporters reestablish their

narrative authority and how they may shape the relative salience of conflicting tales.

Fragmentation

The idea that news fragments our social reality is common enough
among scholars of media and politics.[3] However, these scholars often
underestimate just how fragmented the news is, especially when it
comes to representing our past. When political scholars read the newspaper, they often read only the news: the front section, the metro section, and occasionally the business section. But the newspaper is more
than this. Beyond the spot news, the political news, and the news
analysis are feature stories and travel stories, reviews and profiles, and
much more—stories that offer a richer picture of community life.
References to the past appear in any and all of these places, and they
follow no fixed pattern in either space or time. Both journalists and
their audiences are likely to be unaware that conflicting stories about
the past survive, since no one person reads the entire content of the
paper every day.

The fragmentary quality of the news has a number of sources,
including the ways that information is gathered and assembled and the
expectations that we, as consumers, have about news. The traditional
division of labor among reporters tends to support the continued survival of multiple, often conflicting narratives of the past. Reporters
gather information on selected subjects according to a pattern known
as the beat system (Fishman 1980; Tuchman 1972). The news they
produce is consequently fragmented (Bennett 1983)—a large number of
disconnected stories held together (if at all) only by the fact that the
events they report happened on the same day. As readers, we expect this.

For decades, beats were defined primarily by geography—the police
beat, the White House beat, the court beat, and so on—and journalists
were responsible for reporting events that occurred at a particular location.
This system prevailed during both the Watts riots and the 1968 Democratic
National Convention, and subtle differences in contemporary reporting
of the two events reflect the influence of the beat system. South
Central Los Angeles was not a beat for the national media, and may not
have been even for the local papers. When riots broke out, lacking

assigned beats or an organized ritual for gathering information, reporters and editors seem to have pooled the fragments they collected to produce stories containing a variety of conflicting narrative elements that they did not attempt to reconcile. Reporting on the Chicago convention looks very different in part because there was a well-established beat system for covering it. The result is a much more fragmented account of events in Chicago, with sharp distinctions between the political events occurring at the Amphitheater and the events occurring in the parks and streets. The established, perhaps even ritualized patterns for covering the news seems to have discouraged pooling information. The convention and protests are reported as two separate events, with only the weakest of connections between them. In 1969, established patterns of news gathering encouraged further fragmentation of the story of the convention as court reporters came to Chicago to cover the trial of the Chicago Eight.

The nature of news beats has changed in the last thirty years. Although there is still a great deal of validity to geographic descriptions of news beats, many beats now resemble areas of reporter expertise as much as information location. Environmental or real estate reporters do not collect information from a place so much as they report on a narrowly defined aspect of public life. Some beats, however, are a product of both expertise and location, so police and courthouse beats are still staples of journalism.

Even as the beat system changed, the potential for fragmented memories of these two social breaches remained. The Watts riots is alluded to by reporters covering race relations, by reporters covering the communities of South Central Los Angeles, by business reporters describing economic change and growth, and by reporters discussing the real estate market in the city, among others. The Chicago convention is referenced by feature reporters covering the ongoing exploits of the Chicago Eight, by political reporters discussing changes in procedures for delegate selection, by culture writers describing the events of 1968, and by media critics arguing over the relationship between reporters and the events they cover, to name a few.

Our cultural definition of news also promotes fragmentation. Walter Benjamin's phrase "homogenous, empty time" aptly describes the way news media handle information. Stories in the paper are related to each other only because they are printed on the same day, and in the case of spot news, because the events they tell of occurred on the same day. We do not expect that the stories on the front page will be connected to each other in any meaningful way. Since we do not expect to see a relationship between individual articles in the paper or individual stories in television news, not only are we unlikely to be surprised by contradictions between them, we are unlikely to be aware of them. These expectations are quite powerful, even when the event is "big" enough to warrant the attention of several reporters whose stories appear simultaneously, which is a boon for reporters producing stories on a tight deadline. They do not have time to read each other's work or to coordinate their stories.

The fragmentation produced by the beat system is especially prominent in remembrances of the Chicago convention presented in the *New York Times*, which retained the three stories of the convention it had established in 1968 for decades. One is the story of delegate selection reforms. During 1980 and 1984, news stories that refer to the Chicago convention are dominated by discussions of the impact of the Chicago convention on the primary system, though mention of the credentials fights which encouraged the reform process are almost nonexistent. Later, when the Democrats again proved competitive, this story took a slightly different form, tracing the rise of the boring convention to the chaos of 1968. However, the story of the impact of the convention on the nominating process remained an important part of convention memories in the *Times* for many years.

A second story revolved around the continuing exploits of the Chicago Seven (as they were now usually called, unless Bobby Seale was specifically mentioned). In this story, the central tension revolves around the guilt of the seven men accused of starting the riots. The *Times* followed the eventual "taming" of former radicals Jerry Rubin and Tom Hayden and the later career of the apparently untamed Abbie Hoffman. The paper's evaluation of the Chicago Seven would change over time, but critical here is the fact that acts of the Chicago Seven *during* the convention are almost never mentioned in these stories. The trial is presented as an event separate from the convention. The convention usually merits a one line mention, as in "the 'Chicago Seven' who were tried for conspiracy to disrupt the Democratic National Convention in 1968" (*New York Times* 1988b, 31).

The story of what did happen on the streets in Chicago during convention week is usually narrated as a case of violent police reaction to demonstrators. Frequently, the presentation is quite evenhanded, as in "Recall the 1968 Democratic Convention, when young protestors rioted against the Vietnam War and the Chicago police rioted against the protesters" (*New York Times* 1986b, 22). These three stories coexist in the *New York Times* for more than twenty years.

In some cases, even commemorations that bring a variety of conflicting narratives together have a fragmentary quality. Cohen and Murphy's (1966) "instant" book on the Watts riots, for example, encapsulates conflicting stories in separate chapters. The *Los Angeles Times*'s fifteenth-anniversary commemoration of the riots exhibits a similar kind of fragmentation. A series of stories with the overall logo "Watts: 15 Years After" appeared on the front page of the paper for ten nonconsecutive days, each story focusing on a different aspect of life in Watts, and was followed by several letters to the editor and an editorial. In some ways, this coverage made their remembrance more accessible, since audiences had more opportunities to catch a part of the series. However, the resulting remembrance was also fragmented in ways that the single section produced in 1975 was not, especially because the stories appeared on an irregular schedule.

On August 31, 1980, the last day of the series, three profiles of people whose lives were touched by the riots appeared. Marquette Frye, the wife of a fireman killed during the riots, and the wife of a man shot by police a year after the riots are separately profiled. Their stories preserve a variety of perspectives on the riots through the mechanism of fragmentation. Each story is coherent, but the perspectives are incompatible. The fireman's widow, Mrs. Tilson, resurrects the lawlessness narrative, since she believes that the Watts riots were the fault of those who participated (*Los Angeles Times* 1980b). Marquette Frye's story, on the other hand, portrays him largely as a victim of the past. The article briefly recounts his arrest but dwells far longer on his miseries in the years after the Watts riots. He is described as "like a child star grown old." Famous once as "an example of the anger and frustration of tough ghetto life," he is now avoided as a "troublemaker." (*Los Angeles Times* 1980b, 3, 24) The story of the widow whose husband was shot by the police invokes a weakened version of the police brutality narrative, since it describes the trial and acquittal of the officer who killed him.

The value of fragmentation as a means to avoid adding fuel to a fire becomes even more apparent in the series' coverage of police brutality. The fifteenth anniversary of the riots was observed at a time when police brutality was once again an issue. Officers of the Los Angeles Police Department had shot and killed two people in the Watts area within months of the anniversary. Police brutality stories continued to be denigrated, but once again, proved impossible to ignore. The episodic nature of the 1980 series makes the police brutality narrative easier to miss. It does not appear in every article of the series. Nevertheless, the recent shootings and the anniversary of the riots did prompt the *Times* to make police brutality the focal issue of one day's stories in its series. Whereas most days, one article appears as part of the series, the police brutality focus places two stories side by side. One describes the situation in black neighborhoods from the perspective of police, the other from the perspective of the citizens who live there. The story from the police perspective is the one that is labeled "Eighth in a series" (Secter 1980). As one might expect, both stories subtly favor the view that the police are merely doing their jobs under difficult circumstances, with the exception of a few bad apples. However, the anger of the community is not, and perhaps cannot be, entirely dismissed. Stories of police abuse are related. Although the anniversary of the riots provides a news peg for these police brutality stories, the Watts riots are not explicitly used as an analogy.

Commemorative stories illustrate the limits of fragmentation as a means of dealing with a troubled past. Where the past is commemorated, remaining contradictions between stories that claim to account for that past are difficult to hide. In the absence of commemorations, however, the fragmentary quality of news and the fact that we, as audience members, do not expect the news to make any kind of holistic "sense" enables contradictory stories to pass unnoticed. The pressure to tell "the" story of what happened eases as other processes that lay the groundwork for "the" story simultaneously unfold.

The Implicit Past

Although fragmented news can preserve a variety of perspectives whose contradictory qualities pass under the radar, such news can still draw criticism from social actors and audiences who reject that particular version of the story. Conflict is one of the basic qualities of news, but much of the conflict that actually appears in the news is limited and essentially ritualistic. Partisan conflict, the ritual combat of trials, corporate competition, and so on all represent conflict in manageable forms that can be handled with existing story structures. When handled according to standard news-making practices, such stories are unlikely to attract what Edward Herman and Noam Chomsky (1988) term "flak": negative responses to the news that may take the form of letters, phone calls, cancelled subscriptions, or pulled advertising. Social breaches are different. They represent a kind of unlimited and unmanageable conflict that is difficult to convert into narrative. Any story that is told threatens to incur the wrath of stakeholders to the conflict who may claim that the story is untrue. Since the central claim of journalism as an institution is that it is a source of truth about public events, such complaints strike to the heart of the profession. With officials, eyewitnesses, interest groups, and the public divided over what happened and what it means, how do reporters tell stories about an event that is too big to ignore?

The simple answer is that they leave out a great deal of it. One of the most noticeable aspects of stories that refer to either the Watts riots or the Chicago convention is their failure to describe what actually happened. While this might be expected in historical analogies or contexts because of their focus on current events, it happens in commemorations as well, sometimes even when the commemorations are quite elaborate. Take the 1975 retrospective of the Watts riots published in the *Los Angeles Times*, for example. Ten years after the event, the paper's reporters and editors do not provide any description of the riots themselves in their multipage commemoration. On those occasions when reporters do describe the event itself, they typically let a small collection of uncontested (often officially derived) facts stand in for a much larger whole. For example, the number of people who died (34), the number of days the riots lasted (5), the fires, and the race of the rioters stand in for the details of the Watts riots. Since the Chicago convention never receives anniversary coverage until the mid-1990s, its facts remain obtuse as well. Here again, sketchy facts stand in for the whole: large scale and violent protests took place, the Democratic Party was divided, and the Chicago Seven were tried for inciting riots. The convention is often characterized as "tumultuous" without further elaboration. Other references to the convention are equally enigmatic to those unfamiliar with the event itself. In a one line mention of the convention in 1987, the *New York Times* made the following connections: "Anyone who survived Vietnam, Afghanistan, and the 1968 Democratic National Convention ought to be able to handle these corporate intrigues quite well" (*New York Times* 1987, 78). While the reader can get a general sense of CBS's durability, those unfamiliar with the convention, and especially with anchor Dan Rather's experiences there, will miss much of the point.

Several scholars have noted that journalists frequently assume a regularly reading public that is caught up on current events and needs little reminding of previous events,[4] and in the immediate aftermath of a social breach of the scale considered in this study, that seems like a safe assumption. However, when no narrative of what happened appears in stories that commemorate the event ten or more years later, the assumption is much harder to justify. Indeed, the first recountings of the actual events of the Chicago convention and the Watts riots do not appear until about twenty years later.

Even as details of the events themselves are added back into representations of the past, a subtle shift in grammar results in another aspect of the past becoming implicit in news stories: agency. Early news coverage of these social breaches is quite recognizable to the modern news reader. Each story told represents, among other things, an attempt to affix blame. The lawlessness stories that were central to both the Watts riots and the Chicago convention place the blame for the events on the residents of South Central Los Angeles and the protestors who came to Chicago. Such crime stories, according to Stuart Hall and associates (1978) and Todd Gitlin (1980), are some of the most basic in news. Police brutality stories, also essential components of each event, place the blame for what happened on the police. Beyond these main themes, there are stories of incompetence and poor leadership. Sometimes these are encapsulated in quotations of ill-conceived phrases such as Chief Parker's "monkeys in a zoo" comment or Mayor Daley's "shoot to kill" order. Sometimes, questionable decisions are highlighted: Mayor Yorty's decision to leave the city during the riots to honor speaking engagements elsewhere, Lt. Governor Anderson's delay in calling out the National Guard to respond to the riots. Perhaps there is a natural human impulse to hold someone responsible for these kinds of social disasters. Perhaps it is a uniquely American predilection. Regardless, the desire to hold someone accountable is a familiar one.

Stories that affix blame are bound to be resisted by those who are blamed for as long as they can gain access to the media to contest the story. As was noted in the previous chapter, sometimes people lose their access to the news and with it the ability to resist responsibility, but something else happens as well. Over time, the past comes to be described in a passive voice that glosses the questions of agency that seemed so vital in the immediate aftermath of the event. Here is an example from later stories of the Watts riots: "When the riots finally ended, 34 people were dead...and 1032 were injured. About $40 million worth of property was damaged or destroyed" (Dawsey 1990, B1). Gitlin (1980) argues that news coverage featuring statistics about arrests and property damage feed crime frames, but after twenty-five years, the news sounds rather different. The writer could just as easily be describing the aftermath of a hurricane or tornado as a massive outbreak of assault, vandalism, looting, and arson. The social disaster is described in the same kind of language that would be used to describe a natural disaster, where agency is not an issue. Chicago convention stories take a slightly different form, but once again, the key element of agency is missing: "The chaos that wracked America was evident for everyone to see as they watched the mob scenes of the 1968 Democratic National Convention" (Creighton 1993, 19). Rather than a natural disaster, this description parallels the kinds of stories that might be told in the wake of an economic or health crisis, but as in the previous example, the sentence includes only victims and elides agents.

Shanto Iyengar (1991) has demonstrated that the media distract citizens from social problems by creating episodic stories that attribute personal responsibility for problems. He contrasts these with thematic stories that emphasize the social nature of problems and the responsibilities of government in coping with them. The stories of the past that elide agency, however, are neither episodic nor thematic. They do not focus on individuals, nor do they construct problems as social. Instead, they deny that the events qualify as social problems by denying that they could have been prevented. Malcolm Spector and John Kitsuse (2001) argue that social problems are created in claims that life circumstances can be ameliorated by social action. Stories that elide agency while at the same time considering a wide scope of human affairs claim the opposite—that what happened was an unavoidable disaster.

A belief that no one is really to blame, that the events had a kind of terrible inevitability to them, is also one of the defining characteristics of a tragic narrative. Tragedies turn on the fatal flaw of a central character, and a well-told tragedy is filled with foreshadowing—hints of the doom to come—both of which are dramatically appealing ways to narrate stories of the past. While full-fledged tragic narratives do not appear in connection with either of these events, elements of tragedy do appear in the stories. Some stories involve a kind of Cassandra complex—the storyteller insists that he or she knew what was coming, but no one would listen. City authorities are described as having fatal flaws that caused them to make catastrophically poor decisions at critical moments. Yet in the early stages of the development of the tale, these are not tragic stories. They are stories about government incompetence. Only with the distance of history do they acquire the kind of wistful, "if only" aspect that is necessary to perceive them tragically. Here, too, in an odd way, the very inevitability of the mistake that flows from such a flaw absolves the errant actor from blame. Taking the question of blame off the table, so to speak, helps reporters cope with a troubled past and opens space for the negotiation of a collective memory because those with a stake in the story no longer need to defend their reputations.

Representations of the past that leave out factual details and elide agency do not resolve the narrative conflicts that were present in the original reporting of the event. Rather, they result in open texts that can support a variety of narratives. This helps reporters deal with troubled pasts in at least two ways.

In his work on the discursive forms of history, Hayden White (1987) distinguishes between annals and narratives. Annals, he says, are lists of events—there was a battle; there was a famine; the following people died. Narratives, on the other hand, transform events into full-fledged stories whose chief characteristic is that they have a moral. Moralizing stories have heroes and villains; they place both laurels and blame. By structuring their accounts of the past as annals, or lists of facts, rather than as stories with protagonists, antagonists, and morals, reporters avoid the problem of having to draw conclusions about what happened when such conclusions remain in dispute. Instead, the open structure of the annals allows readers to supply their own narrative (and with it their own moral) for the story. Reminding them that there were large-scale protests does not dictate whether they construct the demonstrators as troublemakers or outraged citizens. Associating the Watts riots with the then-current state of race relations leaves the door open for readers to bring their own ideas about such relations to the text. Work such as that of Nicholas Valentino (1999) and Martin Gilens (1999) suggests that shared schemas for understanding the social world may prompt a majority of readers to "close" open texts in a particular way. However, one reason that these texts are constructed in such open ways may be that overt closure is (or is believed by journalists to be) unacceptable to some group or groups capable of making public its rejection of such a story, which means that more than one viable narrative survives somewhere in the public. Moreover, since public perceptions can be dynamic over time, the way a text is closed can be, too.

The implicit quality of the events themselves in stories that recall the Watts riots and the Chicago convention also serve to enhance reporters' authority to interpret these events over the long run. Shortly after an event, public memory may indeed function in the pluralistic ways Schudson (1992) describes. Large proportions of the public have personal memories of the event. Over time, however, the proportion of the public able to check public memory against personal memory declines, and the authority of journalists expands. Neglecting to describe the event itself gives reporters power over people who do not personally remember the past in at least two ways. First, it reminds these readers that the journalist knows more than they do. Second, it tells the readers little about what happened, so it can pass on conclusions and characterizations that lack the substance required for critical consideration. Indeed, incidental evidence for this appears in materials collected for this study. In 1996, a *New York Times* writer referred to William Jennings Bryan's "cross of gold" speech as an example of "ideological passion" (Rich, A19). It is doubtful that most readers, even of the *Times*, have any idea what Bryan was so worked up about.

When reporters do not regularly remind their readers of the underlying facts that support their uses of history, the possibilities for remaking the past expand. Readers have no regular access to their past through journalistic remembering, so they have only their personal, increasingly distant memories or whatever collective memories they develop interpersonally to resist the retellings presented to them by news (or by the media more generally). As Schudson (1992) points out, other social forces, such as alternative networks of memory and professional historical investigation and documentation, can still prevent the wholesale rewriting of the past. However, it is likely that the relative power of media to influence public memories increases over time since the material necessary for readers to draw their own conclusions about the past is often missing. To the extent that journalism's use of history is like its reporting of most major public issues, quite standardized across news outlets, this growing power to assign meaning to a controversial past will further the process of consolidating a collective memory.

Managing Salience

Media and politics scholars working in both the agenda-setting tradition and the framing paradigm agree that one of the most important functions of media for public discourse is managing the salience of issues and perspectives. Each theory explains the mechanisms by which the media manage salience differently, however. Agenda-setting theory suggests that through the repetition of material, mass media pass on their representations of salience to the audience. The more coverage an issue or perspective gets, the more salient it becomes to the audience. Framing theory suggests that repetition is less important than the narrative structure of a story. Issues and perspectives that are integrated into the narrative structure of a story will be more salient to an audience than will information that, while included in the article, is not incorporated into the narrative. The news media's representations of the past illustrate just how difficult it can be to separate these two mechanisms in practice. However, regardless of whether framing or agenda setting is at work, there is evidence that reporters help to shape collective memory by managing the salience of both events and narratives of those events.

The most obvious mechanism for managing salience is journalists' use of lists in their references to both the Watts riots and the Chicago convention. Lists are similar to annals (White 1987) because they lack the sense of causal connection that is part of narrative. Nevertheless, the lists give shape to the past in what they include, what they leave out, and the situational definitions they imply. Moreover, they take on distinctive and recognizable forms as very similar lists are repeated throughout the news.

Lists associated with the Chicago convention tend to downplay its importance. Embedding the convention in a list of events that occurred in 1968, they render the convention as just another event in a highly eventful year. Here are some classic formulations of the list:

- From the *New York Times*: "[T]he larger-than-life events of 1968: the assassinations of Martin Luther King Jr. and Robert F. Kennedy, the Tet offensive in Vietnam, the Prague spring in Europe, the demonstrations at the Democratic National Convention in Chicago, the sexual liberation, the drugs, the music, the mood of cultural revolution" (Bernstein 1993).
- From an art exhibit review: "'The Turning Point: Arts and Politics in 1968' is an exhibition based on the politicizing of those artists who reacted to a turbulent period that included the assassinations of the Rev. Dr. Martin Luther King Jr. and Robert Kennedy, the escalation of the war in Vietnam, and the violent clashes between demonstrators and police at the Democratic National Convention" (*New York Times* 1988c).
- From an economist writing in the *Times*: "The year 1968 was among the worst years this century for the United States— assassinations, riots, campus uprisings and the infamous Democratic National Convention in Chicago" (Thurow 1995).

In some formulations, the list expands to cover events of the 1960s more generally:

- From a television review: "From the Cuban missile crisis to the 1968 Democratic convention in Chicago, from the Kennedy assassination to the Vietnam War, the moving images are still riveting, a fixed part of the national psyche" (O'Connor 1989).
- From a book review by the chair of the Medill magazine writing program: "[I]t has been 20 years since 'Sgt. Pepper' and the march on the Pentagon—with assassinations, the

1968 Democratic Convention, Woodstock and the Kent
State shootings waiting in the wings" (Peck 1987).

These lists take the form of annals. They imply no causal connection between the events, nor do they pass moral judgment upon the
actors involved or the events themselves as a narrative would. Thus,
they avoid the problems involved in reconciling these complex and
controversial events into story form. However, they also encourage us
not to fixate on the convention. So much happened in that year, in that
decade, that singling out just one event for special attention seems
inappropriate. The convention is no more important than the Tet offensive or the King assassination or the National Guard shootings at Kent
State University. Paradoxically, each event is so significant that none
seems uniquely significant.

Another kind of list denies even that the 1968 convention is especially memorable by including it as one in a list of Democratic National
Conventions—each unique but none more memorable than the others—or as one of a list of political events that, again, do not suggest the
convention was anything special.

- From the *Chicago Tribune*: "The 1964 convention was
  haunted by President Kennedy's assassination less than
  nine months earlier. Then came the violence of 1968, the
  absurdity of 1972 and the drabness of 1976—when the party
  nominated a winner, Jimmy Carter, it didn't really like"
  (Margolis 1988).
- From a *New York Times* editorial: "President Kennedy was
  killed in 1963. Assassinations of Martin Luther King Jr. and
  Robert Kennedy in 1968 brought legislation authorizing the
  Secret Service to protect Presidential candidates. Delegates
  to the Democratic Convention in Chicago that turbulent
  summer grumbled about the passes they had to insert into
  turnstile slots. This year, Michael Dukakis has accepted pro-
  tection..." (*New York Times* 1988a).

Like previous lists, these take the form of annals rather than narratives.
Note that although the *Times*'s list implies causal reasoning it does
not actually invoke it. The *Tribune*'s list is structured so as to create

equivalencies between the conventions of 1968, 1972, and 1976: violent, absurd, and drab, respectively. In its vagueness about the events of each, it implies that all are equally significant and can be recalled with about equal facility by readers. This list is also a good example of a story that leaves implicit details of the event itself, instead offering an overall characterization. The *Times*, for its part, draws attention to a minor detail of convention week (increased security), but leads the reader to believe that the precautions were taken based upon the King and Kennedy assassinations rather than on the threatened (and actual) disruption of the convention by protestors. Indeed, in this list, the 1968 convention sounds like just another nominating convention.

Another kind of list turns up in the obituaries of convention delegates. In some cases, the people being memorialized served as delegates to multiple conventions. The obituaries list the convention years without distinguishing any of the conventions as unusual: "She was a delegate to the Democratic National Conventions in 1968, 1972 and 1976" (*New York Times* 1990, D29).

These lists distract from the passionate disagreement and controversy of the Chicago convention by suggesting that the event was not all that significant, but they do not tell us much about how the convention might be collectively remembered. The lists associated with the Watts riots, in contrast, offer a glimpse of how disparate narratives are being drawn together to facilitate the development of a shared understanding of the past. The riots have two lists associated with them. One is the previously described list of deaths and damage done by the riots, the vital statistics of the event. The other suggests the evolving shape of collective memory, for while it includes elements from multiple narratives of the event, it makes one more salient than the others. Here are a few examples:

- From a *Los Angeles Times* columnist: "Their [reporters] notebooks were full of resident complaints about no nearby medical facilities, inadequate transportation, police brutality, joblessness—and merchants selling shoddy, high-priced goods" (Boyarsky 1985, 1).
- From a *New York Times* reporter: "The events were considered an explosion of anger and frustration over joblessness, poor schools and services, physical and social isolation

from the city as a whole, and police brutality" (Cummings 1985, A11).

- From a community activist: "'Even a cursory examination of the [McCone Commission] report,' the Rev. H. H. Brookins complained days after the report was made public, 'reveals that the commission does not present workable solutions to the problem of the racial ghetto itself, nor the basic problems of police malpractice, jobs, housing, economic exploitation, education and other factors'" (quoted in Dawsey 1990, B1).

- From a review of a made-for-television movie about the Watts riots: "It takes only a few minutes of television time for their dreams to sour. They meet with police brutality, white thuggery, inadequate schools and job discrimination..." (Goodman 1990, C14).

Despite the wide variety of speakers and venues, the lists are all remarkably similar. Although they do not claim to be, one might take them for a list of causes of the Watts riots. In all of the lists, most of the causes are economic ones, and it is here that we see the power of the list at work. While police brutality is mentioned as a cause of the Watts riots in all of the lists, it is in a sense "drowned out" by the flood of economic and social welfare problems that surround it. Because it is present in the list, the list itself will not draw the ire of interested parties who perceive this as an important aspect of the Watts riots, but as one problem among many, the demand to solve the problem is softened. The position of police brutality on the list is also worth noticing. The *Los Angeles Times* columnist places it in the middle of his list, a position that Norman Fairclough (1995) would argue denies it reader attention. The *New York Times* reporter places it at the end of her list. Although this may make it more salient for readers, because lists are often ordered hierarchically, she implies (whether intentionally or not) that this is the least important of the causes she lists. The community activist and the television reviewer, on the other hand, treat it as the most important. Yet even in their statements, the long list of economic problems balanced against the lone mention of police brutality draws attention away from the latter as an important problem.

The lists associated with the Watts riots could be interpreted from either an agenda-setting or a framing perspective. The lists contain more elements associated with economic deprivation than with police brutality, which should enhance the salience of economic problems relative to police malpractice. At the same time, they promote a problem definition of the Watts riots as a response to poverty and hopelessness, making the single reference to police brutality less salient because it does not fit the frame. The lists associated with the Chicago convention can be tied to the framing perspective in the sense that they encourage the reader to reflect upon "the Sixties" or "political conventions" rather than to fixate upon the 1968 convention in particular. That is, they reformulate "the problem." At the same time, they make the 1968 convention less salient through the agenda-setting mechanism of making it one item in a long list.

Regardless of precisely how they manage the salience of these events and their interpretation, the forms these lists take shape collective memory. Yet because the lists resemble annals rather than full-fledged narratives, reporters do not commit themselves to a story that might reignite controversy. They cannot be accused of leaving out essential aspects of the event, even if the structure of the list subtly favors some interpretations over others. Without appearing to do so, the move toward collective memory continues.

Stories of Continuity and Progress

Commemorations perform a unique function in the development of collective memories because they illuminate surviving disagreements about the meaning of the past. Even when the commemorations take fragmented forms, narrative discord is revealed. Social authorities may be reluctant to commemorate controversial events for precisely this reason: the controversy itself is republicized. However, there are some story forms typical in historical contexts and analogies that reduce the risk of renewed controversy over the meaning of the past because they simultaneously acknowledge past controversy and dismiss it.

Using the past as either an analogy or a context requires establishing a relationship between the present and the past. Such relationships can be complex, but they all involve one basic dimension: constructing the past as similar or dissimilar to the present. George Herbert Mead (1929) uses the terms continuity and discontinuity to describe this relationship between present and past. For contexts, the scope of relationships is narrower still, for they are limited to stories of continuity and stories of progress. Where analogies can construct the past as "not like" the present, contexts must treat the past as "left behind." In cases where the past is represented as being unlike the present, or when it is represented as being rendered obsolete by more recent events, its controversial aspects become safe to recall because they do not matter.

One way that progress and continuity stories affect the shape of collective memory is by changing both the constellation of news sources with an interest in influencing stories about the past and the stories they are likely to advocate. Progress stories may reduce the number of social actors involved in negotiations about the meaning of the past. Once the reputation of an individual or group is no longer tied to public perception of a particular past, that individual or group may lose interest in shaping the story. Continuity stories, on the other hand, encourage individuals and groups to stay involved in the debate over the meaning of the past because their reputations remain bound to it, and they should continue to advocate for a version of the story that preserves or enhances their reputation. Of course, this pattern would be quite different in the case of nostalgic pasts, but in the case of controversial or divisive events, the past is not longed for but rather may be gladly "left behind."

Moreover, turnover in the leadership of organizations does not merely affect which stories have sponsors and which stories do not. It also affects the ability of organizations to represent their relationship to the past in terms of continuity or progress. As long as the same people lead an organization, it is difficult to tell a progress story of dramatic organizational transformation. When leadership turns over, it becomes easier to claim that the organization is changed. Thus, in 1975, after Chief William Parker had died, the Los Angeles Police Department's representatives could talk about how the department had changed since the Watts riots. In contrast, the dynastic politics of Chicago made it more difficult for the Mayor's office to argue that the past had been left behind.

The relationships between progress stories, continuity stories and reputation is, of course, fluid. By 1980, a series of police shootings occurring near the anniversary of the Watts riots had reporters questioning whether the department had really changed its ways. In doing so, they reimplicated the reputation of the police department in stories of the Watts riots. Complex stories of progress and continuity are told about the later exploits of most of the Chicago Seven. In progress stories, reporters face a problem: the reason the story is newsworthy conflicts with the content of the story itself. That is, the Chicago Seven are newsworthy as famous radicals (whether heroes or scoundrels), but the central theme of the stories is that their later lives are conventional, often pedestrian. In some cases, perhaps to enhance the reader appeal of the story, the Chicago Seven's behavior is painted as worse than it was, as in the following headline: "Conversations: Tom Hayden; From Inciting Riots in 1968 To Winning in a Wealthy District." The writer continues, "It has been nearly two dozen years since he was tried and convicted on Federal charges of inciting riots at the 1968 Democratic National Convention in Chicago (the conviction was subsequently overturned)" (Reinhold 1992, 7). The headline convicts Hayden, and the story itself only acquits him with the technicality of parentheses. Yet in general, the stories are about dramatic transformations in the lives of these former radicals. The exceptions to this trend are the unrepentant Abbie Hoffman and, at the 1996 convention, David Dellinger. Hoffman's stories are continuity stories. He appears unchanged from the man who came to Chicago in 1968, and at the 1996 convention, his son Andrew continued the family tradition. David Dellinger, too, came to the 1996 convention as a protestor. Hayden's appearance at the 1996 convention provoked stories that contain complex amalgamations of continuity and progress. Covering his speeches, the newspapers suggest that he seeks to revive the "'60s spirit." However, other stories point out how much Hayden has changed, most notably that he is now middle-aged.

Continuity and progress stories are also told about the social breaches themselves. A common theme in later coverage of the Watts riots is that nothing has really changed since they occurred: a continuity story. In these stories, people are still poor, community services are still lacking, jobs are still scarce, and, in a few stories, police-community relations are still tense. Progress stories about the Watts riots are rare. Following the Chicago convention, both continuity and progress stories were told. When protest groups clashed with city officials at subsequent conventions about when, where, and if they could protest, they sometimes claimed that nothing had changed since 1968. Officials, on the other hand, pointed out how much more effectively they managed demonstrators when compared to Chicago city officials in 1968. As Democrats lost elections choosing candidates with their 1968-vintage delegate selection reforms, continuity stories were told about how they had not had a really successful candidate since 1968. These kinds of stories abruptly disappeared when Bill Clinton won the 1992 election.

Continuity stories emphasize the past over the present, whereas progress stories emphasize the present over the past. Because of this, progress stories reduce the risk involved in rehashing a disputed past: it is safe to discuss because it is over and its effects on the present sharply limited. Continuity stories, on the other hand, suggest that the past is not over at all and in that sense make it more dicey to talk about past controversies. At the same time, progress stories reduce the motivation to negotiate a shared meaning for the past. If the controversy is truly over, there is little need to understand it other than idle curiosity. Continuity stories, on the other hand, make the past important to the present and give social actors incentive to understand "what really happened" in the interests of preventing it from happening "again" or in order to resolve the problems that it represents. Progress stories may help to make collective memory possible, but it is continuity stories that make it seem necessary.

Progress and continuity stories may have another kind of effect on the debate over the shape of collective memory. It is rare for either type of story to be actively contested, but where they are, it is not the representation of the past that is contested but that of the present. Thus, when protestors object to permit regulations and convention organizers tout their system, the clash is not over how protestors were treated at the 1968 convention but whether or not the new system is different from the old one (in other words, whether a progress story or a continuity story is warranted). When questions arise over whether the LAPD has mended its ways since the Watts riots, there is no real argument over whether or not its ways needed mending. Thus, historical contexts, like historical analogies, take the meaning of the past for granted. Where collective memory has been established, the received meaning of the past is reinforced. Where no collective memory exists, the past

that emerges in these contexts reveals surviving remnants of conflicting narratives.

The Social Environment

Whether or not representations of the past will reignite controversy
depends not only on the continuing presence of conflicting stories and
agents to sponsor them but also on the public's perceptions of both the
specific past and social life more generally. Although the relative power
of journalists and political leaders to influence the shape of collective
memory may increase over time, they are never writing public memories onto a blank slate. In the immediate aftermath of an event, they are
limited by the personal memories of audiences who, even if they did
not personally experience the event, remember the disputes over what
it meant that appeared in the media. Kurt and Gladys Engel Lang
(1989) and Thomas Johnson (1995) demonstrate that these readers
have stronger opinions about the past than those with no personal
memories of the event itself, and Schudson (1992) points out the
importance of personal memory as a check on historical revisionism.

These personal memories may delay the development of collective
memories because of their diversity. Yet even as the cohort with personal memories of an event is replaced by a cohort without them, the
power of media and officials to rewrite the past is limited in other ways
by people's expectations about social reality. These expectations can be
dynamic over time and are sometimes included in the collective memory literature as a form of "presentism," the idea that the social context
in which a past is recalled affects what is recalled about it.[5] Schwartz
(1991), for example, describes how changing perceptions of American
national identity affected which representation of Abraham Lincoln the
United States sent to London and which they bestowed on Cleveland.

The relationship between public perceptions of the social world
and specific collective memories is a complex one, since memories of
specific events may, over the long term, influence people's values and
beliefs. For example, the specific events of the civil rights movement
helped to reshape public attitudes about race relations. A second complicating factor is that public perceptions of social reality are influenced
by political and social elites as they work to achieve organizational and

policy goals, which may include altering public memory. Recent scholarship has attempted to disentangle the degree to which public opinion operates as a constraint on leaders' behavior and the degree to which public opinion is a product of leaders' manipulation. Lawrence Jacobs and Robert Shapiro (2001) offer compelling evidence that political leaders work to shape public opinion, manufacturing public support so that they can enact the policies they and their allies favor.

Nevertheless, there is a reasonable basis for treating broad changes in public perceptions of political and social life as an environment in which collective memory operates. First, the changes considered here affect wide swaths of contemporary public life, not just memories of the past. Second, these changes were not directly spurred by the events under consideration. Indeed, in both cases, the social disturbances were more likely to hinder than to help change public opinion in the directions that it ultimately moved. Third, to the extent that political leaders sought to move public opinion, it is highly unlikely that they did so in order to revise public memory. In the instances reviewed here, much more immediate political goals offer much more plausible explanations for elite efforts to modify public attitudes. Yet these changes in public perceptions of the political and social world also influenced collective memory by creating parameters that limit the kinds of stories that will be believable and socially acceptable.

Public opinion regarding race has transformed since the mid-twentieth century. In the early twentieth century, traditional racism that was based upon beliefs about white racial supremacy and African American racial inferiority and supported Jim Crow segregation dominated public opinion about race. In the 1950s and 1960s, this belief system eroded. While some argue that these views have not disappeared, most would agree that it is no longer socially acceptable to publicly express such views, and measures of traditional racism in public opinion polls show a dramatic decline in support for the perspective. Even as this perspective faded, however, there was evidence of public opposition to government activism to promote racial equality. Sometimes called symbolic racism, or modern racism, this constellation of opinions supports the idea of racial equality (favoring racial integration in schools or equal opportunities for jobs, for example) but opposes policies that would foster such outcomes (opposing busing or affirmative action). These opinions are often accompanied by perceptions that African Americans are responsible for their own disadvantages, that, for example, they are lazy, sexually promiscuous, or otherwise fail to uphold middle-class, "American" values. Many white Americans appear to believe that African Americans could solve their own problems if they wanted to.[6] Some have linked these more recent racial attitudes to the traditional American values of egalitarianism and individualism. Giving someone special consideration, even to help them overcome decades of discrimination, is said to contradict the fundamental principles of equality that underlie the concept of civil rights itself[7].

Changing public attitudes about race would have an impact on the social acceptability of various stories about the Watts riots. Of course, it required some effort of construction to treat the riots as "about" race since at the time of the Watts riots, northern cities were not typical targets of civil rights–related protests. Indeed, most journalists reporting on the Watts riots noted that African American civil rights organizations had very little presence in northern cities. Further, civil rights advocacy at the time was only just moving on from a focus on voting rights and desegregation to broader programs of equal opportunity. The Voting Rights Act of 1965 had only just been passed when the Watts riots broke out. However, the federal action to address urban minority poverty that coincided with the Watts riots helped to associate the riots with race as well as with poverty.

Once the connection was established, the demise of traditional racism would make some contemporary formulations of the Watts riots socially unacceptable to repeat. The animal metaphors of Cohen and Murphy (1966), for example, express traditional beliefs about African American racial inferiority. Suggestions that the African Americans living in Watts had gone collectively insane or been unable to control their impulses would also express a brand of belief about racial inferiority that has since gone out of fashion, although the representation of widespread criminality in the black community is not at all unusual in contemporary media discourse.[8]

A second development in public opinion may also have had an impact on the evolving story of the Watts riots. Gilens (1999) has documented Americans' belief that most African Americans are poor. African American poverty had been largely invisible in the media prior to the 1960s (Edy and Lawrence 2000), but after the Great Society programs were implemented, the association between welfare and urban minority poverty became well established in public opinion (Gilens). This link may have strengthened the viability of the economic deprivation story of the Watts riots. Since African Americans are associated with poverty, once the Watts riots are linked to race, an explanation of the Watts riots that foregrounds poverty as a motivating factor makes sense. Much research on memory demonstrates that stories that "make sense" have a great deal of appeal, even when they aren't "right."[9]

For the Chicago convention, the relevant public opinion dynamics are in public perceptions of the Vietnam War. However, the connections between opinions about the war and memories of the convention are more difficult to make out. While contemporary observers no doubt knew that the war was a vital convention issue, initial newsmagazine coverage was quite traditional in its devotion to the political machinations that had resulted in Humphrey's nomination. Coverage of the protests was, as Gitlin (1980) would expect, devoted to the activities of demonstrators rather than the causes that had moved them to come to Chicago. Only later would the demonstrations come to be associated with the war. A further complicating factor is that unlike race, which remains a "live" issue in American politics, the Vietnam War has itself passed into the realm of collective memory and thus, recent public opinion about the war is only infrequently measured and studied.

Many point to the loss of American public support for the war in Vietnam as a major reason for the withdrawal of U.S. troops from the field. By 1968, public opinion had already turned against the war, though this did not lead the American public to express support for the protests in Chicago. A poll taken immediately after the convention (Robinson 1970) showed that most Americans felt the Chicago police had not used enough force to quell the demonstrations. No ongoing polling can tell us about changing attitudes toward the Chicago demonstrators. Recent polls regarding other demonstrators suggest that Americans still generally disapprove of public demonstrations, but most of these measures involve public tolerance for demonstrations opposing policies that the majority favors or has no strong opinion about, which makes them quite different from demonstrations against the war in Vietnam.

Although it was a divisive issue at the time, postwar attitudes regarding the war in Vietnam have proved quite stable. Steady majorities have felt the United States should not have gotten involved in the war in the first place,[10] and large majorities have said that the war was not only a "mistake, it was fundamentally wrong and immoral."[11] Recent softening of attitudes measured in these two questions may represent a certain softening of public opinion as the generational cohorts with personal memories of the Vietnam War are replaced by younger generations who rely on collective memory alone, but this generational replacement has not affected overall evaluations of the war. Interestingly, the younger generation would appear to be confident in its collective memories of Vietnam. As the years go on, the proportion of people who say that they are uncertain about the outcomes or lessons of Vietnam remains relatively constant. Not only is American opinion about the Vietnam experience relatively unified in the sense that people perceive it as a mistake (though the basis for this perception is typically left murky in measurements of public opinion), but when they were asked in 1995 about divisions over the Vietnam War, 38 percent said there were none and another 34 percent said that divisions over the war were healing.

During convention week in 1968, evidence of social divisions over the war in Vietnam would have been everywhere even though they were glossed over in contemporary newsmagazine coverage of the meeting. Once the war was over, those social divisions began to fade. Pressures to support one's nation during wartime—regardless of the wisdom of U.S. involvement—and divisions over whether the problem was being caught in an unwinnable war or whether the problem was an insufficient level of commitment to the war became moot. Once that happened, new narrative possibilities emerged for the events of convention week. Like the connection between the Watts riots and racial issues, however, the connection between the convention and the war would have to be made. There were many other issues that influenced the events of convention week, most notably delegate selection, which brought with it overtones of race and gender in addition to youth. Almost all of the links in the news between the convention melee and the Vietnam War are made post hoc, and the Vietnam War did not become the dominant motif in *New York Times* coverage until well into the 1990s. However, once stories about the convention became linked to stories about the war, apparent public consensus that the war was a mistake could help foster a collective memory of the convention that could prove tenable, as long as the tensions about *why* it was a mistake remained unremarked.

There are several mechanisms by which public perceptions of social reality might influence stories of the past. V. O. Key (1961) describes a how social actors attempt to anticipate and manage what he calls "latent opinion." Latent opinion, he says, is essentially the constellation of predispositions that cause an attentive public to respond to an emerging issue in a particular way. The impact of latent opinion is dependent on the size and composition of the attentive public and the ways that public connects its values to the issue at hand. In early phases of memory development, we might expect large attentive publics that use personal memories to evaluate proposed versions of the past. Later, we might expect smaller attentive publics that use contemporary norms and values to evaluate stories that claim to account for the past. At any given time, we might expect rational political actors to take their assessment of latent opinion into account in their representations of the past.

Elizabeth Noelle-Neumann (1984) argues that people have a sense of what kinds of opinion (or in this case stories) are socially acceptable and which will result in social isolation. She argues that people with acceptable opinions express them easily in public while those who embrace alternative points of view are reluctant to share them. The result is that public discourse is dominated by one point of view. While her theory has proved problematic in some tests of individual willingness and reluctance to speak out, one might expect that profit-oriented organizations like news media would be quite sensitive to what audiences would accept or reject as plausible representations of the past. E. E. Schattschneider (1975) argues that social actors attempt to manage the scope of social conflict in ways that give them the best chance of prevailing. Decisions about whether to expand the scope of conflict or to limit it are made partly on the basis of how easy it will be to recruit allies from among those currently uninvolved. Where one's views are popular in the public, one may seek to publicize those views in order to win over supporters. Where one's views are likely to be resisted, one may choose to keep them private. Translating these theories about the shape of political discourse into the realm of collective memory, narratives of the past that fit well with current public beliefs would be told and retold while those that failed to match present-day perceptions of the social world would be rarely related. Schattschneider, like Key, also argues that regardless of the way an audience *actually* reacts, social actors base their behavior on how they *expect* an audience to react, even if those expectations happen to be wrong in the event. Thus, versions of the past might fade from public discourse either because the audience would not accept them or because those who might be tempted to narrate the past in this way assume that the audience would not accept them.

Conclusion

Whether one considers the journalistic "peacemaking" described in this chapter to be a good thing or a bad thing depends very much on one's point of view. On the one hand, in the aftermath of violent social discord, media representations of what happened have the potential to harden social divisions into longstanding feuds or even spark renewed violence. Thus, a circumspect approach to representing the past seems appropriate. On the other hand, many scholars have pointed out that journalists avoid real controversy and entangle themselves in minor, unimportant issues, leaving the public without a good understanding of the choices they face.[12] Such avoidance behaviors may also leave people with an impoverished understanding of their past. Furthermore, when telling stories of the past seems likely to reignite painful social conflict, people may live silently with their differences and never acquire the shared stories that are a vital part of national identity.

Several of the processes by which journalism renders the past safer to talk about in public spaces foster the development of collective memory but have no apparent impact on its form. Fragmentation serves to keep a variety of narrative threads alive in public discourse, and the bare-bones representations of the actual events that took place can support multiple narrative interpretations. Other processes may influence the form of collective memory, although they take place in a social environment whose parameters are established by what the public will believe (or what public actors expect they will believe). The salience of particular interpretations of the past can be subtly adjusted even in the absence of a full-fledged narrative by the content of annals of events. A lack of specific historical detail leaves both reporters and officials with more room to interpret the past in ways that selectively account for the actual events and limits the ability of the public to scrutinize such interpretations. Both progress stories and stories that elide blame for what happened can shape collective memory by altering the constellation of interested parties trying to influence it.

For what it is worth, most of these processes seem to unfold in the absence of any kind of conscious intention. Fragmentation is a product of individual journalists telling stories of current events and drawing upon the narrative resources that seem relevant to them. Only when it appears in commemorative journalism does it appear to be used intentionally as a device to manage conflicting narratives. The implicit quality of the past in many stories is as easily attributed to the limited attention reporters pay to the past when telling stories of the present as it might be to some lingering concern about reigniting old controversies. Stories of progress or of continuity no doubt seem to reporters to be commonsense representations of current events, a conclusion bolstered by the responsiveness of such stories to changes in the social environment. Lists can be both an efficient storytelling tool and a simple way to acknowledge all parties to the controversy without apparently siding with any of them. There is no evidence here of reporters (or anyone else) actively working to create collective memory. Yet collective memory is indeed a byproduct of these social processes, and its form is considered in more detail in the next chapter.

CHAPTER 5

Building Collective Memory

Story Integration

T HE PAST PROVIDES A WEALTH of materials for telling stories. When a moment in time is controversial, every narrative possibility seems to be offered up to account for events. Such richness cannot survive for long. In the news, there is no room. New events will fill limited space, and the past must shrink to fit its niche in a genre that is focused on now. Social relations of power will trump some stories out of existence, if such stories are ever publicly related in the first place. But more even than this, our own beliefs about the nature of reality mitigate against the survival of multiple, competing stories about the past. The past is, or was at least, an objective reality. There must surely be a "true" story of the past to tell—a description and an explanation of what "really happened." This chapter considers how stories about the Watts riots and the 1968 Chicago convention have evolved over time and how various versions of the stories have been integrated with each other and with more recent social and political events to become the stories about the past that we recognize today. It also considers how such stories spread through the media system and the characteristics that such stories share.

Available scholarship offers little guidance about where to look in news texts for signs of story integration. Scholars like Hayden White

(1981, 1987) and Jack Fulford (1999) have described the narrative impulse in both history and journalism, the desire to render real events coherent and meaningful by telling a story about them. James Fentress and Chris Wickham (1992) demonstrate the importance of narrative structure to remembering: the story helps to order facts sequentially and provides cues to fill in any blanks that may exist. Walter Fisher (1985) and David Snow and Robert Benford (1992) argue that the most powerful stories are those with fidelity and coherence. From White's perspective, the struggle to render the past as narrative is a struggle over the moral valence, perhaps over the moral "lessons," of that past. His explanation of how stories function dovetails with the framing approach used in scholarship on media and politics.[1] Yet while these theories help to explain what stories about the past do and what the characteristics of powerful stories are, they tell us little about how such stories develop.

Scholarship on journalism and collective memory offers little guidance about such processes either. Critical scholarship generally explains news production in terms of the power of political elites to shape the news, but as we noted earlier, the relationships between leaders and institutions becomes complicated over time in ways that are not directly addressed by critical theory. Work in media sociology describes the ways that news of current events is produced, but its descriptions of reporting and storytelling techniques do not extend to how reporters integrate conflicting stories of the past. Barbie Zelizer's (1992) study of journalists' role in creating collective memories of the Kennedy assassination demonstrated that they work to develop stories that reinforce their authority as witnesses and storytellers. Kevin Barnhurst and Diana Mutz (1997) demonstrated that the recent trend in journalism is toward placing events in historical context, but they do not discuss how such contexts are created. Theories of collective memory often emphasize the ways that the present affects the past,[2] but they do not explain how conflicting stories of the past are integrated.

Further afield, however, there is a model that provides at least a methodological wedge for identifying what should be key elements of the integration process. In 1947, Gordon Allport and Leo Postman published their now-classic study on rumor propagation. Bringing the rumor mill into the lab, they showed their subjects a complex and ambiguous drawing for a brief time, then asked the subjects to describe the drawing to another person. That person was asked to repeat the description to another person, and so on through several generations. Allport and Postman watched as the original drawing's content was transformed in the stories that were told about it and described the principles that governed the transformation, emphasizing processes of assimilation that brought the drawing's conflicting details together.

There is, of course, good reason to imagine that Allport and Postman's findings will fail to map effectively onto stories of the past that appear in the news. For one thing, they were not studying collective memory, and the psychological processes of recall they examined may be substantially different from social or institutional practices for remembering. Further, there are substantial differences between the way interpersonal communication works and the way mass communication works. Then there is the fact that Allport and Postman's subjects could not refer back to the original source, whereas journalists can and indeed are often required to check their facts. Yet at its heart, there are important similarities between Allport and Postman's experiment and the problem posed by mediated collective memory of controversy. The complex and ambiguous original event cannot be recovered. All that remain are the scars and the stories. Although their motives may be different, the goals of journalists and others who seek to make use of or remember the past in public spaces are much the same as those of Allport and Postman's subjects: to tell a story that captures the essence of the original and yet is simple enough to be easily recalled. At the very least, Allport and Postman's theory of rumor propagation gives us a place to start in that it describes processes for imposing narrative structures on "real" events.

Allport and Postman found that the loss of detail across even a few iterations of the picture descriptions was dramatic, a process they refer to as "leveling." They explain, "As a rumor travels, it tends to grow shorter, more concise, more easily grasped and told. In successive versions, fewer words are used and fewer details mentioned" (1947, 75). The decline in detail is sharpest in the early reproductions. Once the story becomes short enough to hold conveniently in short-term memory, the decline levels out and the story is consistently repeated with almost no changes. This pattern is more or less repeated in journalism, where the details of the event soon become implicit in news stories both because reporters assume their audiences keep up with the news (Manoff and Schudson 1986) and because repeating the contested details of these controversial events fuels the crisis. However, in the news, the details of the past can be and sometimes are eventually recovered. Commemorative coverage of both the Watts riots and the Chicago convention reintroduced details about the original events some twenty years after they occurred. Nevertheless, the actual events of the past often remain in dispute long after a meaning for the past has been largely settled. One finds evidence of this in the contingent language, such as "alleged," "accused," or "claimed," that continues to appear in stories that relate the contested events.

A second phenomenon Allport and Postman observed among their subjects was "sharpening": "The selective perception, retention and reporting of a limited number of details from a larger context" (1947, 46). Odd wordings, familiar symbols, large objects, numbers, and movement are prone to sharpening. Of course the catch phrases of both the Watts riots ("Burn, baby, burn") and the Chicago convention ("The whole world is watching") have survived in popular culture, as have key numbers such as the thirty-four who died in Los Angeles and the Chicago Seven tried for instigating the convention disruptions. The Watts riots, especially, are often characterized with a short and consistent list of key details that are typical of the sharpening phenomenon. However, some familiar symbols, such as the Vietnam War or the civil rights movement only later became strongly associated with stories of these pasts.

Allport and Postman believed that the most important process in explaining the development of a rumor was assimilation. Through assimilation—applying a cognitive and emotional context to the material presented—storytellers attempted to produce a better "gestalt," a more coherent story. They argue, "The change is toward simplicity, symmetry, good configuration" (1947, 100). This description parallels Fentress and Wickham's (1992) description of how narrative structures affect memory: facts that fit the narrative are remembered while those that do not fit the story are not. It is this process of integrating the conflicting details of real life and contradictory explanation that is our main interest here. According to Allport and Postman, assimilation can take any of several forms. Assimilation to principle theme occurs when details are "twisted in such a way as to render the story more coherent, plausible, and well rounded" (101). In assimilation to expectation, "when an actual perceptual fact is in conflict with expectation, expectation may prove a stronger determinant of perception and memory than the situation itself" (104). Collective memory researcher Fred Davis observed a similar phenomenon as subjects in his experiments assigned historical events to the decade they "belonged to" rather than to the decade in which they actually occurred (1984). Allport and Postman liken assimilation through condensation, the third form, to stereotyping. Separate items are "fuse[d] into a single general category" (103) that stresses common characteristics and eliminates differences.

To explore the processes of story integration, each newspaper's stories about each event were examined in temporal order. The original reporting of the Watts riots and the 1968 convention were used as the benchmarks to which more recent transformations of the story were compared. These transformations are considered in terms of how they enact various assimilation processes. Assimilation processes help explain how stories of the past acquire the characteristics of good stories, narrative fidelity, and coherence, and how stories are modified in light of more recent events. They reveal the survival and demise of narrative threads, but also how such threads are blended into stories all parties to the past can live with.

Remembering the Watts Riots

Many remembrances of the Watts riots occur in various kinds of commemorative coverage. The *Los Angeles Times* carried anniversary coverage on the tenth, fifteenth, twentieth, and twenty-fifth anniversaries of the riots. Commemorative events such as the Watts Games (a high school sporting competition) and the Watts Festival (an arts festival), memorial dedications, and obituaries also offer opportunities to recall the riots. The Watts riots also provide historical context for changes and consistencies in community life, but they are rarely used as an analogy for other events until civil unrest again broke out in Los Angeles in 1992. Public memories of the past look very similar in the *Los Angeles Times* and the *New York Times*, although the *Los Angeles Times* contains a great deal more coverage and a greater degree of detail, so the evolution of the story is described here without distinguishing between the two papers.

The first few years following the Watts riots saw the disappearance of most of the city officials who sponsored law-and-order stories of the Watts riots. In their absence, the federal government's preferred narrative of economic deprivation came to dominate the ten-year anniversary coverage even in the *Los Angeles Times*, the paper that should be most sensitive to the perspective of local leaders. At the same time, details of the Watts riots were adjusted to improve the fit of stories that described the riots as part of the 1960s push for African American civil rights. The most prominent example was the rehabilitation of Martin Luther King. When King came to address the neighbors of South Central Los Angeles in 1965, they rejected him. Both the national newsmagazines and the city's African American newspaper, the *Los Angeles Sentinel* (Strohm 1999), printed quotes from residents that insulted him and resisted identifying with the mainstream civil rights movement. Of course, it is difficult to imagine a 1960s civil rights story in which Martin Luther King's leadership is scorned, but the process of connecting King to South Central Los Angeles seems to have begun by accident. After the riots, rebuilding in South Central moved at a snail's pace. One of the few lasting improvements made to the Watts/Willowbrook area was the construction of a hospital. Initially, it was to be named for Charles A. Drew, the famous African American physician, but ground was broken for the project within days of King's assassination in 1968, and a last-minute decision was made to name the hospital in his honor. The hospital became a focal point for media coverage about the community, so the fact that it was named for King and built following the Watts riots appeared repeatedly in the *Los Angeles Times*.

The trend continued. King's name was subsequently attached to streets and shopping centers in the area. A new community library was approved to be built on the site where King supposedly addressed the neighbors of Watts in the aftermath of the riots. No mention was made of his reception (Tobar 1991). At a shopping center in Watts, a memorial to King was unveiled in January 1992. The journalist reporting on the ceremony argues that the riot "was the first in a series of urban insurrections that shed light on the plight of blacks in America's major cities." One of his sources, the director of the Watts Tower Cultural Center, says that "the riots were a pivotal place in the civil rights era" (Tobar 1992, B1). Since King himself was a central symbol of the civil rights movement, this assimilation (whether to principle theme or to expectation) built a bridge between the Watts riots and the civil rights movement and created a story with better "gestalt" than the original version in which King's address was a failure.

Another group whose reputation had undergone considerable change by 1975 was the Black Muslims. The profile of the organization that appeared in the *Los Angeles Times*'s special anniversary section was, on the whole, positive. It contrasted the success of Black Muslim businesses in the inner city to the failure of many large-scale federal government programs that had, according to the article, failed to live up to their promises. The story expressly constructed a discontinuity between the old Black Muslims, "considered a radical black racist cult" (Durant 1975, 7) with the new Muslim creed, which the writer said no longer stressed hatred of whites but instead emphasized self-determination for blacks. Without the Black Muslims as instigators, conspiracy stories about the Watts riots became even less plausible than they had been when the McCone Commission Report debunked them, and they are not revived in the 1975 commemoration. At the same time, folding the Watts riots into the broader program of the civil rights movement emphasizes the symbolic rather than the literal qualities of words like "revolt" and "insurrection," as is the case in the quote from Hector Tobar's story above (1992). Where such terms are used in the 1975 special section, they are typically put in quotation marks or otherwise qualified in ways that suggest they are not meant to be taken literally: "The Watts riot, or Watts revolt as some prefer..." (Kendall 1975, 1).

As was noted in Chapter 3, the 1975 retrospective section in the *Los Angeles Times* was more an evaluation of the War on Poverty than it was a commemoration of the Watts riots. The fact that the War on Poverty was considered a failure but economic deprivation remained the dominant narrative of the Watts riots demonstrates the potency of this story as a public memory of the Watts riots. It also makes evident the ongoing power of political elites to establish meaning through the actions they take in response to events.

In 1980, the police brutality story reappeared in the *Los Angeles Times*'s retrospective, demonstrating its continued vitality when current circumstances, like the then-recent police shootings in South Central Los Angeles, made it seem relevant. However, the two articles in the commemorative series that discuss contemporary accusations of police brutality deal with current problems in South Central Los Angeles and do not directly mention police malpractice as contributing to the Watts riots. Meanwhile, the headline over a profile of Marquette Frye, whose arrest began the riots, depicts him as an instigator rather than a victim of police violence: "The Man Who Started the Riots Can't Live It Down" (*Los Angeles Times*. 1980a, 3)

Another profile in the 1980 series, of an African American widow whose husband was shot by police in 1966, raises the issue of police brutality but confounds it in odd ways, not least because the events they describe occurred a year after the Watts riots. The article explains that the officer who shot him was acquitted. Mrs. Deadwyler also lost a civil suit against the city, despite being represented by Johnnie Cochran, later famous for his defense of O. J. Simpson. However, rather than blaming the police, the widow is described as blaming her unborn son for her husband's death: "Only now is Barbara Deadwyler able to stop blaming her son for the death of her husband.... [H]er man died by a police bullet as he was driving her to the hospital for Michael to be born" (*Los Angeles Times* 1980c, 3). Thus, the police brutality narrative is still present, but it is not embraced as an explanation for the Watts riots as the economic deprivation story is. Indeed, the 1980 anniversary stories have a fragmented quality that suggests incomplete processes of reconciliation. Spaced out over several days as an irregular series, the stories also capture different perspectives on the riots in different articles, suggesting that they cannot yet be integrated.

Although the police brutality story emerged on odd occasions, the economic deprivation story remained the most commonly told and dominant story about the Watts riots. One simple way to appreciate its dominance is to see how many stories in the *Los Angeles Times* refer to both the Watts riots and jobs, the most common symptom of economic problems reporters associated with inner-city Los Angeles. Of 278 stories referring to the Watts riots published between 1985 and 1991, 125 (45 percent) of them mention jobs as well. In contrast, only eighteen of those stories, or six percent, mention the police in conjunction with either brutality or malpractice.

As political times changed, the economic deprivation story was adjusted to fit them, rather than abandoned. Much has been made of the "Reagan revolution," but in many ways it proved less a policy revolution than a revision in political discourse about public problems. In 1980, the change began to affect public memories of the Watts riots.

In the Great Society era, the dominant political rhetoric treated poverty as a structural phenomenon and governments and communities as responsible for alleviating social problems, particularly in the area of race relations where legal discrimination—still in the process of being dismantled—prevented people of color from succeeding. Early coverage of the Watts riots had highlighted a law-and-order view of events, but when stories of economic deprivation did appear, reporters wrote of the white community and its leaders' neglect of the African American community, and of the African American community's obligation to "take care of its own" (The negro after Watts 1965).

Reagan-era political rhetoric emphasized personal responsibility and suggested that poor individual choices rather than social or systemic factors were to blame for social problems. The *Los Angeles Times*'s fifteenth-anniversary coverage of the Watts riots brings this revised perspective to bear on life in South Central Los Angeles. For example, an interview with community resident Leroy Grigsby places the blame for conditions in the inner city squarely on the individuals who live there: "The biggest problem in Watts today is in the home! A place where the man has left the wife and the kids.... Their mamas lay in bed till noon, and they don't care. So all the kid knows how to do, finally is to rob and steal—what else is he gonna do?" (Stumbo 1980, 28). Others interviewed for the series cite similar problems, and the stories themselves support these contentions. Where they focus on individuals, they tend to be profiles that emphasize individual efforts rather than systemic causes to explain events.[3] Where they focus on institutions, such as the King/Drew Medical Center, the stories are about attempts to save the community from itself. The theme of personal responsibility rather than systemic failure that assimilated the past to fit with more recent explanations for social problems such as poverty and unemployment has never left narratives of the Watts riots.

A second transformation permanently confounded the causes of the Watts riots with their outcomes. The 1965 riots became a community benchmark, and "since the Watts riots" became a familiar concept used to document the slow pace of change in the area, but the line between "since" and "because" is a thin one. Evidence of post-hoc-ergo-propter-hoc reasoning appears in the narratives that describe the War on Poverty as a response to the Watts riots. Although the Great Society programs had been planned long before the Watts riots broke out and were already in the process of being implemented, they were reinterpreted as a response to the riots, leading reporters to draw the conclusion that the riots had been a violent reaction to poverty and hopelessness. A similar sort of backwards logic that confounds "since" with "because" appears much later in coverage that uses the Watts riots to mark time in South Central Los Angeles. In this case, since poverty and economic decline had engulfed the community "since the Watts riots," they must have been caused by the Watts riots. Readers unaware that poverty, joblessness, and a lack of community services predated the Watts riots are left with the false impression that these conditions were not the causes of the Watts riots but rather its consequences:

- "Since 1965, hundreds of millions of dollars...have been spent on the problems of south-central Los Angeles. There have been some successes. But, for the most part, Watts, like the South Bronx in New York, remains a symbol of the country's failure to deal with some of its urban problems" (Lindsey 1980, 24).
- "The new $6.5 million structure that opened in the Watts section of Los Angeles last month, for example, is described by city and Y officials as the first major private development completed in the area since the riots of 1965" (Tomasson 1984).
- "Several miles away, the Westminster Neighborhood Assn. will break ground Tuesday in Watts for 130 attractive townhouses—the biggest low-cost rental project to be built in that struggling area since the Watts riots tore up whole neighborhoods in 1965" (Stewart 1988).
- "The Crenshaw district is part of a nearly 50-square-mile area of South and Central Los Angeles that has been virtually abandoned by major food chains since the Watts riots in 1965" (Shiver and Mitchell 1989).

One of the places that this confusion is most evident is in *Los Angeles Times* stories that connect the Watts riots to a phenomenon known as "white flight," in which white families leave inner city neighborhoods for suburban ones. Here are some examples of stories that create the impression of causality:

- "The 39-year-old Crenshaw Shopping Center, which—like the apartments in The Jungle—began to deteriorate with the so-called 'white flight' following the Watts riots in 1965" (Ryon 1986).
- "Since then, however, the community has experienced a number of changes, including white flight after the Watts riots in 1965. Low-income families replaced the middle-class tenants and many merchants moved out" (Mitchell 1987).
- "Cannon, in the months following the Watts Riots, tried to explain how blacks felt about 'white flight.' In one speech, he said: 'When a white neighbor puts up a "for sale" sign and you know you're not so far apart financially and educationally, it's very hard. You realize they're not at all certain what they ought to do. Suddenly, they feel they have to leave because a black-faced person has moved in. Childhood myths overwhelm them'" (Ramos 1988).

A reader savvy to the mechanics of "white flight" and the history of Los Angeles can read around these passages. Such a reader can spot the stereotypes in John Mitchell's story, which implies that white people are middle-class whereas black people are poor. In point of fact, middle class African Americans also left the inner city for the suburbs. Such a reader can also identify the alternative cause for "white flight" implicit in George Ramos's story: the restrictive covenants that had limited black home ownership to particular neighborhoods were outlawed in the 1960s, which meant that white people who sought to avoid black neighbors now moved to avoid them rather than refusing to sell them houses. Of course, not all of the *Los Angeles Times* stories blame "white flight" solely on the riots, but the temporal connection between the riots and the social migrations offer an almost irresistible opportunity for assimilation by condensation—the chance to tell a simple story with good gestalt that dovetails with widespread beliefs about social life.

The subtly altered story of the Watts riots in which economic deprivation was the consequence rather than the cause of the Watts riots was also a good fit with the Reagan-era rhetoric that held individuals responsible for their own fates. By rioting, the people of South Central Los Angeles had destroyed their own community. Rather than being abandoned, the economic deprivation story of the Watts riots has been adapted to fit modern political discourse about poverty and its causes.

Remembering the Chicago Convention

There is virtually no purely commemorative coverage of the Chicago convention, although it is one element on the list of events recalled in 1993 anniversary coverage of 1968 as a whole. Instead, the Chicago convention tends to be recalled in the context of current events. The table in Chapter 4 shows that in the *New York Times*, the convention is primarily recalled as a political event, with the number of references to the convention peaking in presidential election years. In the *Chicago Tribune*, there is no easily discernable pattern to the remembrances. This difference in pattern is also an indicator that the convention is, for many years, recalled differently in each paper. Moreover, with no com-memorative coverage to bring them together, the separate threads of convention recollections stay more or less separate for many years, although each within itself experiences assimilation processes that make for a more coherent story than the one that was told at the time of the events themselves. Just as there had been when the convention was initially covered, there were three separate kinds of stories told about the convention: stories of events inside the International Amphitheater, stories about the street demonstrations, and stories about the trial of the Chicago Seven.

In the New York Times

By 1984, the *New York Times*'s 1968 convention stories about events that had occurred in the convention hall itself had developed two main emphases. The most prominent of these was the delegate selection reforms attributed to the party's experiences at the convention. The convention is used as historical context, a time marker (Lang and Lang 1989) for the rise of the modern primary system for selecting conven-tion delegates. The second emphasis was on Democratic disunity. Writers recalled the discord over the Vietnam War plank of the party plat-form or McCarthy's refusal to back Humphrey until late in the campaign. This story was typically used as a historical analogy to assess party unity in the current election cycle, with 1968 as a kind of worst-case scenario. Condensation processes, then, had reduced the complex story of politicking in the convention hall to two simple, prominent themes.

These stories were further simplified in that while they provided a historical backdrop for current events, they themselves lacked historical context. The credentials fight waged by southern delegations seeking to break the hold of white segregationist governors on the delegate selection processes in their states is not recalled, nor is breaking the unit rule. Sometimes, the reasons for the Democrats' disunity in 1968 are not recalled either, and the actual content of the Vietnam War debate at the convention never appears. Whether reporters omitted these elements because they assumed their audience was familiar with them or because the details of the convention still seemed too hot to handle, the result was that conclusions about the convention were presented without analysis.

After 1984, one finds that stories about Democratic disunity in 1968 undergo a subtle transformation. Rather than using the convention as an analogy to measure party unity, the *Times* begins to use it as a context to mark the rise of the "boring" convention. The 1968 convention is recalled as the moment when both parties learned that presenting a positive face to the television cameras was vital and the convention itself became a media event rather than a working meeting. In 1992, the Democrats selected a winning candidate, Bill Clinton, and stories about the delegate selection reforms (which typically dwelt on how they had hobbled the Democrats' ability to pick a winner) disappeared almost overnight. Because it made possible a progress story about the Democrats' political fortunes since the '68 convention, Clinton's electoral success paved the way for a single story of events inside the convention hall, one that traced the rise of the modern, boring political convention to the "lessons" of 1968.

The story of the street demonstrations in Chicago went through several transformations. The *New York Times* was in a tight spot. Officials were divided over the convention violence in Chicago. There were early hints of some political leaders' distaste for some police officers' behavior, such as the pressure on Humphrey to retract his statement of support, but some of the demonstrators were tried for their behavior. The Walker report was controversial, as was the verdict in the Chicago Seven trial. Opinion polls taken immediately after the convention revealed broad public support for the actions of the Chicago police (Robinson 1970), but journalists had been injured—and some believed they had been targeted—in clashes with police. There was very little guidance available from any of the typical sources about what kind of story to tell.

The resolution that had begun to emerge by the early 1980s was that the demonstrators, as a group, were victims of police violence. Versions of this story that appear in the 1980s sometimes support the claim of police malpractice by mentioning Daley's "shoot to kill" order issued during the riots that followed Martin Luther King's assassination in April. Such stories also emphasize the protestors' youth. Reporting on an investigation into police brutality in Chicago, the *Times* noted, "Minorities in Chicago have complained of police brutality for years, but the issue did not gain widespread attention until the Democratic National Convention in 1968, when scores of young people were beaten by police" (Sheppard 1980a, A16). In many cases, as in this one, the *New York Times* assimilates to principle theme by neglecting to mention the provocative behavior of some demonstrators. At this point in time, the *Times* also typically fails to explain what the protestors were doing in Chicago in the first place.

The story of the street demonstrations in the early 1980s calls into question what we know about crime frames as they are applied to social movement activities. Many of the truisms about contemporary coverage fail to hold up over the long term. The previous chapter demonstrated that over time, references to damage and arrests acquire the quality of a natural rather than a social phenomenon, and the absence of an agent undermines crime frames. Another important principle of social movement theory is that in order to avoid crime frames, demonstrators must be entirely passive. Gitlin (1980) found that reporters would seize upon any provocative behavior by demonstrators, using it as a justification for far more violent response from officials. David Garrow (1978) found that the passivity of the Selma marchers was a key to their success. Yet here, the *New York Times* remembers the violence of the police and forgets the provocation of the demonstrators. Gitlin argues that crime frames are hampered where movement activities are described as politically meaningful. Yet the *Times*'s coverage quoted above belies this as well, for it makes no mention of why the activists came to Chicago. All of this suggests that the ways social movements are covered in their own time may be poor predictors of how their activities are later remembered in the press. Whether this is because public opinion "catches up" with the demonstrators' cause, or for some other reason, is unclear. The impact of these memories on coverage of more recent demonstrations is also unclear. Collective memory may be nothing more than closing the barn door late, but it may also offer a kind of "leg up" to contemporary protestors to be compared to memories of demonstrations past.

By the late 1980s, the *Times* finally began to include reasons for the protests in its stories about the street demonstrations at the Chicago convention. The paper regularly identified them as antiwar, another moment of assimilation by condensation that eliminates the many and complex causes that were protest targets in Chicago. One rough indicator of this change is the increased use of words such as "antiwar" and "Vietnam" in stories that referred to the convention. Between 1980 and 1984, only 28 percent of *New York Times* stories that referred to the 1968 convention included the words "antiwar" (with or without the hyphen) or "Vietnam." Between 1985 and 1989, that proportion jumped to 38 percent, and between 1990 and 1995 it rose again to 44 percent.

Mayor Daley continued to be directly connected to the behavior of his police force, and the actions of the police were still described as brutal or unjustified. Reporting that the Democrats might hold their 1996 convention in Chicago, the *Times* reminded its readers what had happened the last time: "The late Mayor Richard J. Daley was seen on national television during the 1968 convention cutting off irate delegates and defending the brute force used against Vietnam War protestors by his police officers" (Berke 1994, A8). From the perspective of critical scholars such as Gitlin, this must seem a mixed blessing. Though finally constructed as meaningful activity, the protests were stripped of their more radical content and connected with an issue that was now part of the past itself. It is also worth noting that in this passage, Richard Berke connects events inside the convention hall to events in the streets, although not in ways that major social actors are likely to approve. Nevertheless, this blending of events is not far distant from the single narrative that would ultimately be offered in the weeks leading up to the 1996 convention.

No existing theory of collective memory offers a clear explanation for the late identification of a target for the protests. Allport and Postman's (1947) theory explains the loss of detail, not its revival. Other theories, such as those of Barry Schwartz, Yael Zerubavel, and Bernice Barnett (1986) and Bernard Lewis (1975) describe the recovery of memories at a time when they are especially needed by a culture, but there is no obvious event that triggered a need to understand the Chicago protests in the context of the Vietnam War. One clue may be offered by the timing of the addition. Like descriptions of the actual events of the Watts riots, descriptions of the demonstrations as antiwar protests become commonplace about twenty years after the original event. In other words, one generation passes before these kinds of details are added back into stories about controversial events. Karl Manheim (1925) suggests that generational effects are important to understanding collective memory because people's responses to public life are especially influenced by public events that occur when they are in their late teens and early twenties. In his theory, "generations" are defined by the public events that dominated their early adulthood rather than by the amount of time it takes for children to become parents themselves. After twenty years, about one quarter of the population would have had no personal memories of the original events, and it is at this point that the selective details corresponding to the emergent collective memory reemerge in public discourse.

As the image of the Chicago protestors as a group was rehabilitated, the Chicago Seven's checkered past was preserved. Prior to 1985, the *Times* recalled the trial with uneasy precision, using terms such as "allegation" and "accusation" and often mentioning the acquittals. In 1980, the *Times* described the "Chicago Seven trial, in which a separate group of antiwar activists was accused of plotting the disorders that occurred during the 1968 Democratic National Convention here" (Sheppard 1980b, A18). The trial became famous for what the defendants were *accused* of. Their behavior at the trial is rarely described, and their acquittal is usually noted during this early period. They remain connected to the demonstrations rather than the wider causes they supported. Even the passage above, an early example of linking the demonstrations to the war in Vietnam, misses the richness of the causes supported by the Chicago Seven (which, because of the political nature of the trial, were not themselves necessarily representative of the causes protested in the streets of Chicago during convention week).

In the later 1980s, the *Times* was no longer so careful to mention that the defendants were acquitted of some charges, but the stories remained ambivalent as the label "Chicago Seven" was often delegitimated with quotation marks and adjectives such as "so-called." The *Times's* portrayal of the Seven could vary dramatically. In September 1986, the paper reported, "Mr. Hoffman [was] one of the so-called Chicago 7 protestors arrested at the 1968 Democratic National Convention in Chicago.... He was cleared of charges of organizing violence at the 1968 convention" (*New York Times* 1986a, C13). Five months later, the *Times* noted,

> Eventually, Mr. Hoffman and four other defendants were convicted of some of the charges against them which grew out of antiwar demonstrations at the Democratic National Convention in 1968. The defendants were also cited numerous times for contempt of court and Mr. Hoffman received an eight month prison term. (Wald 1987, 1)

Both of these presentations are mixed. In the first, Hoffman's acquittal is prominent and the label Chicago Seven is called into question, but the violence at the convention is meaningless. In the latter version, the protests are meaningful, but Hoffman is guilty.

By the 1990s, ambivalent had begun to lean decidedly negative, sometimes at the expense of the facts. In May 1996, the *Times* described "State Senator Tom Hayden, a Los Angeles Democrat who knows something about rebellion, having been a member of the Chicago Seven, the antiwar group that led demonstrations in Chicago during the 1968 Democratic National Convention in Chicago" (Ayres, A12). The story describes the Chicago Seven as an antiwar organization, when at best they were a group only in the sense that they were codefendants. In 1995, a story in the arts section of the paper reported, "Mr. Kunstler...made his name in 1969 during the famously raucous trial of the seven men who disrupted the 1968 Democratic National Convention" (Weber, B3). This story suggests that the seven did all the damage themselves. But ambiguity can still be found. Jerry Rubin's obituary said of the seven, "They were the subjects of Federal indictments for conspiracy to disrupt the 1968 Democratic National Convention in that city, where the police beat and tear-gassed protestors on the streets" (Pace 1994, D21). This sentence illustrates the different trajectories of the Chicago Seven stories and those of the street demonstrations. While the street demonstrators tend to be innocent victims of police violence, the Chicago Seven tend to be blamed for the convention chaos.

These three narratives continue to exist more or less separately until the middle 1990s, when possibilities for integrating them and for reconciling the *Times*'s version of the story with the *Chicago Tribune*'s began to emerge.

In the Chicago Tribune

The *New York Times* devotes a substantial number of references to the 1968 convention to discussing its national political ramifications. The *Chicago Tribune*, in contrast, remains focused on the local story of the convention, which means that its references to the convention typically involve events in the streets. Despite the editorial change that was announced in 1969 towards more balanced news pages and editorial stances confined to the editorial pages (Wendt 1979), one finds that the *Tribune* takes a consistently dim view of both the protestors and the Chicago Seven and remains concerned about the impact of the 1968 convention on the reputation of its city.

The *Tribune*'s articles are far more condemnatory of the Chicago Seven than are the ambiguous stories of the *New York Times*. On September 30, 1987, *Tribune* columnist Bob Greene described "Jerry Rubin—when he was the bearded, angry leader of the Yippies during the street riots at the 1968 Democratic National Convention in Chicago. With his wild looks, painted face, and revolutionary rhetoric, he became an instant media celebrity" (1). Two weeks later, the paper reported that Abbie Hoffman was protesting mandatory drug testing. He is described as a "perpetual protestor," a leader of Yippie demonstrators at the convention, and a "leading light" of the "notorious Chicago Seven" who turned the 1968 convention into a "three-ring circus of the absurd" (Clark 1987, 3). The following summer, a *Tribune* headline announced, "Tom Hayden the Man Who Turned Chicago Upside-Down 20 Years Ago Says He Is Now a 'Born-Again Middle

American"' (Galloway 1988, 1). Like the late coverage of the Chicago Seven in the *New York Times*, this headline exaggerates Hayden's personal responsibility for the disturbances in a way that seems almost literary. The *Tribune*'s doubt about Hayden's reform is also apparent.

This pattern of reporting about the Chicago Seven does not change much. The *Tribune* does not typically mention that the accused were acquitted of some charges. The men are generally depicted as having behaved outlandishly at the trial and the convention, and the paper's stories of the reform of the Chicago Seven contain a note of dubiousness. Connecting these men with the protests delegitimates their current activities. When his comments on Richard Nixon's death were reported, Hayden was credentialed as "a California state senator and one of the Chicago Seven prosecuted by Nixon's Justice Department after the riots at the 1968 Democratic National Convention" (*Chicago Tribune* 1994a, 1). The *Tribune* also keeps the memory of the Chicago Seven trial alive through its daily almanac. Almost every year, the almanac entries note the day the indictments were handed down, the day the trial began and the day the verdicts were announced.

If the difference between the presentation of the Chicago Seven in the *Times* and the *Tribune* was basically one of degree, the difference in characterizations of the protests was nearer to being of kind, for the *Tribune* tended to blame the demonstrators for the violence. Sometimes, the police were entirely absent from the story, as in a description of "ugly street theater in Chicago, as protestors rioted during the Democratic National Convention" (Breo 1986, 1). The *Tribune* recalls the demonstrators' militancy, forgotten in the *Times*: "During that riotous convention week, during which Illinois National Guardsmen and Chicago police aggressively kept the demonstrators from getting near the convention center, war protestors came wielding bottles, rocks and a heady passion for change" (McRoberts 1988, 3).

In the late 1980s and early 1990s, the *Tribune*'s stance toward the demonstrators softened to something approaching the even-handedness of preconvention newsmagazine coverage. In 1992, a reporter considered the possibility of a bid to host the 1996 convention: "It could help wipe away the stain left in 1968, when liberals and shaggy-haired anti-war demonstrators sought a confrontation with Richard J. and got one at the end of the billy clubs swung by his police" (Kass 1992, 1).

This version of the story has no heroes. Critical scholars might argue that such even-handed treatment subtly privileges authority, since official violence is sometimes legitimated while citizen violence almost never is. Contemporary opinion polls about the Chicago convention certainly bear out this observation in the short run. In the long run—and given current public attitudes towards the Vietnam experience—it is difficult to know for sure, and the softening position of the newspaper is clear. At about this time, the *Chicago Tribune*, like the *New York Times*, also begins to regularly identify the protestors as antiwar.

Throughout this period, the alternative version of the story in which demonstrators are the victims of police violence is kept alive in the work of columnists and letter writers. Interviewed for a feature story on ideal dinner guests, Studs Terkel described a companion as "teargassed, pursued, astonished, with me as his companion, he, middle-aged, frail, somewhat battered, was envisioning and pursuing his ideal" (Carroll 1986, 15). A reporter reminiscing about old Comiskey Park recalled, "I hid my own liberal feelings during the 1968 Democratic National Convention while police were beating long-haired protesters" (Sakamoto 1990, 17). A debate over the relevance of comparing police behavior at the convention to that of Chinese officials during the Tiananmen Square demonstrations sprang up in letters to the editor published in late June and early July of 1989.

By the late 1980s, then, the *Tribune* was in many ways closer to a unified narrative of the Chicago convention than the *Times* was. While the *Times* preserved several distinct stories corresponding to the original fragmentation of the convention coverage, the *Tribune* focused on the street demonstrations and the subsequent trial of the Chicago Seven. The *Tribune* also told a relatively consistent story of the city's attempt to uphold law and order in the face of rowdy demonstrators spoiling for a fight. But in the middle 1990s, it became apparent that the national press would return to Chicago to cover another Democratic National Convention, and the story that worked for local audiences in Chicago was unlikely to dovetail well with the stories told by the national press. Audiences in Chicago would be exposed to conflicting claims about what "really happened" in 1968—claims that would call into question the authority of news organizations whose stories would not match. A hint of the coming conflict is revealed when, after reporting an alderman's comment that the upcoming convention gives the city a chance to repair its reputation, *Tribune* staff writers observe that "A *national* inquiry called the street fighting a 'police riot' where law enforcers battered Vietnam War [protestors]."[4] To preserve its journalistic authority as a source of the "true story" of what "really happened," the *Tribune* needed a narrative of the past that would not contradict the stories in other news media. The *Times*, for its part, still had conflicts in its three stories to resolve.

From Many, One?

By the time the Democrats returned to Chicago in 1996, the stories of the Chicago convention looked as though they might never be resolved. In the absence of anniversary-style commemorations, the *Times*'s three stories of convention week were never juxtaposed, and the *Tribune*'s stories for its local audience were never compared to the alternative versions in the national paper. In spite of the ongoing fragmentation in the *Times*, the "gestalt" of each of the stories did improve. Each was more coherent than the stories told at the time of the convention itself. The mixed presentation of the demonstrators at the time of the convention had been resolved into two tales: demonstrators as victims, the Chicago Seven as culprits. The broad agenda of the demonstrations had been narrowed to one of anitwar activism, added later to the story. Events inside the hall were represented as giving rise to modern primaries and modern conventions, though the reasons for the interparty strife were not typically preserved.

There had been some articles printed in the papers that had potential to unify the stories told about the convention, but early versions were damaging to the reputations of powerful institutions and often failed the "good gestalt" test. The most common connections linked the chaos in the hall to the chaos in the streets. In a *New York Times* story that identified the 1968 meeting as the birthplace of the boring convention, the reporter observed, "After the Democratic blood-letting of 1968, it became clear to strategists of both parties that neither could conduct an ugly eye-gouging fight in front of the [television cameras]" (Weaver 1984, 3). Here, the linkage between events in the hall and events in the streets is seamless but vague. Like many early stories, it expects the reader to apply some background information in order to make any literal sense of the story.

Four years later, R. W. Apple connected events inside and outside the hall in a story about delegate selection reform: "Since the Democratic National Convention of 1968, when tensions within the Democratic Party exploded into riots on the streets of Chicago, American political parties have been tinkering with the methods by which they choose their presidential nominee" (1988, A12). But this story both damages the reputation of the Democrats and fails the "good gestalt" test. It seems impossible that the protests could have become so violent over an issue as esoteric as delegate selection reform, especially since the connection between the reforms, the Vietnam War, and the expansion of civil rights almost never appears in the *Times*.

In the early 1990s, as stories about events in the hall became less concerned with delegate selection following Clinton's election, a new connection was made: "The 1968 Democratic National Convention in Chicago became a symbol of a party torn apart over Vietnam" (Toner 1993, A16). This connection was available because by this time the street demonstrations were regularly linked to the Vietnam War, and it had better gestalt than a story that suggested that there had been riots in the streets over delegate selection. However, it still did not capture the underlying struggle over democratic values such as representation and meaningful electoral choice. It was less harmful to the Democrats' reputation now that the war was over, but it still suggested a damaging tendency to disunity.

The *Tribune* offered a different version of a unifying story that absolved everyone of responsibility for what had happened in Chicago. The earliest version appeared in 1988: "The events surrounding the 1968 Democratic Convention have come to symbolize a national political and social cataclysm that erupted from the unrest over the Vietnam War" (Foerstner, 57). In this narrative, neither the Democrats nor the city of Chicago nor the demonstrators are to blame. They are the visible symptom of a national malaise that they did not create and could not control. In 1994, the story acquired a powerful sponsor and a new twist. It was at about this time that serious discussions began about the possibility of Chicago hosting a national party convention. In May, responding to questions about how the experiences of 1968 would affect the city's bid to host the 1996 Democratic National Convention, Mayor Richard M. Daley said, "We don't have anything to apologize for.... We had the convention here in 1968. If it was somewhere else, it would have happened there." Daley cited other national events of 1968, including the Kennedy and King assassinations and the Vietnam War in arguing that his city was just unlucky in hosting the convention that year (Daley 1994, 3). Daley's version of the story absolved the city and the party of blame for the violence. Like later references to the Watts riots, this narrative structured the Chicago convention as a kind of natural disaster. That summer, Chicago had been in the path of a tornado of civil unrest that could not have been prevented.

As a unifying story, this had a great deal to recommend it. It absolved key groups of blame: demonstrators, police, city officials, the Democratic Party, even the Chicago Seven. The disturbances were an expression of the national divisions over the War in Vietnam. With no guilty party and a national struggle safely bound in the past, this story seemed a prime candidate for widespread adoption as the coherent interpretation of the Chicago convention. Instead, it was delegitimated. The *New York Times* first told the story this way:

> The Mayor...became somewhat defensive about 1968 in an interview today. "It could have been any place in the country," he said. "It was the right place but the wrong time, 1968, with Vietnam, the Kennedy assassination, the King assassination."...That convention was thrust into turmoil when the police attacked thousands of Vietnam War protesters who had come to Chicago from around the country. (Berke 1994, A8)

It was the source of the story that the reporters doubted. Daley had a vested interest, both as the mayor of Chicago and as the son of the former mayor, to present the most positive story of the convention possible. Professional values dictated skepticism of interpretations offered by interested parties. The *Chicago Tribune* also cast doubt on Daley's version of events, referring to his interpretation as a "mayoral outburst" rather than an attempt to understand the past (Locin 1995).

The mayor's advocacy of a unified story had finally brought concentrated attention to this narrative, for he offered this story to whoever asked him about the events of 1968. Perversely, his advocacy made the story seem less satisfying as a means of understanding the disturbances than it had when sometimes offered by other commentators on odd occasions over the years. Whether this unified story of the 1968

Chicago convention would become the accepted narrative of events was unclear when the Democrats returned to Chicago in 1996.

Telling a Good Story

It is worthwhile to note that none of the stories told about either the Watts riots or the Chicago convention could be described as factually inaccurate,[5] although there is a certain amount of literary license taken in some of the stories about the Chicago Seven. While their exploits are sometimes exaggerated, there is a fact pattern that all versions of the convention story agree upon and account for: that the convention occurred in 1968, that it nominated Hubert Humphrey, that police and protestors clashed violently, that no one died, that eight men were indicted for conspiracy to incite riots, and so on. The same is true for the Watts riots: thirty-four people died, many buildings were burned, many stores were looted, African American people were involved, and the affected neighborhoods were inhabited by poor people. Of course, memory is selective, and no memory ever accounts for each and every aspect of the past. However, the stories told about controversial pasts differ less in their recounting of the events themselves (which is often absent altogether) than in the meaning they assign to the past.

Then why these meanings? What made these stories preferable to other stories? One way to explain the outcomes is in terms of how the stories serve the needs of those in power, and indeed the needs of the powerful are effectively served by the narratives that come to dominate. The economic deprivation narrative of the Watts riots certainly suited the federal government as it implemented Great Society programs in the 1960s. A story that represented the Chicago convention as a concentrated expression of social divisions over the Vietnam War certainly suited the Democratic Party by attaching the convention unrest to the historical moment rather than to the Party itself. Yet this explanation for the outcomes is in some ways unsatisfying.

First, these complex social events do not involve a unified social authority but rather several levels of social authority that are sometimes at odds with one another. In particular, local governments are in both cases best served by a law-and-order narrative of events in which city officials competently protect citizens from the violent criminality of strangers ("outside agitators" who come to the city to foment trouble). In both Los Angeles and Chicago, local and federal officials collide over the meaning of events. In Los Angeles, a federal narrative comes to dominate fairly quickly. In Chicago, the local newspaper and the national newspaper preserve different stories, with the local paper remaining responsive to local authorities and the national paper maintaining several narratives. Critical scholars recognize these kinds of divisions among elites as a necessary component of controversy in the news media, but the negotiation process by which that controversy is settled is less remarked. In Los Angeles, the likely reason for the federal government's dominance is the turnover in city government, but in Chicago the explanation must be different. The integrative story must satisfy the needs of two different authorities.

A second issue to consider is that even as the needs of social authorities change, the narrative about the Watts riots remains relatively stable (on this point, less can be said about the Chicago convention because an integrated story develops so late in the process). In the more conservative 1970s, as the Great Society is declared a failure, the economic deprivation narrative of the Watts riots remains stable rather than being replaced by an alternative story. In the Reagan era, the economic deprivation story is modified to match the contemporary emphasis on personal responsibility, but the story is not itself abandoned in favor of the ultimate personal responsibility story: an account of the riots as an act of lawlessness.

The most impressive evidence of the stability of the Watts riots story appears in connection with the 1992 Los Angeles riots. When the acquittal of the police officers who assaulted Rodney King in the process of arresting him sparked civil unrest in South Central Los Angeles, the opportunity arose to resurrect almost any of the stories initially told about the Watts riots: police brutality, economic deprivation, or lawlessness. King, like Frye, was beaten by police during the process of his arrest, offering clear connections to the police brutality story of the Watts riots. The subsequent violence offered an opportunity to revive the lawlessness story of the Watts riots, for strong similarities existed: most notably that many of the same neighborhoods were affected and residents burned and looted "their own" neighborhoods. The economic deprivation story also seemed applicable to the 1992 events, for while the triggering incident for the disturbances in both cases was an accusation of police malpractice, the nature of the violence that followed suggested that economic issues were an important force driving events. The communities most affected were inner-city neighborhoods where poor people lived.

If the past serves the powerful, one would expect that the lawlessness story of the Watts riots would be revived under these circumstances. Of all the stories that were initially told about the Watts riots, this one has the most potential to bolster the authority of local officials. Federal officials, furthermore, no longer had an interest in justifying massive social programs to alleviate poverty. Yet that is not what happened. Although the 1992 unrest was covered from a law-and-order perspective in its own time,[6] the stories about the more recent unrest that drew parallels to the Watts riots did not invoke the lawlessness story of the 1965 event. Of course, it was quite possible in that election year for Democrats like Bill Clinton to score political points with a story about how Republican neglect of inner-city poverty that had existed for decades had produced this civil unrest; therefore, the economic deprivation story of the Watts riots could serve the purposes of some authorities as well. Yet it is important to note that the struggle between local and federal officials over the meaning of the Watts riots was not reopened during the 1992 unrest.

The evolution of a collective memory of the Watts riots shows that social actors, including social authorities, treated the past as a preexisting interpretive structure that could be used to supply meaning for current events rather than using current events as a justification for radically reinterpreting the past. One useful way to make sense of this stability even in light of changing elite needs is to observe the economical way in which power is used. Revising a story of the past requires effort and an expenditure of resources, and it is likely that the more radical the revision, the more effort and resources are required. Often, the story of a past controversy evolves without much official intervention, and the evolving story is typically subject to minor modifications rather than radical overhauls. The demise of the Great Society may have made the economic deprivation story useless, but it did not make changing the story worthwhile. Making the story fit the Reagan-era paradigm of individual responsibility did not require fundamentally altering the narrative, only changing the responsible agent (and it seems worthwhile to point out that the work done to make this change seems to have required very little direct intervention from authorities). In the context of the 1992 unrest, it surely made more sense to concentrate efforts on defining the present rather than on redefining the past. Thus, during the 1992 unrest, the story of the Watts riots as it had developed by 1992 was picked up by people who found it useful in the construction of analogies or contexts to the current unrest. They used it as a "factual" resource, much as poverty statistics or community demographics might have been. In other words, the story of the past came to stand in for the past itself. None of this is to say that if redefining a past seemed sufficiently important to the achievement of the goals of powerful social actors, its meaning might not be radically altered to suit current exigencies, but only that the expenditure of resources required to redefine the past mean that much of the time the past is likely to be used "as is," rather than retailored to fit.

Yet in recognizing the limits of official influence, we are still left with the question, Why these stories? A notable feature of the stories that ultimately succeed is that they offer something to all groups who are stakeholders in the event, even if it is only absolution from blame for the event itself. Take the economic deprivation story of the Watts riots. It was initially sponsored by the federal government and met the needs of the administration as the White House rolled out the Great Society. However, supporting the federal government's narrative also supplied the city government with largesse to distribute along with a compelling story about how it restored devastated neighborhoods, which in many ways would serve the local government's needs as well as a lawlessness story. Community leaders might be most basically concerned with the policing of their neighborhoods, but after decades of neglect, an economic deprivation story of the Watts riots offered—in conjunction with the Great Society programs—both government programs and a rationale for arguing that more needed to be done. The only immediate stakeholder in the Watts riots that did not directly benefit from the economic deprivation story was local law enforcement, but they at least were absolved of blame for the violence and for their methods of policing the community. In many ways, the economic deprivation story of the Watts riots was initially bought by the federal government, but its continuing usefulness to a variety of social actors kept it healthy long after the money ran out. It could be used to make a case that money was being wasted, that more money was needed, or that money should be allocated differently and so remained a useful story for those engaged in debate on a variety of issues involving race and class in Los Angeles and beyond.

The story of the Chicago convention that was emerging at the time of the 1996 Democratic National Convention had fewer rewards for stakeholders, but it did successfully transfer blame from individual actors to the era itself. Neither the city of Chicago, the Democratic Party, the Chicago Seven, nor the demonstrators were to blame for what had happened in 1968. Instead, a perfect storm of political and social chaos had converged in Chicago. It could have happened anywhere and involved anyone, but now that the era was over, there was little chance that it could happen again. The future utility of this story might be in doubt, but at least it would lay the past to rest.

These stories of the past, then, are like water following the path of least resistance. To continue the metaphor, they also have a certain amount of surface cohesion. That is, the stories hang together reasonably well. Assimilation processes pull together the details that make sense with the larger theme and leave behind inconvenient facts (although in journalism, factual inaccuracies are quite rare). The stories simplify, resonate, and make sense, taking on the qualities of good narrative and functioning as Hayden White (1981) suggests we want history to function: assigning to real events the comforting coherence of a story.

Spreading the Story

This chapter has focused on how disparate narratives of controversial pasts are winnowed and integrated to create a collective memory, but alternative versions of the past can be preserved in news as well. This raises the question of whether and how integrated stories of the past might appear in other newspapers. We have already seen some evidence of pressure to resolve discrepancies between the stories told by different news organizations. The gap between the convention stories of the *Chicago Tribune* and the *New York Times* would be revealed when the national media came to Chicago to cover the 1996 convention. While the *Tribune* serves a local audience, that local audience also has access to national television news broadcasts that might challenge the *Tribune*'s version of the convention story in the course of covering the 1996 nominating convention. News claims to present the truth objectively, which should mean that there can be only one "right" version of the story. To present more than one damages the credibility of at least one and perhaps all news organizations.

To explore how stories of the Watts riots and the Chicago convention were presented in other newspapers and mechanisms by which stories presented in one venue might reappear in others, we can look at some of the other newspapers that are available on the Nexis database using the standard search terms developed for searching the *Los Angeles Times*, *New York Times*, and *Chicago Tribune*. Many papers were added to the database in the early 1990s, and this creates the opportunity to choose papers that are regionally and editorially diverse and to make sure that each paper is owned by a different organization. However, because the papers do not appear in Nexis until the 1990s, it is impossible to trace the development of collective memory in them but only to consider whether the narratives that developed in the three newspapers examined so far also appear in other newspapers. For the Watts riots, the search for stories was expanded to the *Atlanta Journal/Constitution*, the *Houston Chronicle*, and the *Chicago Sun-Times*. For the Chicago convention, the coverage in the *Atlanta Journal/Constitution*, the *Houston Chronicle*, and the *Seattle Post-Intelligencer* was compared to that of the *Times* and the *Tribune*. Because an integrated story of the Chicago convention was still in development, we might expect to see considerably less consistency across newspapers in this case than we would for the Watts riots, where the economic deprivation story has dominated for decades.

The *Atlanta Journal/Constitution* serves the South, is owned by Cox newspapers at the time of this writing, and operates under a joint operating agreement in which the *Journal* and *Constitution* share some news copy and printing facilities but maintain separate editorial identities. The *Journal* supports Democrats; the *Constitution* supports Republicans. Copy from both newspapers is uploaded to the Nexis database. In this analysis, they are treated as one paper because documentation of which paper carried what stories is uneven, and in most cases where the documentation is clear, the relevant story was carried in both papers. The *Houston Chronicle* serves the southern Midwest and the Southwest, is presently owned by Hearst Publishing, and supports Republicans. The *Chicago Sun-Times* serves the upper Midwest, is currently owned by the Hollinger group, and supports Democrats. All three of these cities have substantial minority populations, and several experienced racial tension or even unrest in the period under study. The *Seattle Post-Intelligencer* is owned by Hearst Publishing at the time of this writing and supports Democrats. It replaces the *Chicago Sun-Times* in the convention case study because the *Sun-Times* is a local paper in Chicago and because the first large-scale antiglobalization protests occurred in Seattle.

Remembering the Watts Riots Elsewhere

The pattern of distribution of references to the Watts riots in each of these newspapers compared to the *New York Times* is displayed in Table 5.1. The *Times* contained eighty-four articles referring to the riots between 1991 and December 31, 2000. The *Journal/Constitution* contained fifty and the *Chronicle* sixty-eight. The *Sun-Times*, not available on Nexis until 1992, contained twenty-three. While it is true that the numbers found in regional newspapers are consistently smaller than those of the *Times*, the more remarkable finding is that the numbers are as high as they are. The *Times* devotes extensive space to national and world news and for years was accused of slighting the interests of local New Yorkers by neglecting news about their city. In contrast, the local papers in Houston, Atlanta, and Chicago serve audiences that are regional at best. Distributions of references to the Watts riots in these papers is also quite similar to that of the *Times*: a spike in 1992 during the civil unrest following the so-called Rodney King trial subsides, leaving a soft echo that lasts for about three years. The slightly elevated number of references fades before the fifth anniversary of the 1992 unrest, and there is no second spike in the number of references in 1997. As is the case in the *New York Times*, references to the Watts riots appear throughout these papers in the national news and editorial sections; in television, book, film, and art reviews; in the sports section; and even, occasionally, in the local news.

Both the *Atlanta Journal/Constitution* and the *Chicago Sun-Times* strongly resemble the *Los Angeles Times* and *New York Times* in their treatment of the Watts riots. The story of the Watts riots is that of a crisis in race relations brought on by economic and social deprivation in the African American community. In these newspapers, one of the

Table 5.1: Number of Stories Referring to the Watts Riots in Four Newspapers by Year

YEAR	Atlanta Journal (N=50)	Houston Chronicle (N=66)	Chicago Sun-Times (N=23)	New York Times (N=80)
1991	4	1		5
1992	29	35	10	40
1993	4	5	3	5
1994	4	4	1	7
1995	4	4	1	7
1996	1	2	0	5
1997	2	5	2	3
1998	0	2	3	1
1999	2	3	2	2
2000	0	5	1	5

Note: All editions of each newspaper are included. Search term is "Watts" within 50 words of "1965." The *Atlanta Journal* and the *Houston Chronicle* are available on Nexis beginning January 1, 1991. The *Chicago Sun-Times* is not available on Nexis prior to January 1, 1992.

mechanisms by which the story spread also becomes apparent. While the *Los Angeles Times* has a large metro reporting staff and the *New York Times* has a large national staff—both of which supply their respective papers with a great deal of original copy—the regional papers are more dependent on wire services and syndication to provide them with news and views about distant events in Los Angeles, both past and present. Papers that are regional need not be provincial: they have access to the news created by national wire services like the Associated Press and to the copy of their sister papers elsewhere, especially when those papers are owned by the same organization. It is reasonable to imagine that as the story develops among national reporters and the local press in Los Angeles, it trickles down to other regional papers via the news services. For example, although the documentation of its wire copy is not entirely clear, it appears that approximately ten of the twenty-three articles in the *Chicago Sun-Times* that refer to the Watts riots came from news services.

The *Houston Chronicle*, although it too contains a good deal of news service copy (twenty-one of the sixty-eight stories are documented as including material from news services or are syndicated columns that appear in other newspapers in this analysis), little resembles any of the other papers analyzed here. The difference is not of subject matter but of emphasis. The *Chronicle*'s references to the Watts riots are unlikely to attach any sort of meaning to the events. These kinds of references can be found in other newspapers. In some cases, they are what Lang and Lang (1989) refer to as "yardsticks"—comparing the present to the past, as in "the worst incidents of civil unrest since the 1965 Watts riots." In other cases, they are a means of credentialing a source as worthy to speak on a subject, as when a Houston transportation coordinator argues that as a witness to the Watts riots, he recognizes the symptoms of a crowd about to get out of hand. In still other cases, these references are simple time markers for the beginning of some kind of trend. The *Houston Chronicle*, like many other newspapers, includes a "this day in history" feature that informs readers on August 11 that the Watts riots began on this day in 1965, killed thirty-four people and damaged 634 buildings. These references lend no particular meaning to the Watts riots, for they offer the reader no clues about why the riots might have occurred.

Where the meaning of the Watts riots is explored, the *Chronicle*'s list of possible explanations is much richer than that of other newspapers. The explanations are not novel: all were present in the news media when the riots occurred in 1965 and most still make occasional appearances in the other newspapers. However, the large number of empty references to the Watts riots and the diversity of explanations present in the few articles that do assign some meaning to the Watts riots make patterns difficult to discern. Nevertheless, it is worth pointing out that the *Houston Chronicle* does not present an alternative narrative to the one that dominates mainstream news elsewhere. Rather, it preserves the narrative chaos that other newspapers subsequently resolved into a coherent collective memory.

A second open question is why the *Houston Chronicle* is so different from the other newspapers included in this study. The most plausible answer is that it is the only conservative newspaper that does not serve the local community. However, the *Chronicle* does serve a region more like Los Angeles than any of the other papers in the analysis, so it remains curious that it is so unlike the also conservative *Los Angeles Times*. It is also possible that editorial practices unique to the *Chronicle* are responsible for the differences.

Remembering the 1968 Democratic National Convention Elsewhere

The distribution of references to the Chicago convention in the *Atlanta Journal/Constitution*, *Houston Chronicle*, and *Seattle Post-Intelligencer* compared to those of the *New York Times* are displayed in Table 5.2. The *Houston Chronicle*'s distribution pattern most resembles that of the *Times*, but the distribution in the other two papers is odd. The *Seattle Post-Intelligencer* was no more likely to carry stories that mention the 1968 convention when the Democrats returned to Chicago in 1996 than it was in any other election year, though the elevated number of stories in election years is apparent. The *Journal/Constitution* carried more stories about the 1968 convention in 1996 than in any other year, as one might expect. However, the pattern of increased references in presidential election years does not appear in the *Journal/Constitution*. Instead, the second largest number of references occurs on the twenty-fifth anniversary of the convention, and the decline in references following the 1996 convention is precipitous.

While regional newspapers' retrospective coverage of the Watts riots offers clues as to how a common story of the past might spread from one news organization to another, their retrospective coverage of the 1968 convention demonstrates how elements of the past can be kept alive in the regional press. In both *New York Times* and *Chicago Tribune* coverage of the Chicago convention, several important elements of the event persistently turn up missing. In its own time, one of the most important aspects of the 1968 Democratic Convention was the large number of credentials challenges that occurred before it began. African Americans in Southern states, protesting the then-current delegate selection system, sent their own opposition delegations to the convention. At that time, governors or other high-ranking state officials handpicked state delegations. Segregationist Southern governors

Table 5.2: Number of Stories Referring to the 1968 Convention in Four Newspapers by Year

YEAR	Atlanta Journal (N=78)	Houston Chronicle (N=93)	Seattle Post-Intelligencer (N=62)	New York Times (N=229)
1990			5	8
1991	6	2	1	15
1992	7	8	10	28
1993	13	7	3	16
1994	6	7	6	22
1995	9	6	3	16
1996	21	37	10	56
1997	3	4	1	9
1998	6	7	7	27
1999	4	8	4	8
2000	3	7	11	24

Note: All editions of each newspaper are included. Search term is variations of "Democrat" and "convention" within 50 words of "1965." The *Atlanta Journal* and the *Houston Chronicle* are available on Nexis beginning January 1, 1991. The *Seattle Post-Intelligencer* is available on Nexis beginning January 1, 1990.

selected their states' representatives to the convention, and it was these delegations that the protestors sought to unseat. The most famous credentials challenge was to the Georgia state delegation, when an eloquent speech by Julian Bond, televised and warmly greeted by other delegations, convinced the credentials committee to split Georgia's convention votes between the official and opposition delegations. Several of the regular Georgia delegates walked out of the convention and became Republicans, and Bond's name was put into nomination for the vice presidency. These credentials challenges— along with the fact that antiwar candidates who had won delegates in primaries still had no realistic shot at the nomination, even though Humphrey had not run in any primaries—were a motive force in creating the primary system we have today.

While the memory of Bond's challenge and that of Charles Evers (brother of Medgar Evers) to the Mississippi delegation has not been preserved in the *New York Times* or the *Chicago Tribune*, it is an important element of the 1968 convention in Georgia's *Atlanta Journal/ Constitution*. Many members of Bond's rump delegation went on to hold statewide office or become prominent citizens, and their role in the Chicago convention is mentioned in their obituaries. The defection of the five members of the regular delegation as a result of the challenge is mentioned in the obituaries of two members who have since passed away and in a profile of a prominent local family. Other members of the regular delegation also sometime have that fact mentioned when their names appear in the news. Profiles of Bond, a prominent Georgian, mention his role in the convention as well. Overall, thirteen of seventy-eight convention-related stories (17 percent) appearing in the paper between 1991 and 2001 mention the credentials fights or Bond's nomination. Despite this, the goals of enfranchisement and equal representation that the rump delegations of 1968 represent are still never mentioned in *Atlanta Journal/Constitution* stories that report or comment on the current primary system. Thus, the memory of these struggles remains undervalued, even in the newspaper that remembers them best.[7]

Although the *Seattle Post-Intelligencer* has the smallest number of articles referring to the convention of any of the papers included in this study, it, too, preserves convention events that are largely lost to the rest of the media explored here. For example, two stories recall the invasion of Eugene McCarthy's campaign headquarters by Chicago police on the last day of the convention and one recalls that his hotel suite became a makeshift clinic for wounded demonstrators on the most violent night of the convention, both rarely recalled events. Stories also recall Lyndon Johnson's attempts to manipulate the convention, an aspect of the event also rarely remembered.

As one might expect given the unsettled quality of narratives about the 1968 convention, the unifying story of the convention that was offered in 1996 does not dominate discourse in the regional press. Instead, the conflict between the *Times*'s representation of the 1968 convention and the *Tribune*'s representation is replayed. Stories in the *Post-Intelligencer* typically blame the police or Daley, personally, for the violence at the convention rather than the demonstrators. In some cases, the treatment appears balanced. When demonstrators are blamed for the violence, it is in the context of editorials or columns. The *Journal/Constitution* takes a much dimmer view of the protesters than the *Post-Intelligencer*, blaming demonstrators for the violence in both news and commentary. In the *Journal/Constitution*'s version of the story, Daley plays a minor role. The *Houston Chronicle*'s references to the Chicago conventions are more likely to describe events in the streets than events in the hall, and it repeatedly points out the damage done to the reputations of major actors, including the Democratic Party, Mayor Daley, and the city of Chicago. It describes "clashes"—or, more rarely, "skirmishes"—between police and demonstrators. Like the *Times* and the *Tribune*, these newspapers typically identify the protests as antiwar.

For all that the regional press does not show signs of developing a narrative that might be considered mainstream, there are signs that some issues have been resolved. For example, the protestors are now identified as antiwar, as they are in the *Times* and, more recently, the *Tribune*. Further, the point of contention has been reduced to whether the demonstrators or the police were to blame for the violence. Complex questions about delegate selection reforms and the connection between events in the hall and events in the streets no longer appear in stories that refer to the convention. This is the same issue that divided the *Times* from the *Tribune*, suggesting that even though these regional papers preserve aspects of the past that are lost to both the national paper and the local paper, they do not preserve novel narratives or frames. Nevertheless, the memories offered of the Chicago convention do not have the "settled" quality that memories of the Watts riots do.

Although by 1996 a unified story had not yet been established for the Chicago convention and not every regional paper embraces these stories in exactly the same form, in both of the cases examined in this study, the movement is toward simplicity, narrative coherence, and a story whose outlines are recognizable across a variety of media sources.

Conclusion

Stories of the past remain dynamic. As so many collective memory scholars have remarked, the present makes an impact on how the past is remembered. Yet the evidence here shows that the dynamism of this remembrance is limited. While Reagan-era politics and Democratic Party electoral fortunes have left permanent marks on the stories told about the Watts riots and the 1968 convention, the complex and con-flicting stories told about these events at the time that they occurred have slowly resolved themselves into relatively simple stories whose forms are modified but not transformed by more recent events.

Moreover, the stories reveal signs of the social practices and pres-sures that created them. As collective memory scholars would predict, more recent events have played a part in how the past is remembered, but other factors have been important as well. The stories exhibit a steadily improving gestalt that demonstrates the influence of narrative expectations. The stories make better sense, meaning they both better meet our expectations of how a story should go and fit reasonably well with the other stories we tell ourselves about both the past and the present. In other words, they resolve the narrative crisis that the social breaches instigated. Yet it takes more than good gestalt for narrative threads to survive. When sponsors survived, the story elements that were important to them survived as well. Stories that lost advocates, in contrast, disappeared from memory. The integrated stories that devel-oped and took hold were those that offered benefits to major stake-holders in the original event who retained their media access. Such stories were unlikely to meet with focused resistance from individuals or groups whose reputations might be damaged by other kinds of tales.

The next chapter considers how the collective memories that had developed affected public discourse about more recent events. The Watts riots helped to structure the discourse about the 1992 civil unrest that broke out in Los Angeles following the acquittal of Los Angeles Police Department officers who had beaten an African American motorist, Rodney King, during the course of his arrest. The 1968 Chicago convention was repeatedly referred to during the Demo-crats' 1996 nominating convention, the first to be held in the city in twenty-eight years.

CHAPTER 6

Using Collective Memory

The Role of the Past in the Present

I SN'T IT IRONIC THAT THE one thing for which most people remember George Santayana is his observation that "those who cannot remember the past are condemned to repeat it?" The idea that history repeats itself is as perilous as it is seductive. Human affairs are complex, and knowing the past can make them more understandable, more predictable. But while the future is contingent on the past, it doesn't really repeat it. World War II wasn't just a reprise of World War I; South Korea wasn't the next Czechoslovakia; and the 2003 Iraq War didn't just resolve the unfinished business of the 1991 Gulf War. And if forgetting is bad, inappropriate remembering may be even worse. But what tempts reporters and public officials to use the past, and how can they use it well?

The Refuge of the Past

In the process of describing and analyzing public affairs, both everyday and epic, invoking the "lessons of history" is a constant temptation for political leaders and journalists alike. The future is always uncertain, and the outcomes of political action are never entirely knowable.

Consulting the past appears to offer a measure of predictability for those who must make decisions. Indeed, Bruce Smith (1985) argues that the very act of prediction, right or wrong, makes people more comfortable with taking action.

While the use of the past in political discourse has much in common with the use of condensation symbols (Edelman 1964) and news icons (Bennett and Lawrence 1995) in its potential to crystallize an issue or problem, its perceived power to predict makes it unique. The narrative of the remembered past contains an element of emplotment that can be used to suggest that the course of the future will resemble the course of the past. The fact that the past event "really" happened (regardless of its subsequent interpretation and reconstruction and the plausibility of its comparison to the present) makes it seem a better predictor than the guesswork—no matter how educated—of officials or experts. The past appears a neutral prognosticator as well, unlike educated guesses, which may have an agenda behind them. Yet this perspective neglects the possibility that the past itself may have been reconstructed in order to support an agenda.

The idea of the past as predictor also draws on one of the most basic narratives about the past: the idea that history repeats itself, a notion constantly reinforced by the regular repetitions of natural cycles. This belief about the essential qualities of the past emphasizes continuity over change and history as a "natural" rather than a social phenomenon. Analysis in the preceding chapters demonstrates just how misguided this belief is. The "real" events of the past are enfolded into a narrative which, as White (1987) points out, only exists because the potential for other narratives exists. Narrative always involves choices about which facts to leave in, which facts to leave out, and how to endow facts with meaning. As we have seen, the development of collective memory about these pasts was a complex and lengthy process, and the interpretations that prevailed did not necessarily do so because they were "right."

Using the past to predict the future involves yet another complex permutation. In order to apply the "lessons of history," one must not only construct a meaning for the past but also build a connection between past and present. The appearance of similarity between past and present is not simply there—it is created, and it is as much a product of the way the past is remembered as it is a function of the way current events are understood.

Much has been written about how political leaders use history, but the social processes that produce collective memories have been largely ignored in these works. Critical scholars have described self-serving invocations of the past designed to shore up leaders' authority or legitimate their chosen course of action.[1] These works, which essentially treat the past as a rhetorical tool of leadership, appreciate the distinction between the real past and the remembered past, but they tend to treat the remembered past as something controlled by political leaders. The foregoing analysis here has shown that the remembered past—at least in these cases of controversial events—is the product of complex social negotiations. The past can neither be invented nor reinvented at will. Further, leaders do not always use the past in self-serving, purely rhetorical ways. Scholars such as Schwartz, Zerubavel, and Barnett (1986) and Michael Schudson (1992) showed that there are other reasons to turn to the past: for comfort in times of trouble, and for information and inspiration when one does not know what to do.

In 1986, Richard Neustadt and Ernest May wrote a book designed to help policy makers use history more effectively in their decision-making processes. They proceeded from the assumption that the past was more than a tool for persuasion—that the lessons of history could enhance leadership. However, other than considering the pitfalls of oversimplification, they did not consider that there might be a gap between the past as remembered and the past as it was. For them, there is no distinction between facts and meaning; the remembered past is real rather than constructed. To really understand how leaders' use of the past affects their handling of current issues would require a perspective that incorporates both the ontologically real and the socially constructed aspects of collective memory and that appreciates leaders' limitations in both recalling and rewriting the past.

Much less has been written about how journalists use the past, perhaps because we imagine "news" to be the opposite of "history." Yet the past holds many of the same temptations for reporters that it does for politicians. Like political leaders, reporters place a high value on being able to predict the future. Robert Entman and Benjamin Page (1994) observe that journalists value sources of information who are able to predict or influence the outcome of a policy debate. Many other

researchers[2] have observed journalists' tendency to focus on the outcome of electoral contests rather than the issues involved. Entman and
Page describe how elite informants fulfill this predictive function. In
electoral contests, polling technology is used to predict outcomes.
When collective memory is invoked, the past may be used to predict
the future.

Journalists, like leaders, can also appeal to the past as a neutral
prognosticator. Under typical circumstances, reporters are highly
dependent upon political leaders for information and "news." When
they accept this information, they also accept the framing, or "spin,"
that politicians and press secretaries attach to it. Reporters are aware of
this, but the professional norm of objectivity sets severe limits on their
abilities to resist elite framings. Introducing perspectives that lack
"legitimate" sponsorship into the news violates their professional values.[3] But it does not appear to violate objectivity norms to bring up the
past. Despite the potential of collective memories to serve as frames for
current events, many of the historical analogies and contexts examined
in this study were first introduced by reporters. Perhaps this is because
past events carry the mantle of objectivity: they really happened and so
qualify, in journalistic parlance, as "facts." Because a socially shared
memory is invoked, the meaning attached to the past appears transpar-
ent, and the choice involved in selecting a past to include in the reporting is no more problematic than the selection of facts and quotes that
reporters engage in every day. Since they appear to be neutral commentators, collective memories can allow reporters to resist elite framing and present alternative perspectives on current events even when
those perspectives are missing from elite debate.[4]

Although the precise motive or combination of motives that leads
public officials or journalists to turn to the past is probably impossible
to untangle in real-world settings, the fact that they use the past often
is not at all hard to demonstrate. Earlier portions of this analysis have
shown that references to both the 1968 convention and the Watts riots
are commonplace in the news. Neustadt and May (1986) offer many
more examples of moments when political leaders' decisions were
informed by references to the past. Indeed, they describe some historical analogies as "irresistible."

Many pasts represent extraordinary temptations for leaders and journalists, but there are undoubtedly moments when leaders, and perhaps

reporters too, wish they could leave the past behind, which brings us to Santayana's warning about what will happen if they do. He might be referring to literal forgetting of history, but this seems unlikely. Of course, we do lose elements of the past altogether. Documents, artifacts, knowledge: all can be lost to decay, disaster, and disruption. Libraries burn; everyday items are discarded; communities are disrupted by war or slavery or some other catastrophe and their oral traditions are lost. But many losses of this kind cannot be helped, and in many ways the past is more difficult to forget than it is to lose. Research in psychology has shown that the more people try to avoid talking or thinking about a past event, the more likely they are to remember it (Pennebaker and Banasik 1997).

A more plausible reading of the famous saying is that people fail to see the relevance of the past to the present and therefore "repeat" the "same" mistakes. Some pasts seem safely behind us—we are unlikely to return to the gold standard. Other pasts simply seem irrelevant: the great fire in London in 1666 was spectacular, but does it really have anything to tell us about modern life? Santayana's aphorism implies that the past is never safely left behind and that the truly wise are able to appreciate the complex connections between then and now. However, the constructed nature of collective memory makes the past a double-edged sword. Collective memory can be an invaluable resource for progress if it helps us identify and avoid mistakes. It can also lead those who use it astray if they fail to appreciate the difference between the past as it was and the past as it is remembered or if they ignore the fact that the relevance of the past to the present is not found but made.

Santayana's observation and Neustadt and May's book are classic expressions of the importance of the past in public life, but both miss the crucial aspect of history that emerges in this study: the past is not an empirical given. Its ontological essence is dressed in social constructions that render it meaningful and memorable. Labeling a response to foreign aggression as "appeasement" is not just a descriptor: it connects events, imagines motivations, and evaluates policy in the space of a single word. Even public actors who consciously follow the advice of Neustadt and May to evaluate presumptions and to be as aware of differences as they are of similarities are still bound to the past not as it was but as they remember it.

This chapter examines the ways that the 1968 Democratic National Convention and the Watts riots were used to think about more recent events, refracting these classic perspectives on the role of the past in the present through the prism emerging from this study: the realization that the remembered past is a product of social processes as well as empirical fact.

Ashes to Ashes: The Watts Riots as a Thinking Tool

In 1992, the neighborhoods of South Central Los Angeles exploded in violence, and the parallels to the Watts riots proved irresistible for reporters and officials. A year earlier, white officers of the Los Angeles Police Department had arrested African American motorist Rodney King. They had struck him more than fifty times with their batons in the process. They claimed that he had refused to follow their directions and that they had reason to believe he posed a threat. Videotape shot by a passerby and aired repeatedly on national television seemed to tell a different story.[5] On April 29, 1992, a jury acquitted all of the officers involved in the beating, and that night, neighborhoods in South Central Los Angeles erupted in violence. In three days and nights of civil unrest, 51 people died, 2,328 were injured, and damage was estimated at $717 million according to contemporary press reports (Braun and Russell 1992).

The Limits of the Empirical Past

The plain facts of the Watts riots—the number of dead and injured, the amount of property damage, the numbers arrested, the time of day the violence occurred, and so on—were a source of historical analogies that helped journalists and officials represent the scale of several later events, including the 1992 unrest. Kurt and Gladys Engel Lang (1989) refer to these as "yardstick" uses of the past. In the case of the 1992 civil unrest, comparisons to the Watts riots led to the conclusion that the events of 1992 were more serious: more people died, more people were injured, and more property was destroyed. The violence was more widespread, it continued day and night, and the participants were better armed in 1992. The only person to contest this yardstick was Los Angeles Police Chief Darryl Gates, who argued for another yardstick: more effective policing, he said, meant that the 1992 unrest ended sooner than the 1965 riots had (Sipchen 1992). Perhaps because these kinds of yardstick uses of the past leave open the question of what the Watts riots actually meant, these were some of the first uses of the Watts riots as a resource for understanding—appearing as early as 1966.

Yet even these uses of brute fact rely to some extent on the development of a shared narrative about the past. Without at least an implicit story of what an event means, how can one know what sorts of events it is comparable to? When brute facts lead thinking astray, as Neustadt and May (1986) expect they will, the fact that they are infused with implicit meanings is revealed. As the previous chapter demonstrated, by the 1990s, the narrative potentials of the Watts riots had been resolved into a story about an African American community's angry response to poverty and hopelessness. Using the Watts riots to think about the 1992 unrest in Los Angeles, then, encouraged reporters to focus on African Americans' involvement in both events despite the fact that the 1992 violence was multiethnic and most of those arrested were Hispanic (Smith 1993). In this instance, the inevitable blending of fact and meaning combine to have important impacts on the representation of the 1992 unrest without the constructed nature of collective memory ever becoming apparent: the Watts rioters' African American identity is perceived as essential rather than their status as poor people or Angelinos or any other shared status they hold. Collective memory is like psychological memory in that our retention of and use for disconnected facts is extremely limited, so while the Watts riots are ontologically real events, this reality is hopelessly bound up in our memories with the meaning we have created for them.

The real power of the Watts riots in representations of the 1992 unrest did not come from these kinds of yardstick comparisons between the present and the past. Rather, it came from the shared meaning that had developed over the course of a quarter century through a variety of complex negotiation practices, but, like the yardstick uses of empirical fact, was treated by those who used it as self-evident historical truth. And while the admonitions of scholars like Neustadt and May will rescue users of history from false analogies between the ontological facts of present and past, they will require adaptation in order to save reporters and decision makers from mistaking the past as remembered for ontological reality.

The Potentials and Pitfalls of the Meaningful Past

By 1992, the economic deprivation story of the Watts riots predominated to such an extent that even though the events surrounding King's arrest offered opportunities for reviving various versions of the Watts riots stories, alternative stories rarely appeared. Perhaps the strongest sign of this was that even the powerful parallel of accusations of police brutality against Marquette Frye and Rodney King was not enough to revive the police brutality story of the Watts riots until after violence had broken out in 1992. Only four stories published in the *New York Times* and thirteen stories in the *Los Angeles Times* mentioned both King's arrest and the Watts riots before the violence broke out in the wake of the officers' acquittal, compared to thirty-eight stories in the *New York Times* and 194 stories in the *Los Angeles Times* that mention Watts from the time the unrest began until the end of the year.

Once violence did break out, the Watts riots played a prominent role as journalists and officials of both political parties tried to describe and explain the 1992 unrest. The first very first news cycle after the violence began found *New York Times* reporter Seth Mydans (1992) drawing parallels between the erupting violence in South Central Los Angeles and the Watts riots. Three *Los Angeles Times* stories from that day reference the Watts riots in the context of the unfolding unrest: in all three, the journalists introduce the comparison to the past. A keyword search of the *New York Times* for 1992 reveals that nearly 8 percent of all stories on the Los Angeles violence also mention the unrest in 1965. A similar search in the *Los Angeles Times* shows that nearly 6.5 percent of its coverage of the 1992 unrest published in the year it occurred referenced the Watts riots. These percentages undervalue the importance of collective memory of the Watts riots in interpreting the more recent violence, for many of the stories that mention the 1992 violence alone are mere news briefs that make no attempts to explain events. For example, many of the stories turned up by the searches only report the cancellation of performances or sporting events due to the unrest. By contrast, stories about the Los Angeles violence that contain references to the Watts riots are almost always centrally concerned with interpreting current events.

As a tool for representing the 1992 civil unrest in Los Angeles, collective memory of the Watts riots constrained the debate over what had happened and what to do about it. On the surface, officials and reporters sometimes (but not always) did a reasonable job of obeying Neustadt and May's (1986) injunction to be aware of similarities and differences between the past and the present: "In South Los Angeles, the core economic problems have not changed since 1965, but the population has—as evidenced by a large immigration of Latino residents" (Clifford 1992, A1). However, they made these comparisons within the overarching perspective of thinking about the Watts riots as an African American community's response to hopeless destitution. When they thought with the Watts riots, their attention was captured by the economic conditions in South Central Los Angeles, and they made three key assumptions that limited public discussion of what was happening and what to do about it. First, they assumed that the causes of the violence were the same in both 1965 and 1992; second, they assumed that the cause was unrelenting poverty; and third, they assumed that proposed policy responses in 1965 and 1992 were comparable. With these assumptions in place, public debate over the effectiveness of policies—past and potential—and analysis supporting those evaluations raged, but debate over *why* the civil unrest had occurred in the first place was largely absent from stories that referenced the Watts riots.

What made the Watts riots an irresistible analogy was not that conditions in South Central Los Angeles by 1992 were as bad or worse than they had been in 1965. It was how easily the Watts riots as a historical analogy could be confused with the Watts riots as a historical context. Had the 1965 riots occurred in another city (or another part of Los Angeles), their status as an analogy—a comparative case—should have remained clear, even in the face of remarkable similarities to the 1992 unrest on every other dimension. But the Watts riots were more than a historical analogy: as part of the history of Los Angeles, they could be seen as one of the circumstances that led to the 1992 unrest—in other words, as a historical context. The fact that poverty and deprivation were sometimes represented not as causes of the Watts riots but as outcomes of them[6] made the temptation to use them as a historical context even greater.

Because their historical status was blurred in this way, it was possible to conflate claims that "something *like* this" had happened before with claims that "*this*" had happened before. This blunted the contingent nature of the predictions derived from historical analogies: if "this" had happened before, it was possible to describe (rather than merely to predict) what came next. Possible outcomes began to appear certain:

- "Brown's lieutenant governor, Glenn Anderson, hesitated in calling out the National Guard and also lost re-election. At Mayor Tom Bradley's request, [Governor] Wilson quickly activated the Guard shortly after violence erupted Wednesday night...but his image still could be tarnished if he is found to be partly responsible for the Guard's slow deployment while killers, looters and arsonists ran amok" (Skelton 1992, A3).
- "If what happened after the Watts riots is any indication, many frightened people could begin abandoning the city for good" (Corwin and Gordon 1992, B1).

This is a pitfall that Neustadt and May (1986) do not consider, in part because they do not treat the punctuation of events as problematic.

Perhaps the best example of blurring historical analogies with historical contexts during the civil unrest in Los Angeles was presidential spokesman Marlin Fitzwater's claim, made on May 4, that the Great Society programs of the 1960s had *caused* the 1992 civil unrest. Collective memories of the Watts riots had made the War on Poverty and the Great Society seem relevant to the 1992 civil unrest because the programs were, by 1992, perceived as a response to the riots. Other commentators had used the programs as a historical analogy to address the question, "What do we do?" Understanding the failures of other, comparable solutions could increase the odds of successful response in this case. Commentators (with the exception of Joseph Califano) agreed that the programs had failed to meet their goals of rejuvenating inner-city Los Angeles, but they continued to debate the reasons why. Conservatives argued that they were poorly conceived, designed, and managed. Liberals argued that effective programs had been gutted by funding cuts during the Reagan and Bush administrations. Fitzwater, in contrast to these commentators, used the debate to address the question "how did we get here," making the Watts riots a historical context. The failures of past solutions had created the conditions that led to the current crisis.

Benjamin Page (1996) demonstrates how public deliberation processes quickly rejected the explicit historical context contained in Fitzwater's claim. However, Fitzwater's claim was rejected on the narrow ground that the Great Society programs did not *cause* the 1992 unrest: most commentators agreed with the broader, underlying argument that the Great Society had failed. Further, the perceived importance of and debate over the Great Society, along with its use (by analogy) as a predictor for the success or failure of various responses to the 1992 unrest, continued before and after the Fitzwater flap. Those predictions were given heft by the implicit contextual claim that the "same thing" had happened "again."

Since the predictive value of the Watts riots was based on the belief that the causes of the riots were the same in both cases, news stories that refer to the Watts riots usually describe policy solutions that address the economic problems faced by inner-city residents. In 1992, the War on Poverty became an example of what not to do, and policy advocates took pains to distinguish their programs from those of the 1960s: "In 1965, (after the Watts violence) we essentially gave people fish by throwing money at the community. This time we must teach people to fish, implementing a building trades apprenticeship program that will train hundreds of unemployed members of the community..." (Silverstein and Lingre 1992, D1). Sometimes programmatic differences were described as structural; sometimes they were motivational. Corporate involvement was frequently a part of the structure of proposed policy solutions to inner-city poverty, and corporate leaders promised to do a better job "this time" (Weinstein 1992a; Weinstein 1992b; Rivera 1992).

Other, gloomier predictions relied on analogies to the Watts riots to suggest that nothing could resolve the problems of inner-city Los Angeles. These dark prophecies observed that when the Watts riots broke out, the government could afford to spend vast sums of money on inner-city revitalization and had the political will to do so. If this sort of government largesse could not repair the inner cities, then no program enacted in the conservative, cash-strapped 1990s would ever do so.

The Watts riots seemed to teach other lessons about what it would take to successfully address African American urban poverty "this time." The memory was used to support a sense of urgency. Reporters, officials, and citizens all argued publicly that action must be taken quickly to address the (economic) conditions that had provoked the violence.[7] They observed that unless policies were enacted immediately, momentum would be lost and with it the chance for real change. They based this conclusion on the outcomes of the Watts riots, contending that after a brief "golden age" when national attention was focused on central Los Angeles and money and support poured in, interest in the inner city waned and funding dried up before any significant change could take hold.

Although the more immediate cause of both the Watts riots and the 1992 unrest would appear to be police malpractice, the Watts riots were not generally used as a thinking tool for publicly airing the issue of police reform. Of the over two hundred stories appearing in the *Los Angeles Times* during 1992 that mention the Watts riots, only about ten percent discuss the role of police brutality in provoking the 1965 riots. The dominance of economic perspectives on the Watts riots is also indicated by the fact that comparisons between past and present allegations of police malpractice are typically made in editorials, columns, op-eds, and news analyses. The police brutality aspects of the Watts riots appear in the realm of "opinion" while economic aspects of the Watts riots appear on the newspaper pages devoted to "fact."

Where connections between alleged police malpractice in 1965 and 1992 were made, they were diluted in a variety of ways. Mentions of the Watts riots in connection with allegations of police brutality do not appear at any time during the trial of the LAPD officers accused of beating King, nor do they appear during the civil disturbances themselves. When mentions of police brutality do occur, they often appear as part of a long list of community grievances said to have fueled the Watts riots, which defuses their impact. In other cases, obvious connections never quite get made. For example, a week after the disturbances, in a series of long articles that comprised a special section of the paper, the *Los Angeles Times* traced the city's history leading up to the events of the previous week. One article briefly mentions the LAPD's "reputation...for brutalizing black suspects" (*Los Angeles Times* 1992a, 4) as one of a long list of complaints African Americans might have against the city. In another story, Marquette Frye's arrest is briefly described: "A scuffle broke out, and Frye's brother and mother were arrested. The crowd grew angry."[8] The connection between the LAPD's reputation and Frye's arrest is never made.

A few columnists used the Watts riots to make predictions about the potential success of police reform rather than the success of economic reforms. Here, the key point of comparison was the work of the McCone Commission as it might predict the success or failure of the Christopher Commission, appointed to evaluate the LAPD following the King beating. Most were not optimistic. As one interviewee explained, the people who had been in charge of implementing the McCone Commission recommendations were still more or less in charge. Since the McCone Commission, he argued, had failed in its mission, Christopher's probably would, too (Gray 1991). Columnist Bill Boyarsky, however, expressed hope that Christopher's personal power and the narrower scope of his committee's charge would make this commission more successful at identifying causes and implementing solutions than McCone's had been (1991).

Using the Past Well

Using the Watts riots to think about causes and solutions for the more recent unrest clearly left room for debate. There were arguments about what had caused the failure of those social programs that were enacted after the 1965 disturbances. There were arguments about how best to avoid the pitfalls that had plagued earlier attempts to redress the problems of the inner city. There were debates over whether the problems of inner-city poverty could ever be resolved. But these debates rested upon fundamental assumptions that constrained the topic of debate in key ways: assumptions that the Watts riots were a response to poverty and hopelessness, and that the grievances that had been expressed in 1965 were the same grievances that exploded into violence in 1992.

Looking only at news articles that refer to the Watts riots cannot give a general sense of the public debate that surrounded the 1992 civil unrest—only a selective slice of it. Regina Lawrence's (2000) work, which looks at a wider selection of coverage of the civil disturbances, suggests, for example, that discussions of police reform were a significant element of the overall coverage. Nevertheless, it is possible to build on Neustadt and May's (1986) advice to decision makers using history. As they themselves would have observed, the Watts riots needed to be used with caution as a historical analogy. Much had changed since 1965. The neighborhoods involved were no longer pre-dominantly African American: they were multicultural, and many Hispanics were involved in the unrest. Their grievances and cultural experiences may very well have been quite different from those of the African American community. The shops that were in the "riot zone" were often owned by people considered to be outsiders to the neigh-borhoods, but in 1965, those "outsiders" were typically Jewish. In 1992, the most prominent shopkeepers—in the media at least—were Korean. In 1965, the violence had remained localized in South Central Los Angeles—people burned "their own" neighborhoods, and they did it at night. In 1992, violence occurred in other neighborhoods, too, both day and night. Neither African American civil rights nor government antipoverty programs were especially high on the national government's agenda in 1992. Dozens of other similarities and contrasts might be drawn on the basis of these ontologically "real" aspects of the two events. In some cases, the media and the leaders they quoted were careful to make such distinctions, in other cases less so, particularly with regard to the multiethnic aspects of the riots.[9]

While Neustadt and May's (1986) advice could easily warn reporters and officials away from these kinds of mistakes, it is more difficult to adapt their advice to cope with the changed perceptions of what the Watts riots *meant*. The ontological "facts" of the Watts riots are not what misguide; rather, it is the acceptance of socially constructed meaning as empirically derived fact. Tracing the develop-ment of meaning—as this study does—makes it obvious that the story that was told about the Watts riots in the mainstream media before and during the 1992 unrest isn't the "truth" about the Watts riots. They were a complex event that could support a number of different inter-pretations, and no single social actor was really able to impose a mean-ing on them. The story that had shaken out by 1992 was the product of negotiation between several actors, and it had been changed by inter-vening historical events. It should not have been treated as "truth" in news media's representations of the 1992 unrest, but it was.

The meaning of the Watts riots was never really contested as lead-ers and journalists latched onto it in 1992. Everyone seemed to accept that the truth about the riots was known, even if the details of Frye's arrest remained murky. As one might expect of leaders and journalists using the past as a tool to represent a current social crisis for the public, their focus remained on the present. While their public statements were somewhat careful in recognizing how times had changed, these statements did not tend to reflect the fact that the story of the past handed down to them offered a limited perspective that may have been detrimental to efforts to address, or even identify, the problem at hand. Perhaps the best evidence of this failure is the relatively minor role of the police brutality theme in stories that mentioned the Watts riots. It may seem obvious now that police brutality should have been recalled when reporters remembered the Watts riots, but we have 20/20 hindsight—to reporters and officials who used the Watts riots analogy, it apparently did not.

Another issue that Neustadt and May (1986) do not deal with is how to avoid confusion between historical analogies and historical contexts. How does one avoid blurring the line between civic and policy histories and essentially ahistorical analogies between past and present? It seems clear that leaders and journalists who think with history will have to expand their list of cautions. They must treat meaning as cautiously as they do fact. To avoid conflating contexts and analogies, they must be conscious of their use of the past to make predictions. Using the past to predict the future creates a historical analogy, regardless of whether the same past will serve as a context or not.

Finally, one should note that from a critical perspective, thinking with the Watts riots had its benefits as well as its problems. While the most radical interpretation of the Watts riots—that they were simply a reaction to the long-standing problem of racist police abuse—played a minor role in the public discourse about the 1992 unrest, the lawlessness perspective never appeared at all in stories that referred to the Watts riots. Analogies to the Watts riots suggested that the violence, both in 1965 and in 1992, was a meaningful response to poverty and deprivation rather than a mindless burning of one's "own" neighborhood. Again, one cannot say with these data whether that view of the 1992 civil unrest prevailed elsewhere, but to the extent that it was available, the Watts riots helped leaders and journalists construct interpretations that framed the later disorders as meaningful political action.

Building a Past that Won't Repeat: Chicago Then and Now

Santayana's concern was different from Neustadt and May's—not that leaders would be tempted or seduced by analogies to the past, not that they would use the past without reflecting upon it, but that they would fail to use the past at all. But why? Neustadt and May describe some uses of the past as irresistible, but they become irresistible only because of the *way* we remember them. What if some pasts are remembered in ways that make them seem irrelevant to the present, that make them seem useless as tools for making sense of the present? This may be the fate of the 1968 convention, and it may be the kind of forgetting that Santayana worried about.

Discussion about holding the 1996 Democratic National Convention in Chicago was first broached in 1992, and the convention was awarded to the city in 1994. Bill Clinton's nomination and election, and now potential reelection, had an important impact on memories of the 1968 convention: now his renomination convention would attempt to seal its fate as a relic of the past.

The 1968 Convention as Historical Context

Although the Chicago convention remained controversial for many years, a historical context was invoked without raising hackles as early as 1972. The Chicago convention was identified as the birthplace of the modern primary system, a claim that is not entirely accurate since important changes to delegate selection rules were also made in 1964. Nevertheless, the McGovern Commission report produced in response to the credentials debacle at the 1968 convention did result in a major overhaul of the Democrats' delegate selection system that was emulated by the Republicans soon afterward. The essence of the change was the creation of meaningful primaries that elected delegates bound to vote for a particular candidate at the convention. In combination with the demise of the unit rule that required state delegations to vote together—which was shouted down at the 1968 convention— the changes produced the presidential nomination process we recognize today.

This past is typically used as a historical context rather than a historical analogy. Reporters (and scholars) writing about the primaries often note their origin in the fallout of 1968, which is one reason for the pattern that appears in newspaper references to the 1968 convention. Invoking historical contexts carries different opportunities and risks than creating historical analogies, but the ultimate source of these opportunities and risks is the same. Whether it is used as an analogy or a context, the relevance of the past to the present is socially constructed. The risks of historical analogies include ignoring essential differences between the past and the present and the temptation to use the past to predict the future—flaws that appeared in thinking with the Watts riots in 1992. Historical contexts sometimes spring from faulty causal reasoning, but a more subtle risk—and one that affects collective memory no matter how it is used—is that the limited meanings for the past that survive in the present fail to capture the true richness of the past. This risk affects both the empirical and the socially constructed aspects of the past, and it has garbled memories of the 1968 convention.

Both scholars and journalists use collective memory of the 1968 convention as what Lang and Lang (1989) call a "time marker." Journalists trace the history of the boring convention to 1968, describing two major changes that they attribute to post-1968 reforms. First, before the McGovern Commission reforms, the identity of the nominee was (technically) an open question until the night of the vote. With meaningful primaries, the nominee is chosen long before the convention even begins. Second, the 1968 convention, like many of its predecessors, was a kind of free-for-all, an unscripted meeting of the party faithful where issues were debated. These conventions produced plenty of what reporters recognized as "news." Not only was the identity of the nominee unknown, but crucial platform planks remained to be worked out, as the Vietnam War plank was in 1968. Speeches often went long, with floor debate lasting into wee hours of the morning (Humphrey's acceptance speech went off at 2:00 A.M.), and there was only a limited sense that the party was performing for the cameras. Because of the Democrats' experiences in 1968—so the established wisdom goes—conventions became scripted affairs meant to appeal to television audiences. This turns out to be somewhat weak causal reasoning: the Republicans' 1964 convention in San Francisco had its chaotic elements;

their 1968 convention in Miami was reputed to be exceptionally dull (Mailer 1968). However, 1968 continues to be perceived as a watershed year, and the Chicago convention is often portrayed as the last to be truly newsworthy. As Chicago Tribune columnist Mike Royko, a major proponent of this perspective, put it in 1988, "Wouldn't you rather watch a fat cop chasing Abbie Hoffman and Jerry Rubin?" (3).

Journalists were also given to evaluating the "effectiveness" of the McGovern Commission reforms. As Tom Patterson (1993) might predict, their assessments often turned on the new system's ability to produce a winning candidate. By 1989, a chorus of complaint was beginning to swell. Tom Wicker of the *New York Times* sang lead:

- "After the 1968 Democratic Convention...Democrats set up a commission...to make the nominating system more representative of the results of primaries—and less representative of party bosses' personal preferences—and to increase the participation of blacks and women. The Democrats have periodically tinkered with the rules since then.... They want their system to be representative but they also want it to produce winners" (Dionne 1989, 5).
- "Well, a candidate chosen in an open convention, whether an old or a new face, could not possibly do worse than the losers put forward by the primary system..." (Wicker 1991, 11).
- "Democratic Party 'reforms' since 1968 have all but guaranteed that [Clinton's] primary victories...will insure his nomination on the first ballot. Some Democrats—dourly contemplating the loss of four of five Presidential elections since the reform era began after 1968—have had enough of this 'automated' process" (Wicker 1992, 34).
- "Our presidential nominating system was designed by Rube Goldberg in his most inspired state of convolution" (Schmuhl 1994, 27).

By this time, complaints against the modern primary system were widespread for many reasons. Warren Weaver of the *New York Times* wrote an extended critique of modern primaries and conventions in 1984 using the 1968 convention as a time marker. Reiterating the claim that modern conventions were dull, he added that "the five-month election-year primary marathon killed off many competitors early; only winners could afford the sport for long" (3). In 1993, scholar Thomas Patterson would refine and extend this argument in a carefully researched critique of the American electoral process. Patterson's chief allegation against electoral institutions is that they result in an interminable election process that both bores and disillusions voters.

In these analyses, the 1968 convention is used as a historical context, a time marker delineating the transformation to a new (and ill-conceived) candidate selection system. Left out of virtually every story is a description of the concerns that produced the system. E. J. Dionne's description (above) is exceptional in its inclusion of a major motivating factor for the McGovern Commission: the credentials fights staged in 1968 by insurgent Southern delegations seeking better representation of African Americans in Democratic Party politics, themselves partly a product of reforms enacted in 1964. Like the reporters, Patterson skips over the credentials struggle in his history of the modern primary: "Humphrey had not contested a single primary and was associated with Johnson's Vietnam policy; his nomination further divided the party. When Humphrey narrowly lost the election to Richard Nixon, insurgent Democrats demanded a change in the nominating process" (1993, 31–32). Although he does recognize the McGovern Commission's attempt to empower voters, he associates the change (rather ironically) with the strategic concerns of a losing party when he makes the following argument about how conventions should work:

> A brokered convention is no threat to the public's interest. Although individual voters in separate primaries cannot easily sort through a crowded field to make an optimal and informed choice, party leaders in the context of a deliberative convention can perform this task. Moreover, these leaders are at least as adept as the voters themselves in selecting nominees who have the voters' acceptance. (228)

The point here is not that Patterson is wrong, only that he would make a very different sort of argument if he were considering the critiques of democratic practice and the demands for civil rights that were also an important part of the 1968 convention. Julian Bond almost certainly would have disagreed that party leaders should be the ones to pick a candidate. McCarthy's youthful supporters would almost certainly have disputed this as well. Indeed, any single-issue voter who viewed the 1968 election as a referendum on the war and found no peace candidate for whom to vote might doubt the validity of Patterson's claim. For these citizens, the 1968 convention debacle was about much more than losing an election.

Patterson's argument gives concrete shape to Santayana's concerns: unless one appreciates the true complexity of voters' dissatisfaction with the candidate selection process in 1968, one may institute reforms that trade one form of voter dissatisfaction for another. Unaware of the "lessons of history," we may re-create practices doomed to fail us again—a swinging pendulum rather than an arrow of progress. But there is a catch to Santayana's claim: those who denigrate the modern primary system *do* remember the past. They recognize the origins of the current system in the experiences of the 1960s, but it isn't enough. *How* they remember it is everything: instituting primaries in an effort to improve the odds of picking a winning candidate is not the same as establishing them in order to enhance democratic representativeness. In other words, it is not the plain facts of the 1968 convention that are key; it is the meaning that is assigned to those facts.

None of this is to say that the current primary system is a positive force in democratic politics. A critique could be made based upon the democratic aspirations that were so much a part of the discourse at the time and that have been, for the most part, forgotten. The complaint against conventions run by party elites was that they systematically disenfranchised certain demographic groups within the party. Segregationist governors picked white delegations that did not represent the large numbers of African American Democrats in their states. Women and young people were also underrepresented at the convention, so their voices were drowned out when it came to creating a platform and choosing a candidate. Viewed from this perspective, the McGovern commission reforms were an attempt to democratize an antidemocratic process (regardless of their strategic ends), but the changed system has failed to achieve this goal.

Rather than disenfranchisement by demographic group, modern primary voters are disenfranchised by geography. Those in states with late primaries are disregarded by candidates and parties, while those in states with primaries that "matter" influence the choice of the nominee and the platform he or she runs on. Front-loading from this perspective represents a desperate attempt to be included in the group of voters whose choices count. In the 2004 election cycle, there was some talk among cash-strapped state governors about canceling primaries in their states in order to save money because the late primaries would have no impact on the nomination. The degree to which this represents a novel critique of the primary system is indirect evidence of the degree to which the critique of democratic practices in the convention hall and in the streets has faded from collective memory.[10]

Exorcising the Ghosts of Chicago

The 1992 civil unrest in Los Angeles brought the past back to life for reporters and officials trying to cover and cope with the violence. What they understood to be the lessons of history seemed crucial to making sense of the chaos in which they found themselves. But if the civil unrest in Los Angeles seemed like a resurrection of the Watts riots, the 1996 Democratic National Convention was crafted as a burial.

From the time that the 1996 convention was awarded to Chicago, serious discussion arose about whether memories of the 1968 convention could be superseded by the meeting that would renominate Bill Clinton in an atmosphere of partisan unity. Many articles in the local and national press suggest it was the fondest hope of all concerned that memories of the 1968 convention would just go away: "Hoping to erase the stain of the violent 1968 convention from the image of the Democratic Party and the city of Chicago, party officials said today that they had selected this proud Midwestern city as host for their 1996 Presidential nominating convention. Mayor Richard M. Daley is clearly eager to burnish the image of the Daley family and the city itself" (Berke 1994, A8). Whether this began as a product of media expectations or as a genuine campaign by city officials, or both, is unclear.

In its coverage of the bid process, the *Chicago Tribune* did not help much with its constant reminders and its harsh judgment of the way the convention had affected the national reputation of the city and its leaders. In March, covering the World Cup, one reporter observed, "The world's image of Chicago...seems to be dominated by 'repeated flashbacks' of news footage of protesters fighting with police outside the

1968 Democratic Convention" (Kendall 1994, 4). Tracing the history of the city's conventions, a political reporter wrote: "The city went into a slump after the 1968 Democratic convention riot made the city synonymous with political discord" (Hardy 1994, 1). Indeed, throughout its convention coverage, the *Tribune* would return to the question of whether the city could effectively polish its tarnished reputation. However, when the convention was awarded to the city, the *Tribune* (in its editorial voice) crowed that the past agonized over in its pages during the bid process had become a historical relic: "Chicago, the traumatic memories of its 1968 Democratic national convention under the original Mayor Daley now transmuted into history, is exulting over its selection under a new Mayor Daley for a new Democratic convention" (*Chicago Tribune* 1994b, 16).

Of course, it wasn't as simple as that, and one theme of the coverage of convention preparations and of the convention itself was the impact that these events had on memories of the 1968 convention. In order to tell this story, the *Tribune* had to admit to its pages the national impressions of the convention that it had rejected or ignored for the most part during the previous twenty-eight years. Reporters at last lent their own authorial voice to stories that identified demonstrators as victims of police violence, where previously they had couched such stories as claims made by others. However, they remained less sympathetic to the protestors' perspective than the *New York Times* was. If they identified protestors as victims, they tended not to describe the purpose of the demonstrations, failing even to assign the typical antiwar motivation to those who had participated. If they identified the protests as antiwar, they tended to treat the police and protestors as equal opposites. However, in no single year was the *Tribune* as hard on Richard J. Daley as it was in 1996. Ironically, the national story of the 1968 convention emerged in the *Tribune* just as a concerted effort to bury it got underway.

During the two years leading up to the convention, the city undertook civic improvements and staged events that lent themselves to stories whose theme was laying the past to rest. For example, prior to the convention, the Balbo Drive bridge, site of some of the most dramatic clashes between police and demonstrators in 1968, was renovated. In May, the *Tribune* dryly reported, "The rebuilt Balbo Drive bridge over the Illinois Central Gulf railroad tracks, the site of many protests during the 1968 Democratic convention, will be completed in time for

TV reporters to do their standups recalling the turmoil the last time the Democrats came to town" (Recktenwald 1996a, 1). To remember, then, would be to misrepresent, a serious accusation against a professional journalist.

In July, the *Tribune* reported the transformation of the Chicago Police Department. For the first time, the police department seemed prepared to admit that mistakes were made in the way the 1968 demonstrations were handled, but most of the story is devoted to how much the force has changed in the years since the last convention: "'clearly things were not handled the way that they could have been.' But...a lot has changed since 1968. Back then, the demonstrations that upset the convention were spawned by the country's involvement in an unpopular war. At this convention, police are prepared for demonstrators" (Recktenwald 1996b, 1). Like many stories told during this period, this one contains elements of the nationalizing story that links the protests to the war and emphasizes national division rather than poor administration as a cause of the convention violence.

Typically such progress stories were related without criticism or controversy. Only stories regarding the "improved" handling of demonstrators included elements of resistance. Protest groups insisted that little had changed since 1968. The city would not let them protest where and when they wished. In July, the *Tribune* reported, "Protestors are complaining that all of the heavy handling by the city feels like a bureaucratic version of 1968 head-bashing" (Griffin 1996, 6). Tom Hayden's reported activities in Chicago help to explain the resistance to the overall theme of laying the past to rest. Hayden wanted to recraft, not bury, memories of the 1968 convention: "The event...is aimed at 'bringing together a lot of memories and feelings and hopefully [will] also have an effect of resurrecting the idealism that people brought here in 1968,' Hayden said. 'It's about the need to convene a progressive spirit again'" (Reardon 1996, 1).

Hayden's presence, along with that of Dellinger and Abbie Hoffman's son Andrew, had the potential to evoke themes of continuity and reprise, but such potential was not typically realized. Even Hayden was co-opted into events that supported the city's preferred theme. In June, a "reconciliation meeting" took place between Daley and Hayden:

A delegate to this summer's Democratic Convention, Hayden revisited a much friendlier mayor's office this time around—gray headed, softened by the bulges of middle age, and talking about the spirit of healing. Both politicians spent an hour discussing ways of commemorating the traumatic events of August 1968. (Salopek 1996, 1)

The theme of mutual transformation was revisited in Daley's speech to protestors on the opening day of the convention: "'However unwelcome you may have felt 28 years ago,' Mr. Daley the son said, 'you are welcome today'" (Clines 1996, A9). Peace was declared, the past was made to pass, and the convention was on.

Mike Royko, among other commentators, opined that it would be dull as dirt, a prospect that was probably music to the ears of city and party officials: "Remember, this was the last city to have a convention that was truly lively…. Most of the media creatures coming to Chicago are more interested in rehashing the 1968 convention than in yawning through the upcoming one" (1996, 3). The sheer scale of the contrast between the "yawnfest" and the "lively" meeting over a quarter century ago would contribute to the overall sense that the 1960s were an exceptional time that would never come again, safely historical and largely irrelevant.

The *Tribune*'s feature coverage leading up to the convention contained another type of story with no obvious official sponsorship that nevertheless contributed to burying the memories of the 1968 convention safely in the past. These stories related the history of political conventions in Chicago. They made the point that prior to 1968, Chicago had been a popular convention town. The 1968 meeting was not the only controversial convention to be held in the city, just the most recent. Such stories had appeared in the paper on and off for almost twenty years, but they became especially common in the months leading up to the 1996 convention. In May, the *Tribune* observed, "From the nomination in 1860 of Abraham Lincoln to the protest tumult of 1968, Chicago has provided the backdrop for many memorable conventions" (*Chicago Tribune* 1996, 2). Days later, a reporter reminded *Tribune* readers, "Chicago's convention legacy is as rough and rowdy as it is rich. In less uptight times, chaos and lunacy ruled" (Secter 1996, 1). Grouping the 1968 convention as one of many similar events took the edge off the memory—it just wasn't all that unusual an event. It only seemed that way because it was the last of its kind. Like other lists, this one defused tensions by suggesting that the 1968 convention was not, in fact, especially remarkable.

During convention week, the work to lay the past to rest continued. Just before the opening of the convention, Daley retold his nationalizing story[11] and went on to consign it to the past:

> "The last time Democrats met in Chicago to nominate a candidate for president, America was at war, abroad and at home. Our party and our convention reflected the deep divisions of those difficult times," said Daley, mindful of the role his late father, Mayor Richard J. Daley, played during the brutal 1968 convention and its street battles between war protestors and police. "This year, we gather under happier circumstances. America is at peace." (Kass and Heard 1996, 9)

Interviewed during convention week, President Clinton agreed: "I believe we have gone a long way toward burying the ghosts of Chicago" (Neikirk and Tackett 1996, 1). The *Tribune* reported that the demonstrations had "fizzled." A headline read, "Dellinger Is Arrested, but World Not Watching" (Black and Hill 1996, 5). Meanwhile, the Chicago Police Department redeemed itself, at least in the press:

> The police department was blowing away the ghosts of 1968 like so much mist....Even though Chicago has had its share of incidents of police brutality since 1968, the national focus on the issue has moved elsewhere—to Los Angeles, to Philadelphia. This time around, instead of tear gas and bloodied batons, the image of the Chicago police at the convention is the face of [a wounded officer addressing the convention on violence]....In 1996, the cop at the convention cut the figure of a hero. The officer on the street, meanwhile, appeared to be showing restraint and professionalism. (Griffin and Martin 1996, 1)

Postconvention wrap-ups suggested that the exorcism of the ghosts of Chicago had been successful, if not entertaining. The *New York Times*, although it had not focused on Chicago's reputation in its previous remembrances of the 1968 convention, reported the city's claim that its past was now behind it: "Chicago officials say the just-concluded Democratic National Convention may have finally chased the ghosts of 1968 out of town" (*New York Times* 1996, 2). A *Tribune* columnist decried the wholesale renunciation of the past that had just taken place:

> The Democrats just wrote off their own past...and turned the site of the 1968 convention into DaleyWorld, where the cops were concierges and the ubiquitous Host Committee greeters were instructed to smile often and never talk about politics. Their convention was clean, polite, and devoid of personality. (Dold 1996, 27)

It seemed that the boring convention had paid off. It should be noted that one commentator did offer an alternative reading of the meeting's carefully scripted performances, namely, that they were too dull to supplant memories of 1968: "The Daleys can never expunge the stain left by Chicago's 1968 convention debacle, which will be remembered much longer than the just-concluded yawnfest" (Hardy 1996, 4). However, even this commentator agreed that the 1996 convention was a positive step for the city. In general, then, the consensus was that the process of dismissing this troublesome past had worked.

The process was helped along by an evolving collective memory of the convention that distilled the dozens of causes that had brought protestors to Chicago into one: the war in Vietnam. Gitlin (1980) demonstrates how damaging media coverage that denies meaning to protest activities can be to the causes and reputations of social movements, so a story that made the protests meaningful represented an important advance over contemporary news coverage of the Chicago demonstrations. But collective memories of the 1968 convention show that assigning meaning can be a double-edged sword. The protestors who went to Chicago in 1968 had an agenda so diverse it probably did not deserve to be called an agenda. Indeed, David Farber's (1988) history of the convention demonstrations uses separate chapters to distinguish the various groups and their causes. Associating the convention protests (and the disruptions inside the convention hall) with the war in Vietnam was a choice, and a critical one. Julian Bond's eloquent demand for racial justice in the convention hall; the frustrations of the "clean for Gene" youth whose work to win primaries was nullified by

Humphrey's command of the party's infrastructure; the counterculture Yippies' many-faceted street theater illuminating a wide range of mainstream cultural hypocrisies; and even the "poor people's march" (one of the few street demonstrations that obtained permits from the city) were forgotten or subsumed under the mantle of antiwar protests. And the war was over.

Other possible choices would have sustained convention memories as a vital aspect of modern political and social life, particularly the critique of democratic practices voiced by Julian Bond inside the hall and by a variety of groups (including the antiwar protestors) outside the hall. Had the man who won the most votes in the primaries become the Democrats' nominee for president, antiwar protests in Chicago would have seemed either ironic or pointless, for McCarthy was considered a dove. But Humphrey would win the nomination (despite nostalgic memories of open conventions, it had been decades since a second ballot was requited to determine the nominee), and voters who saw the 1968 election as a referendum on the war knew they would be denied the opportunity to choose. The antidemocratic nominating process was, then, an important target for many protestors, including McCarthy supporters, antiwar groups, and even the Yippies, whose first act of street theater in Chicago was to nominate a pig for president in a gag that mocked the flaws of an elite-dominated candidate selection process. The extension of democratic practices—both for better and for worse—remains a key element of public discourse to this day, and had the 1968 convention disruptions been remembered as a demand for democratic representation, burying memories of the Chicago convention might have seemed either harder or unnecessary.

Like most aphorisms, Santayana's cliche is a simplification of a complex idea. Forgetting the past may not be the only thing that "condemns us to repeat it." Failing to recognize the relevance of the past may be just as damaging, if not more so. R. Bruce Dold's (1996) expression, "writing off" the past, is apropos here. During the rituals of the 1996 Democratic National Convention, the past was not forgotten; it was dismissed. Unlike the Watts riots, the Chicago convention seemed to offer no "lessons of history." Transformations in the structure of the presidential nominating process and the association of the demonstrations with a war that had been over for twenty years made the convention melee seem more artifact than legacy. The aspects of convention memory that could have served the function of "lessons of history," the democratic frustrations expressed in 1968, had been lost when the demonstrations acquired the label "antiwar." Public frustration and cynicism about a political system that seems unaccountable and unresponsive to their demands is a past we have been condemned to repeat.

Conclusion

To separate the real past from the remembered past is almost impossible. Even elements of the past that seem purely empirical—things that really happened—are connected to the present only by means of contexts or analogies that construct the past as relevant to the present. Thus, the shape of collective memory matters not simply in the sense of doing justice to the events themselves and the people who took part in them, not simply because of the common ground that shared memory can make possible, but because the way that we remember the past can have impacts on our responses to present dilemmas and crises.

Memories of the Watts riots may have foreshortened debate over what to do about the explosion of violence in South Central Los Angeles in 1992. They focused attention on the economic aspects of social unrest, and they supported arguments that expansive government assistance and involvement could not solve the problem. These memories, then, supported conservative (in both senses of the word) responses to the unrest. However, no official craftsmanship was required to make them so. The story of the Watts riots that attributed them to economic deprivation among inner-city African Americans had entered conventional wisdom decades earlier, and the idea that the Great Society had failed and that individual responsibility was the true key to economic revitalization had been evolving for decades after that. The appeal to the past was all the more powerful because the past "itself" seemed to support the conclusions that public officials were drawing about how to respond to the current crisis. Even when Fitzwater overstepped the boundaries of public acceptance in using the past to explain the present, the value of the Watts riots as an apparent predictor of what was to come was not significantly diminished.

Perhaps the best evidence that a collective memory of the Watts riots had coalesced by the early 1990s emerges from the fact that the police brutality story of the Watts riots was not immediately revived by the events surrounding Rodney King's arrest. Nor did thinking with the Watts riots encourage serious discussion of police misconduct as a social problem. The immediate causes of the Watts riots had been forgotten as the riots themselves came to be defined in terms of the policies that were implemented in their wake. The official craftsmanship that had constructed a meaning for the Watts riots had really occurred in 1965, not 1992.

Not all of the implications of the Watts riots were conservative, however. Collective memories of the Watts riots made it hard to treat the 1992 civil unrest as mindless violence. They gave rise to the possibility that what was going on in South Central Los Angeles was a form of political action, however "misguided." Here again, however, no craftsmanship was necessary on the part of those who sought to express community grievances. The past "itself" was their warrant.

To the extent that collective memories of the Watts riots were used in good faith as a tool to represent the 1992 unrest and to shape public debate on a plan to ameliorate the conditions that led to it, they were not used very well. However, it was not so much a selective remembering of the facts that led reporters and officials to prematurely close off discussions of both problems and solutions. Rather, it was a failure to invoke the rich meanings that the Watts riots could potentially generate. Reporters remembered that the Watts riots had begun with the controversial arrest of an African American man, but they attached no particular importance to this fact. It was sometimes present in stories, but it was not integrated into plot lines. Both reporters and officials accepted the evaluation that the Great Society had failed and the follow-on conclusion that massive government intervention was an ineffective response to poverty, even as they debated the exact reasons for the failure of the programs in terms that suggested that adequate funding and implementation could have made them a success. They took the past they were given as if it were the past as it was.

Like collective memory of the Watts riots, collective memory of the 1968 convention had a conservative quality that probably went undetected as it was developing. Even as associating the 1965 riots with economic deprivation and the Great Society rather than labeling them as meaningless violence seems both forward-thinking and liberal in the short run, connecting the protests in Chicago with the war in Vietnam may also have seemed progressive (in both senses of the word). But the war was over, and even though connecting the protests to it made them meaningful, it also made them seem irrelevant to contemporary American life. Media commentators, and even scholars, seemed to forget that the Chicago convention also expressed citizen frustrations at institutions that appeared to be undemocratic and a sense that political leaders were unaccountable to public demands.

Laying the "ghosts of Chicago" to rest did require some craftsmanship on the part of officials. They staged events, answered questions, and otherwise took an active hand in structuring how 1968 was recalled in ways that, with the exception of Fitzwater's comment, are far more apparent than was the case when the Watts riots were recalled in 1992. Yet they were helped along by the existing structure of collective memory. Had the Chicago convention been connected to democratic dissatisfaction, rather than to a war that was safely over, it seems unlikely that the 1996 convention would have been awarded to the city in the first place. Connected with the war, the convention protests acquired a nostalgic glow perhaps best exemplified in a reporter's description of a middle-aged Tom Hayden. It was possible to associate the protests with a time of youth and innocence that was long past. While the overall tone is one of forgiveness and affection, one of the key features of nostalgia is that it is a longing for an unrecoverable past (Davis 1979).

Although the richness of meaning that emerged from the Watts riots was largely lost, collective memories of the 1965 riots helped leaders, journalists, and citizens appreciate just how long the neighbors of South Central Los Angeles had lived in poverty and at least raised the question of what government could do to help them. It helped angry South Central residents construct their actions as meaningful and political rather than simply lawless, and it remains part of the living past of the city of Los Angeles. In contrast, the Chicago convention has been trapped in the past. Its events have acquired meaning but lost relevance for contemporary public affairs. A consequence of forgetting the broader themes that emerged from those events was that, by 1996, we seemed to have put the past behind us.

While the risks involved in treating the narrow slice of meaning that survives in collective memory as a proxy for the "real" past have become apparent in this analysis, both treating the past as "living history" and laying it to rest carry risks and opportunities as well. A collective memory that seems relevant to present concerns, either as a historical analogy or as a historical context, has the potential to enrich our understanding of the present so long as we take proper precautions to treat it as the social construction it really is. However, a living past that appears to repeat itself can also take on the dysfunctional qualities of traumatic memory, a past endlessly relived without hope of progress or change. The inability to let go of the past may produce vendettas, feuds, and perhaps even genocides. The ability to put the past behind us can enable us to patch social rifts and recognize progress; however, such a past will at the same time become unavailable to us as a tool for making sense of current affairs because it does not seem possible that such times could ever come again. In this respect, they are as Santayana described them: pasts that we do not remember and may therefore be condemned to repeat.

CHAPTER 7

Conclusions

The Future of the Past

ONE OF THE MOST SURPRISING elements of this study is that two relatively minor incidents of the eventful 1960s are still so often remembered in the news. Each has become incorporated into the history of the cities where they occurred. In Los Angeles, the Watts riots are part of the story of urban migration patterns and race relations in a city whose ethnic face is always changing. In Chicago, the 1968 convention has been a kind of millstone.

Does collective memory develop from a troubled past? In the case of the Watts riots, yes. The story that explains the Watts riots as an angry outburst by African Americans frustrated by their poor living conditions has the characteristics we would expect of collective memory. It is consistently told in the news, dominating other potential stories that are subsumed in lists or no longer related. As more conservative political discourse has come to replace the language of the Great Society era, the economic deprivation story has not been abandoned but adapted to a more conservative explanation for poverty and disadvantage. Finally, the story is told, albeit with minor variations, by all of the major social actors who speak about the Watts riots in the news, not just government officials but community leaders and eyewitnesses as well. All of this suggests that the memory of the Watts riots is what we might term "stable." That is, although it remains responsive to the shape of current events, collective memory of the Watts riots is consistently narrated in terms of economic deprivation, and arguments over the meaning of the past develop within that frame rather than over what frame should be assigned to the events. Of course, collective memory is never fixed. Alternative narratives of the Watts riots have not entirely vanished, and just because collective memory of the Watts riots is stable now does not mean that future events will not result in a reframing of the past. Still, the stability of this particular story does suggest that we not only have a collective memory of the Watts riots, it would take some concentrated effort to alter it.

The relative stability of collective memories about the Watts riots supports Michael Schudson's (1992) argument that our ability to alter our memories of the past is quite limited, but in another way, the collective quality of the memory itself does not match his findings regarding memories of Watergate. Schudson makes the case that four versions of the Watergate story have survived and that two irreconcilable versions remain prominently available in public discourse: "the system worked" and "the system almost didn't work." In some ways, the difference between his findings and those presented here is a matter of perception and emphasis, for there are two versions of the economic deprivation story of the Watts riots whose contrasting claims are apparent in the news discourse that brings Watts riots memories to bear on the 1992 unrest. Some argue that the Great Society was a failure because it misdiagnosed the problem as structural poverty when the real problem was a lack of individual initiative. Others argue that social welfare programs were underfunded and the inner city neglected until it was primed to light again. Thus, in some ways, two different versions of "lessons" of the Watts riots survive, and in some ways, only one narrative of Watergate survives in that the struggle over the meaning of that past has been reduced to a debate over whether or not the "system" worked.

There is another difference between Watergate and the Watts riots, however, that may also account for the difference in outcomes. Watergate was a political scandal, and prominent political actors have remained invested in, and divided over, how it should be remembered. In contrast, many political leaders with an interest in how the Watts riots were remembered are dead or no longer have easy access to the news to advocate their views. Further, the Great Society programs that fed the economic deprivation story of the Watts riots functioned to unify political leaders in that they offered both real and rhetorical benefits to federal, state, and local officials. The level of political conflict over the meaning of the Watts riots was thus reduced in a way that political conflict over Watergate was not.

Whether or not a collective memory of the 1968 Chicago convention has or ever will develop is a more complex question. Two stories seem to have the potential to weave together the remaining threads of the convention week stories: one says that the discord within the Democratic Party itself overflowed into street violence, and another says that the divisions within the country, particularly over the Vietnam War, coalesced and then exploded in Chicago. A story that says the country's divisions over the war were coming to a head and that it just so happened the explosion occurred during the Democrats' convention and in Chicago lets all the major social actors off the hook, so to speak, and therefore seems to have potential as a unifying story. A story that links the violence in the streets to divisions in the party is more problematic because it is damaging to the image of the Democratic Party, but the evidence suggests that party electoral successes—which enable it to tell progress stories about its history since the 1968 convention— could still make this a viable unifying story.

Regardless of whether a unified story of the Chicago convention ever prevails in news discourse, the stories that are told about the 1968 convention exhibit a steadily improving narrative coherence that suggests the evolution of collective memory. This progression is particularly noticeable in stories about the Chicago Seven and the demonstrators. Early coverage paints a mixed picture of both the demonstrators and the men indicted for inciting the convention violence. Some of the demonstrators are described as looking for trouble—bearded motorcycle gang leaders riding into Chicago, seasoned demonstrators teaching techniques for resisting police, and so on. Later in convention week, the demonstrators are typically portrayed as victims of police violence. Years later, the street demonstrators in Chicago are usually described as having a cause of action (the Vietnam War) and as abused by violent police officers.

Coverage of the Chicago Seven trial in its own time included a range of perspectives: the defendants as disrespectful, confrontational, and absurd; the judge as humorless, uptight, and biased. In more recent years, Judge Hoffman has all but disappeared from the story, and despite being acquitted of the major charges against them, the Chicago Seven have remained the ringleaders responsible for the convention violence. In their modern forms, these stories preserve the perspectives available during and soon after the convention, but they do so by encapsulating negative perceptions of the protestors in Chicago Seven stories and positive perceptions of the protestors in street demonstration stories, eliminating the contradictions of the early stories. This distinction appears much more clearly and much earlier in the *New York Times* than in the *Chicago Tribune*, which continued to take a dim view of the demonstrators generally until the mid-1990s at least. However, regional papers outside Chicago tend to look more like the *Times*, and when the national media returned to Chicago to cover the 1996 convention, the *Tribune*, too, began to tell the national story.

The story of what happened at the convention itself was never as scrambled as the stories of events in the streets, but it has been through more transformations. Early versions described the convention as the trigger for new delegate selection rules and declining Democratic fortunes. Later, it became the last interesting convention and the one that gave rise to all the dull meetings that followed, partly because the new delegate selection rules meant there was no mystery about the nominee and partly because the chaos in Chicago had taught both parties the value of presenting an image of unity to the television cameras. Oddly, many of the stories that describe the lessons about party unity learned in 1968 do not describe the reasons the Democrats were so divided. In general, the substantive debates over the Vietnam War and the delegate selection rules are poorly preserved in collective memory.

The evidence from these case studies reveals that during and immediately after social breaches, the debate in the news over their meaning is dominated by official voices, as many scholars of media and politics might expect. However, as collective memory evolves over time, no single social actor is able to control its form. Although there are a variety of voices that help give shape to collective memory—including the voices of journalists who both select the sources and occasionally narrate the past without using sources—this study reveals little evidence of an organized effort to define the past once official redressive rituals have ended. Officials may be more interested in their own reputations and those of their institutions, and only incidentally interested in collective memories of events. Individuals are typically granted access to the news only briefly and therefore cannot engage in a concerted program to affect the development of stories about the past. Indeed, many elements of the stories we know of the Chicago convention and the Watts riots seem the unintentional by-products of news production and storytelling processes rather than the product of framing struggles between competing social actors. Instead, stories evolve in ways that do not directly interfere with the more immediate interests of important stakeholders and fit reasonably well with cultural expectations.

The struggle for a good story is an important part of the development of collective memory, although it is difficult to know whether the demands for a such a story are created by audiences, by the professional values of journalism, or by some fundamental aesthetic sense of narrative we all possess as human beings. Since the meaning for the Watts riots and the Chicago convention evolved largely in the absence of descriptions of the events themselves, the development of coherent stories about these pasts does not rely on "goodness of fit" between the events themselves and the stories told about them. A better description of the process would be that meaning develops, and details of the events that fit that meaning are later recalled. Thus, once a civil rights framework develops for the Watts riots, selective details of Martin Luther King's visit to Watts are recalled. As the demonstrators come to be described as victims of the police, their cause comes to be consistently identified as opposition to the war in Vietnam, a cause many Americans now support, though in complex ways. Once the Chicago Seven are consistently described as troublemakers, their indictment comes to define their trial rather than their eventual acquittal. These representations are not false, but they are incomplete, and the pattern of the omissions is governed by the requirements of a good story.

Even where tension between competing narratives remains, the stories that have emerged to account for these social conflicts have become progressively better over the years, using the narrative theorists' most basic criterion: coherence. Coherence amounts to more than the simplification necessary to fit stories of the past into the tight space and time requirements of journalism. Stories of the Watts riots and the Chicago convention initially have uncertain moral valences and lack authoritative voice because so many alternative narratives openly compete to account for events. Later stories have developed clear morals and effectively subsumed or deflected narrative alternatives. The narrative impulse—the desire for a story with a moral—may be one of the forces that drives collective memory processes, even in the wake of social discord. Multiple stories with multiple morals satisfy neither our aesthetic sense of narrative nor our beliefs about the existence of an objective reality. Thus, we seek *the* story of what "really happened." However, the better stories produced by collective memory processes are not necessarily true or right. This is especially evident in the Watts riots remembrances—where Martin Luther King's relationship to the initial event has been misrepresented to create a story that hangs together better— but it can also be seen in the literary license often taken in recollections that feature the Chicago Seven and in other places.

Because our standards for a good story conflict with our acceptance fragmented news, the contexts in which journalists remember the past make a difference in how collective memory develops. Historical contexts and analogies can preserve multiple narratives of the same event because they appear relatively randomly in the news. Contradictions between the stories told about the past glide by unnoticed. Commemorations, however, make apparent remaining discrepancies between stories. In some cases, the contradictions are still elided by publishing a commemorative series of articles over a number of days or encapsulating conflicting perspectives in different articles in a single section. The audience's acceptance of fragmented news can make such techniques a viable way of coping with remaining controversy. Nevertheless, on commemorative occasions disagreements between stories are much more obvious than at any other time. Residual disagreements over the meaning of the Watts riots resurface in the *Los Angeles Times*'s 1980 anniversary series on the Watts riots, for example.

It is impossible to say on the basis of two case studies whether commemoration is necessary for the development of collective memories of controversial events. However, without commemorative coverage, there may be little pressure to resolve differences. In the absence of commemorations of the 1968 Chicago convention, there is little evidence of an integrated story until the Democrats' return to Chicago produced concentrated attention to memories of 1968. While controversy makes an event difficult to commemorate, without commemoration it is difficult to resolve controversy.

What is clear is that we live with the past every day. However, we commonly fail to realize that the past we use in our daily lives is not something we are given but something we have made. In these two cases, reporters and officials searching for ways to make sense of an ambiguous present treated the remembered past as the real past, which had complex implications for the course of current events. In consigning the 1968 Chicago convention to the past, reporters and officials acknowledged the Vietnam War as the demonstrators' chief grievance and painted them as wronged victims of police violence. However, they also failed to perceive the wider critique of democratic practices that was, in many ways, a better explanation of the convention disruptions as a whole. Thinking with the Watts riots in Los Angeles during the 1992 social unrest encouraged thinking about economic issues and debating the effectiveness of antipoverty programs, rather than dismissing the 1992 unrest as mindless violence. However, the common origin of the Watts riots and the 1992 unrest—tension between the police and the community—was overlooked.

One of the advantages of studying how collective memory of controversy and social division evolves is that it makes the processes of collective memory development particularly apparent. Although generalizing from case studies should be done with caution, it is possible to describe some social processes likely to be key to the development of other collective memories, including memories of the September 11 terrorist attacks.

Public Officials, Power, and Collective Memory

Power matters in the development of collective memory, but in complicated ways. In both cases examined here, the power of public officials to manage public perceptions of events was at its greatest during and immediately following the occurrence of events. Real-time newsmagazine coverage of the Watts riots and the Chicago convention reveals that public officials had some influence on the relative salience of stories, but that they could not impose meaning on the events. They could not banish alternative narratives from the news. Most forms of officially sponsored redressive ritual were similarly unsuccessful in authoritatively assigning meaning to the event. Rather, the evidence from these case studies shows that the most effective tool the government had for assigning meaning to events was its policy "response." In contrast to failed or modestly successful redressive rituals, linking the Watts riots to the Great Society programs implemented shortly afterward helped to produce the collective memory of the riots that we still have (albeit in somewhat altered form) today. Since the Watts riots "resulted" in social welfare programs, the Watts riots must have been "about" economic and social deprivation. It seems quite possible that had the verdict in the Chicago Seven trial been more straightforward, it too would have been more effective in assigning meaning to the Chicago convention—if they were guilty, they must have been responsible. Similarly, had the McGovern Commission report been more closely connected to the Chicago convention, it might have been more effective at supplying an interpretation of the convention rooted in ideas about political participation and democratic representation.

The power of policy choices to influence our collective memories suggests that the Bush administration made its contribution to collective memory in its choice to militarize the events of September 11, 2001. Like the Great Society programs, Bush's war on terrorism has retrodictive power to assign meaning to events. If the response to September 11 was to wage war on Afghanistan and Iraq, then the events of September 11 must have been an act of war. Even today, it is difficult to recall the events as, say, a criminal conspiracy, even though this conceptualization has been applied to previous acts of terrorism committed in the United States, including the 1995 bombing of the Murrah Federal Building in Oklahoma City and the previous bombing of the World Trade Center in 1993. Evidence from this study suggests that the Bush administration's policy choice will continue to influence the collective memory of September 11 even after the administration has left office and its power to shape public discourse has faded.

One reason policy responses effectively supply meaning to events may be that they satisfy our narrative expectations. Policy solutions can give shape to policy problems (Spector and Kitsuse 2001), and if we are, as Hayden White (1987) claims, driven by an instinct to assign to real events the comforting coherence of a story, we may reason backward from the ending of a story to make sense of it (Martin 1986). Controversial and traumatic events, such as the cases examined in this study and the September 11 terrorist attacks, may evoke especially strong desires for the comfort and coherence of stories.

Another reason that policy responses are particularly effective in structuring collective memory may be that the policies typically outlast the officials who created them. The war on terrorism and the collective memory of September 11 it implies, for example, might long survive the current crop of public officials who may bequeath both lingering international conflicts and commitments and a restructured military to presidents to come. In contrast, stories that serve the immediate needs of particular public officials may not survive for long. Where individual officials are effective in claiming credit for their leadership, they become personally rather than institutionally invested in the stories they promote, which may then fade after they leave the public stage. For example, Mayor Rudolph Giuliani is held responsible for managing New York City's emergency services during and immediately after the World Trade Center collapse. His laurels are not necessarily bequeathed to his successors, so future mayors may have little interest in supporting collective memories of his leadership. Institutional reputations can also be affected by crisis management, as both the Los Angeles and Chicago police departments were for their handling of social unrest. The New York City Fire Department was lionized for its response to the events of September 11 and that acclaim can be handed down. These complex relationships between officials, institutions, and policies are virtually invisible when one considers only current events and thus have been neglected by scholars of media and politics. However, the passage of time makes clear these distinctions and complicates the role of social power in the development of collective memory.

Another reason that the Bush administration's early decisions about how to respond to the events of September 11 are likely to have a lasting impact on collective memory is that power is not only a characteristic of individuals or institutions. It is also a resource, and even the most powerful individuals and institutions must make choices about when and how to use it. When it comes to negotiating a meaning for the past, it may be that those who have great power to influence the story choose to use that power for other causes instead. Some evidence of this comes from the role of the Watts riots and the Chicago convention in more recent events. When riots broke out in Los Angeles in 1992, the economic deprivation story of the Watts riots was not an ideal past for Republicans running for reelection after twelve years of conservative economic and social policy. Their policies could be negatively contrasted with the Great Society programs that had briefly brought hope to the inner city. While they might (and did) argue that the Great Society was a failure, they would still be vulnerable to critiques that the "Rodney King riots" were the product of the same social problems that had produced the Watts riots—problems they had ignored. Yet faced with the immediate problems of explaining the riots and justifying both their authority and their policies, neither federal nor civic leaders spent their energy trying to redefine the past in ways that might be more congruent with the representation of the current unrest they promoted. Instead, they took the story of the past as given (as the past itself) and tried to work around it as they concentrated on developing meaning for the current crisis. Similarly faced with the problematic past of 1968 at their 1996 convention, the Democrats chose not to revise it but rather to dismiss it as irrelevant. They declined to revisit controversies over the Vietnam War, delegate selection practices, and other key elements of their last Chicago convention.

Other cases may have different outcomes—particularly when political officials are using the past to justify some contemplated course of action—but these two cases demonstrate that leaders are sometimes uninterested in expending their power to redefine the past and instead work with the meanings already available in public discourse. Future administrations may likewise live with the story of September 11 that is handed down to them.

Over time, we might expect the dominance of official voices to fade as the narratives of average people are featured in remembrances of September 11. As they become rarer, those who were eyewitnesses to an event acquire a special kind of authority while many of the sources of authority common to political leaders, such as their power to influence events (Entman and Page 1994) and their status as public officials, vanish. This process may be slowed in the case of September 11 memories, as it was in the case of the Chicago convention, because so many reporters were themselves caught up in the events of the day. However, the shift in perspective from those who managed official responses to the event to those who experienced it directly seems to be a common phenomenon in mediated collective memory, driven perhaps by journalistic norms that value witnessing[1] events. This movement from the realm of political action to the world of everyday experience has been criticized by some as a depoliticization of the past,[2] but in many ways, it is a double-edged sword. While it may personalize and therefore deny the social and political nature of a historical event, it also reduces the event to a human scale that is more easily understood in empathetic ways by those who have no personal memory of the past. It therefore preserves the relevance of the past in everyday social discourse. In the case of September 11, eyewitness testimony may in fact prove very political if the stories told by survivors and victims' families help to shore up support for the war on terrorism.

Audiences, Culture, and Collective Memory

Difficult as it is to imagine at present, personal memories of September 11 will fade. As older Americans pass away and a younger generation is born, the population that can remember where it was that morning will be replaced by one that cannot. For now, personal memories may represent an important limitation on the power of media and political officials to reconstruct the past, although the fact that some people later came to believe Saddam Hussein was involved in the attacks reveals that personal memory is more a limitation than an outright barrier to historical revisionism.

In the aftermath of the Watts riots and the Chicago convention, the news media generally focused on the meaning of the past rather than the actual events that occurred. Reporters typically did not provide audiences with the means to think critically about their pasts. Instead, audiences would have to draw upon their personal memories for evaluating the stories they were told, for details about the events themselves were not typically related until about twenty years after the fact. It is plausible to imagine that the events of September 11 might be more readily related in the media since overt struggle over the meaning of the past is not a feature of the terrorist attacks to nearly the degree it was in the wake of the riots and the convention. Still, whether the details of the past are regularly related or not, we should expect the power of the media to influence representations of September 11 to grow over time. Fewer and fewer people will have personal memories of the event, and the stories that are told should become more and more coherent and therefore plausible, regardless of their relationship to the actual past. Processes of assimilation should make events that dovetail with the meaning assigned to the past relatively more prominent while those that call into question the shared meaning of the past are likely to fade. Already, the attacks in New York City are far more prominently remembered than the bombing of the Pentagon. The religious and ethnic identities of the hijackers have been emphasized while their nationalities have more or less vanished from news discourse. Today, many of us can still recognize the gaps between our own memories and the past as it is represented, but soon, few of us will. Failures of our personal memories, for we are as prone to limited remembrance and assimilation processes as the media,[3] and processes of population replacement mean that this pluralistic brake on the wholesale reconstruction of the past[4] is limited in that over time, it becomes less and less effective. Audience power will give way to media power.

Still, public perceptions of social reality will probably continue to affect stories of September 11 even after personal memories are all but gone. Theorists of memory—both psychological and collective—point out that we bring our current beliefs and values to bear upon our memories of the past. It should be easier to persuade audiences to narratives of the past that square with contemporary ways of thinking. Some evidence of this is apparent in the transformation of the Watts riots story to accommodate the conservative public discourse of the 1980s. We might expect that future perceptions of international relationships, of security threats, of Islam, of Arab peoples, and perhaps other aspects of social reality as as yet unimaginable will influence the evolution of stories about September 11 even as changing attitudes about race and the Vietnam War have altered the narrative potentials of 1960s-era events. Nor should we expect such evolution to cease, for the present does have an influence on the past. However, the evidence of this study suggests that these changes occur incrementally and typically within the context of established meaning. For example, the economic deprivation narrative was not abandoned when the rhetoric of personal responsibility was applied to it. Rather, it was adjusted to fit. When Bill Clinton was elected, negative evaluations of the 1968 delegate selection reforms remained the main narrative of events in the convention hall, but instead of being held responsible for the Democrats' losing streak, they were answerable for boring conventions. Reform is more common than revolution, even when present circumstances offer opportunities for either.

The terrorist attacks of September 11 were not as divisive—at least domestically—as the 1960s events examined in this study. Although the Bush administration has used the events of September 11 as justification for some controversial policies, such as attacking Iraq and passing and enforcing the Patriot Act, opponents with access to mainstream media have not typically called into question the administration's representation of September 11. Opponents of the Iraq War, for example, commonly argued that Saddam Hussein had no connection to the events of September 11 when they objected to the Bush administration using the terrorist attacks as a justification for the war. Those who oppose the Patriot Act's more intrusive provisions do so on the grounds that civil liberties outweigh national security rather than arguing that national security is not implicated in the events of September 11. In other words, even opponents to Bush administration policies do not undermine the meaning that has been assigned to September 11. Instead, their arguments challenge factual details or offer competing values. The same could be said of the aviation industry's resistance to new and more expensive passenger screening procedures—where cost-benefit ratios are typically applied—and to the criticisms aimed at the Department of Homeland Security as an overcomplicated, inefficient bureaucracy.

An important challenging element to the narrative coherence of this story of September 11 comes from those who place blame as much on government officials for disregarding credible threats as upon the terrorists who carried out the attacks. Shifting the responsible agent shifts the frame from one that unites the public and the government as a target of terrorism to one that represents the public as victims of government incompetence. While public cynicism and distrust of government may give this story some staying power, there is evidence in this study to suggest that this narrative may one day be transformed into a tragic story that elides government agency and suggests that the attacks were fated to happen, much like a natural disaster might be.

In thinking of September 11 as a controversial event, one might also be tempted to speak of "global" collective memory and the struggle to define the events of September 11 on the world stage. However, to do so is to stretch the concept of collective memory to its limits, for collective memory theories have always described the phenomenon as emerging from a community that shares common values and a group identity.

The crucial groundwork for collective memory of September 11 is being laid now and will shape its legacy for years to come, perhaps even more than the early discursive struggles over the meanings of the Watts riots and the Chicago convention have shaped the subsequent collective memories of those events. For better or worse, the meaning we are now in the process of assigning to September 11 will be handed down and is likely very soon to be treated not as a story of the past, but rather as the past itself because the narrative processes that went into making it are already fading from public view. The influence of the current political administration has shaped a story of the past that is amenable to present agendas and policy goals, but there is no guarantee that over the long term collective memory of September 11 will reliably serve any political agenda as it emerges in unpredictable analogies and contexts. The evidence from the case studies suggests that the past we make is the past we will live with even as circumstances change. Indeed, this is what makes collective memory an independent force in public life.

Coda: The Power of the Past

One reason the past is so powerful is that as collective memories evolve, they achieve a kind of perfection unattainable by either real life or narrative fiction. They remain embedded in the real events that were their genesis—they tell of real events that really happened. Yet they also acquire a narrative coherence that is impossible for any real event. They resolve ambiguous events and complex characters into simple, moral tales populated by heroes, villains, and fools. In other words, they take on the characteristics of "true stories." Their status as a true story is enhanced by the fact that they seem to have no individual or institutional sponsor nor to serve faithfully any political agenda. Instead, they are embraced by a variety of social actors and institutions who relate them in essentially the same way but use them to achieve different rhetorical purposes. The work that was done to make the story fit the facts and the facts fit the story fades from view; the collective memory appears whole, complete, true.

The disruption of authority represented in social unrest like the Watts riots or the 1968 Chicago convention can be preserved in memory, although in attenuated form, because social and political elites—like the rest of us—typically treat the past as given rather than made. Initially, social unrest produces an open struggle for control of events and their meaning that makes it impossible for political leaders to authoritatively assign meaning to the present. Over time, they lose interest in and authority over the meaning assigned to the past as average people gain increasing authority to narrate their own pasts. Of course, there is a paradoxical quality to this dynamic. Where political leaders remain invested in creating meaning for the past—as may be the case with Watergate and with the Vietnam War more generally—this process may be stalled indefinitely. Where they lose interest in the meaning for the past it may be a sign that they no longer consider it sufficiently relevant to be useful in thinking about current affairs. Still, the fact that political leaders were forced to cope with inconvenient pasts at important political moments of the present does suggest that collective memories can be a resource for challenging social authority in addition to being invoked by elites as rhetorical tools to justify their policy choices.

While they never lose their roots in the real events that spawned them, the implied objective past (Mead 1929; Maines, Sugrue, and Katovich 1983) of burned buildings and stage-managed conventions, these stories of the past become in many ways more symbolic than real. They are myths, used to teach the lessons of history to generations without personal memories of the events themselves. They remain dynamic, for they are recalled in new and unpredictable contexts (Zelizer 1995). However, their dynamism is typically limited to shifts of emphasis within a narrative frame rather than dramatic changes to the narratives themselves. Concentrated effort on the part of powerful political actors or some dramatic cultural shift might be enough to reframe the past, but the work involved will be considerable. With their seamless synthesis of real pasts and good stories, collective memories become part of the cultural repertoire we use to make sense of social reality, and so we are bound by the pasts we have made.

Notes

CHAPTER 1 INTRODUCTION

1. Halbwachs's seminal work on collective memory was published posthumously. Many of his works were published in the 1920s and '30s.
2. For just a few examples, see Hobsbawm and Ranger 1983; Schudson 1992; Schwartz, Zerubavel, and Barnett 1986; Zelizer 1995; Zerubavel 1995.
3. E.g., Petrocik 1996; Ansolabehere and Iyengar 1994.
4. E.g., Gitlin 1980; Entman 1991; Jacobs and Shapiro 2001.
5. E.g. Herman and Chomsky 1988.
6. See Kammen 1978 on the moderation of the Revolution in historical novels.
7. For an example of media framing as an aspect of the text, see Gamson and Modigliani 1989. For an example of framing as a media effect see Iyengar 1991.
8. E.g., Entman 1991; Lawrence 2000.
9. E.g., Entman 1993; Lawrence 2000; Stone 1989.
10. E.g., Baumgartner and Jones 1993; Entman 1993; Iyengar 1991; Kingdon 1995.
11. For an empirical demonstration of this see Protess et al. 1987.
12. See also Schwartz 1991.

CHAPTER 2 REAL-TIME NEWS

1. E.g., Johnson 1994; Strohm 1999; Love 2001; Caldwell 1969.
2. See McCombs and Ghanem 2001; Baumgartner and Jones 1993.
3. E.g., Darnton 1990; Hall et al. 1978; Lule 2001.

4. None of the stories appearing in any of the newsmagazines at this time carries a byline, which was a typical practice at the time (Nourie and Nourie 1990).

5. On the latter point, see Gitlin 1980.

6. See Hall, 1978.

7. See Gitlin 1980.

8. Indeed, a study coordinated by UCLA and funded by the Office of Economic Opportunity found that 75 percent of adult African American men in South Central Los Angeles had arrest records (Cohen 1967).

9. *Newsweek* printed a longer version of this comment in their article "Tough Years Ahead" (1965, 20).

10. The following discussion is based on Caute's (1988) history of 1968 and the *New York Times Index* entries dealing with preparations for the convention.

11. See "Stalag '68," 1968, 12. It is important to note that this language was reminiscent of the language used to describe the Soviet Union's recent invasion of Czechoslovakia.

12. The role of the media in the 1968 Democratic National Convention was a subject of discussion at the time, and this debate has been enfolded into public memory to some extent. However, the self-reflexive nature of these memories raise issues that are beyond the scope of this study, so they are not explored in detail here. Memories of the media's role in the convention are not generally classed with other convention memories in the *New York Times Index*, though they appear regularly in full text searches that mention the convention. In general, the media downplay their role in convention events, as one might expect.

13. See also Robinson 1970.

CHAPTER 3 POLITICAL OFFICIALS AND THE PUBLIC PAST

1. E.g., Sigal 1973; Bennett 1990; Gandy 1982; Lasorsa and Reese 1990.

2. See Gitlin 1980.

3. E.g., Dee 1990; Ely 1994; Kaul 1997.

4. This discussion of the verdict and the appeals was drawn from Ely 1994.

5. E.g., Haas 1975.

6. E.g., Entman 1991; Althaus et al. 1996.

7. E.g., Bennett 1990.

8. E.g., Jacobs and Shapiro 2001; Lawrence 2000.

9. E.g., Patterson 1993; Entman and Page 1994.

10. Capt. Frank Isbell, former LAPD community relations director, quoted in Kendall 1975, 8.

11. Lt. Ron Nelson, then-current LAPD community relations director, quoted in Kendall 1975, 8.

12. See Zelizer 1992.

13. See Entman and Page 1994.
14. E.g., Neustadt and May 1986; Allport and Postman 1947.

CHAPTER 4 DEFUSING CONTROVERSY AND
PAVING THE WAY FOR COLLECTIVE MEMORY

1. An examination of the histories of the individual newspapers analyzed in this study (Cose 1989; Berges 1984; Hynds 1980; Edge 1999; Gottlieb and Wolt 1977; Wendt 1979) suggest that changes in the editorial and business climates of the newspapers are unlikely to have affected the conclusions drawn here. In many cases, important editorial and business model changes predate the time when the newspapers were available on Lexis-Nexis and were thus institutionalized before the analysis really begins. For example, all three newspapers made important changes to their editorial structure in the late 1960s and middle 1970s, years before the newspapers became keyword searchable in the 1980s. The *Los Angeles Times* became a monopoly newspaper in the 1970s (Gottlieb and Wolt 1977) and the *New York Times* established its weekday "software" sections during that decade as well. Overall changes in the industry, such as the increasing professionalization of news staffs and the increasing pressure to turn a profit, may further encourage the development of a uniform, non-controversial story of the past, but they do not necessarily suggest what form that story might take.
2. See Edy and Daradanova 2006.
3. E.g., Bennett 1983.
4. See Manoff and Schudson 1986.
5. E.g., Halbwachs 1950/1980; Schwartz, Zerubavel, and Barnett 1986; Schwartz 1991; Novick 1999.
6. For a thorough discussion of research and perspectives on contemporary racism, see Sears, Sidanius, and Bobo 2000.
7 See Carmines and Stimson 1989.
8. See, for example, Dixon and Linz 2000; Entman and Rojecki 2000.
9. See, for example, Fentress and Wickham 1992; Allport and Postman 1947.
10. 57 percent in 1979, 50 percent in 1991.
11. 72 percent in 1978, 63 percent in 1998.
12. E.g., Bennett 1990; Patterson 1993; Entman and Page 1994.

CHAPTER 5 BUILDING COLLECTIVE MEMORY

1. E.g., Baumgartner and Jones 1993; Entman 1993; Iyengar and Kinder 1987.
2. E.g., Schwartz et al. 1986; Schwartz 1991; Novick 1999; Zerubavel 1995.

3. See Iyengar 1991.

4. Warren and Mills 1994, 1 (emphasis added).

5. Reporters for the *Los Angeles Times*, the *New York Times*, and the *Chicago Tribune* are rarely factually inaccurate. More common are errors or misrepresentations by columnists or news sources. Simple errors of fact are quickly corrected. In 1992, *New York Times* columnist Russell Baker recalled that newsman John Chancellor had been dragged off the floor and arrested at the 1968 Democratic convention (Baker 1992a). A few days later, he wrote a brief apology to his readers: Chancellor had been arrested at the 1964 Republican National Convention in San Francisco (Baker 1992b). His error is an excellent example of assimilation to expectation, but his mistake was the sort of technical one that is frowned upon and fixed in the news (though the *Houston Chronicle* made the same error in 1996 and failed to correct it). More subtle errors by other columnists were allowed to stand. A Clarence Page column argued that at the 1968 convention, diverse groups came together to protest the war and contrasted that with the fragmented protests at the 2000 Democratic convention in Los Angeles. In fact, the demonstrators in Chicago agitated on behalf of a remarkably diverse set of causes, but Page is clearly caught up in the now-common recollection of the protests as antiwar. A Flora Lewis column in the same year made the same mistake in contrasting the 1968 "cohesion" to the World Trade Organization protests of 1999.

Two news stories in the *Seattle Post-Intelligencer* contain notable errors that also went uncorrected. One story claims that Carl Albert, as convention chairman in 1968, stifled unruly antiwar and dissident delegates. In fact, Albert was unable to do so, and one of Daley's aides, Dan Rostenkowski, who would later chair the House Ways and Means Committee, took over the convention chair to put an end to the disruptions from the floor. In another story, a congressional representative makes the dubious claim that the protests at the convention did not harm the reputation of the city of Chicago and cites the resounding reelection of Richard J. Daley to support his assertion. Yet evidence from elsewhere in this study suggests that Chicago was deeply concerned about its reputation. Most of these errors are relatively minor and are ascribed to individual sources or to columnists. In general, the news about the past is factually consistent even if it is never factually complete. It is meaning that develops over time.

6. See Lawrence, 2000.

7. Knowing that additional, sometimes alternative, information about the past is preserved in newspapers that serve audiences and communities with a particular interest in that material might lead one to expect that an alternative narrative of the Watts riots is preserved in the newspaper that serves the African American community in Los Angeles: the *Sentinel*. This turns out not to be the case. Research by Susan Strohm (1999) reveals that the trajectory of coverage in the *Sentinel* closely resembles that of the mainstream media documented in this study. Strohm locates the reason for this in the *Sentinel*'s close ties to traditional black community leaders and their need to negotiate with the dominant white

community and its leaders. Her evidence shows that more militant viewpoints and spokespeople were ignored by the paper in favor of the integrationist philosophies embraced by established community leaders, although she does note that the presence of more militant and "radical" elements in the community can give traditional black community leaders a certain leverage with their white counterparts that they would otherwise lack.

CHAPTER 6 USING COLLECTIVE MEMORY

1. E.g., Hobsbawm and Ranger 1983; Bodnar 1992.
2. See especially Patterson 1993.
3. See especially Bennett 1990.
4. See Edy and Daradanova, 2006.
5. Although not the whole story: see Lawrence 2000.
6. See Chapter 5.
7. E.g., Stevenson 1992.
8. *Los Angeles Times* 1992b, 6; note the elision of agency.
9. See Smith 1993.
10. Patterson's more recent work (2002) has touched on some of these issues, noting that the goal of the McGovern Commission reforms was to put voters in control of the nominating process and describing how the phenomenon of front-loading gives voters in states with early primaries the ability to choose the nominee while voters in states with late primaries are voiceless. His conclusion, however, rejects a return to party-dominated conventions not because they were undemocratic but because there is not the political will to reinstate them (148–149).
11. See Chapter 5.

CHAPTER 7 CONCLUSIONS

1. See Zelizer 1992, 1998.
2. E.g., Frisch 1986.
3. E.g., Bartlett 1932.
4. See Schudson 1992.

References

Abu-Lughod, J. 1989. On the remaking of history: How to reinvent the past. In *Remaking History,* ed. B. Kruger and P. Mariani , 111–229. Seattle: Bay Press.

After the blood bath. 1965. *Newsweek* 66 (August 30): 13–14.

Allport, G. W., and L. Postman. 1947. *The psychology of rumor.* New York: Henry Holt and Company.

Althaus, S. L., J. A. Edy, R. M. Entman, and P. Phalen. 1996. Revising the indexing hypothesis: Officials, media, and the Libya crisis. *Political Communication* 13:407–21.

Ansolabehere, S., and S. Iyengar. 1994. Riding the wave and claiming ownership over issues: The joint effects of advertising and news coverage in campaigns. *Public Opinion Quarterly* 58:335–57.

Apple, R. W. 1988. Tinkering with way parties choose nominees hasn't worked very well. *New York Times,* January 18.

Ayres, D., Jr. 1996. Los Angeles, long fragmented, faces threat of secession by the San Fernando Valley. *New York Times,* May 29.

Back of riots: "Discontent, illiteracty, criminal element." 1965. *U.S. News and World Report* 90 (August 30): 22–23.

Baker, R. 1992a. Observer: The way they were. *New York Times,* August 18.

———. 1992b. Observer: Rendered onto Chancellor. *New York Times,* August 29.

Banks, S. 1985. Watts: The legacy. *Los Angeles Times,* August 11.

Barnhurst, K. G., and D. Mutz. 1997. American journalism and the decline of event-centered reporting. *Journal of Communication* 47 (4): 27–53.

Bartlett, F. C. 1932. *Remembering: A study in experimental and social psychology.* Cambridge, UK: The University Press.

The battle of Chicago. 1968. *Newsweek* 72 (September 9): 24–29.

Baumgartner, F. R., and B. Jones. 1993. *Agendas and instabilities in American politics.* Chicago: University of Chicago Press.

Bennett, W. L. 1983. *News: The politics of illusion.* New York: Longman.

————. 1990. Toward a theory of press-state relations. *Journal of Communication* 40:103–25.

Bennett, W. L., and R. G. Lawrence. 1995. News icons and the mainstreaming of social change. *Journal of Communication* 45:20–39.

Berges, M. 1984. *The life and times of Los Angeles: A newspaper, a family, and a city.* New York: Atheneum.

Berke, R. L. 1994. Democrats pick Chicago for convention. *New York Times,* July 20.

Bernstein, R. 1993. Yale, class of '68: Time to take stock. *New York Times,* May 30.

Black, L., and J. Hill. 1996. Dellinger is arrested, but world not watching; protests smaller, tend to fizzle out. *Chicago Tribune,* August 29.

Bodnar, J. 1992. *Remaking America: Public memory, commemoration and patriotism in the twentieth century.* Princeton, NJ: Princeton University Press.

Bommes, M., and P. Wright. 1982. Charms of residence: The public and the past. In *Making histories: Studies in history-writing and politics,* eds. R. Johnson, G. McLennan, B. Schwarz, and D. Sutton, 253–302. Minneapolis, MN: University of Minnesota Press.

Boyarsky, B. 1985. In Watts, a mayoral race suggests a mutual myopia. *Los Angeles Times,* March 24.

————. 1991. Echoes of the McCone commission. *Los Angeles Times,* May 3.

Braun, S., and R. Russell. 1992. Riots are violent reruns for the veterans of Watts. *Los Angeles Times,* May 4.

Breo, D. L. 1986. July 14, 1966. *Chicago Tribune,* July 6.

Caldwell, D. W. 1969. An analysis of selected newspaper coverage of the 1968 national Democratic convention. Unpublished master's thesis, West Virginia Univ., Morgantown.

Carmines, E. G., and J. A. Stimson. 1989. *Issue evolution: Race and the transformation of American politics.* Princeton, NJ: Princeton University Press.

Carroll, M. 1986. Best guest list: From intellectual ladies to charming men about town, here are the favorite dinner guests of our most notable hosts. *Chicago Tribune,* October 15.

Caute, D. 1988. *The year of the barricades: A journey through 1968.* New York: Harper & Row.

Chicago Tribune. 1994a. A day of mourning declared for Nixon. April 24.

Chicago Tribune. 1994b. The Woodstock generation ages. August 3.

Chicago Tribune. 1996. Tales of political conventions on tap. May 19.

Chong, D. 1996. Creating common frames of reference on political issues. In *Political persuasion and attitude change,* eds. D. C. Mutz, P. M. Sniderman, and R. A. Brody, 195–224. Ann Arbor, MI: University of Michigan Press.

Clark, K. R. 1987. Dear Abbie: Abbie Hoffman, the perpetual protester is out to thwart the latest establishment edict: Mandatory drug testing. *Chicago Tribune,* October 14.

Clifford, F. 1992. Rich-poor gulf widens in state. *Los Angeles Times,* May 11.

Clines, F. X. 1996. Chicago diary; lucky protesters hit the soapbox jackpot. *New York Times,* August 26.

Cohen, J., and W. S. Murphy. 1966. *Burn, baby, burn! The Los Angeles race riot, August, 1965.* New York: Dutton.

Cohen, N. E. 1967. *Summary and implications for policy.* Los Angeles: Institute of Government Affairs, University of California.

Cohn, W. H. 1976. History for the masses: Television portrays the past. *Journal of Popular Culture* 10:280–89.

Commager, H. S. 1965. The search for a usable past. *American Heritage* 16 (February): 4–9.

The compleat delegate. 1968. *Time* 120 (August 30): 19.

Corwin, M., and L. Gordon. 1992. King case aftermath: A city in crisis; many people's view of the carnage is in their rearview mirrors. *Los Angeles Times,* May 2.

Cose, E. 1989. *The press.* New York: William Morrow and Company.

Creighton, N. 1993. When hearts and minds were lost. *Chicago Tribune,* January 30.

Cummings, Judith. 1985. 20 years after riots, Watts still smolders. *New York Times,* August 12.

Daley city under siege. 1968. *Time* 120 (August 30): 18–19.

Daley, S. 1994. '68 convention shades 1996 bid; Clinton's process of selection concerns Daley, allies. *Chicago Tribune,* May 19.

Darnton, R. 1990. *The kiss of lamourette.* New York: W. W. Norton & Company.

Davis, F. 1979. *Yearning for yesterday: A sociology of nostalgia.* New York: Free Press.

———. 1984. Decade labeling: The play of collective memory and narrative plot. *Symbolic Interaction* 7:15–24.

Dawsey, D. 1990. 25 years after the Watts riots: McCone Commission's recommendations have gone unheeded. *Los Angeles Times,* July 8.

Dee, J. 1990. Constraints on persuasion in the Chicago Seven trial. In *Popular trials: Rhetoric, mass media and the law,* ed. R. Harriman, 86–113. Tuscaloosa, AL: The University of Alabama Press.

Dementia in the second city. 1968. *Time* 92 (September 6): 21–24.

Dionne, E. J. 1989. The nation: Again, Democrats agonize over rules. *New York Times,* May 21.

Dixon, T. L., and D. Linz. 2000. Race and the misrepresentation of victimization on local television news. *Communication Research* 27:547–573.

Dold, R. B. 1996. Who's running the show? *Chicago Tribune,* August 30.

Druckman, J. N. 2004. Political preference formation: Competition, deliberation, and the (ir)relevance of framing effects. *American Political Science Review* 98:671–86.

Durant, C. 1975. Black Muslims: Growing economic force. *Los Angeles Times,* March 23.

Edelman, M. 1964. *The symbolic uses of politics*. Urbana, IL: University of Illinois Press.

Edge, M. 1999. And "The Wall" came tumbling down in Los Angeles. In *The big chill: Investigative reporting in the current media environment*, eds. M. S. Greenwald and J. Bernt, 197–213. Ames, IA: Iowa State University Press.

Edy, J. A. 1999. Journalistic uses of collective memory. *Journal of Communication* 49 (2): 71–85.

Edy, J. A., and M. Daradanova. 2006. Reporting through the lens of the past: From Challenger to Columbia. *Journalism* 7:131–151.

Edy, J. A., and R. G. Lawrence. 2000. Archiving poverty: A study in the production of social knowledge. Paper presented at the American Political Science Association Annual Meeting, Washington, DC, August/September.

Ely, J. W., Jr. 1994. The Chicago conspiracy case. In *American political trials*, ed. R. Belknap, 233–53. Westport, CT: Greenwood Press.

Entman, R. M. 1991. Framing U.S. coverage of international news: Contrasts in narratives of the KAL and Iran Air incidents. *Journal of Communication* 41:6–27.

———. 1993. Framing: Toward clarification of a fractured paradigm. *Journal of Communication* 43:51–58.

Entman, R. M., and A. Rojecki. 2000. *The black image in the white mind: Media and race in America*. Chicago: University of Chicago Press.

Entman, R. M., and B. I. Page. 1994. The news before the storm: The Iraq War debate and the limits to media independence. In *Taken by storm: The news media, public opinion, and U.S. foreign policy in the Gulf War*, eds. W. L. Bennett and D. L. Paletz, 82–101. Chicago: University of Chicago Press.

Fairclough, N. 1995. *Media discourse*. London: Edward Arnold.

Farber, D. 1988. *Chicago '68*. Chicago: University of Chicago Press.

Fentress, J., and C. Wickham. 1992. *Social memory*. Oxford, UK: Blackwell.

Fine, G. A. 2001. *Difficult reputations: Collective memories of the evil, inept, and controversial*. Chicago: University of Chicago Press.

Fisher, W. R. 1985. The narrative paradigm: An elaboration. *Communication Monographs* 52:347–67.

Fishman, M. 1980. *Manufacturing the news*. Austin, TX: University of Texas Press.

Foerstner, A. 1988. Watching the news from 1968. *Chicago Tribune*, August 5.

Frisch, M. H. 1986. The memory of history. In *Presenting the past: Essays on history and the public*, eds. S. P. Benson, S. Brier, and R. Rosenzweig, 5–17. Philadelphia: Temple University Press.

Fulford, R. 1999. *The triumph of narrative: Storytelling in the age of mass culture*. New York: Broadway Books.

Fussell, P. 2000. *The Great War and modern memory*. Oxford: Oxford University Press (Originally published 1975).

Galloway, P. 1988. Tom Hayden: The man who turned Chicago upside-down 20 years ago says he is now a "born-again middle American." *Chicago Tribune*, July 19.

Galtung, J., and M. H. Ruge. 1965. The structure of foreign news: The presentation of the Congo, Cuba and Cyprus crises in four Norwegian newspapers. *Journal of Peace Research* 1:64–91.

Gamson, W. A. 2001. Foreword. In *Framing public life: Perspectives on media and our understanding of the social world*, eds. S. D. Reese, O. H. Gandy, and A. E. Grant, ix–xi. Mahwah, NJ: Lawrence Erlbaum Associates.

Gamson, W. A., and A. Modigliani. 1989. Media discourse and public opinion on nuclear power: A constructionist approach. *American Journal of Sociology* 95:1–37.

Gandy, O. H. 1982. *Beyond agenda setting: Information subsidies and public policy.* Norwood, NJ: Ablex Pub. Co.

Garrow, D. J. 1978. *Protest at Selma : Martin Luther King, Jr., and the Voting Rights Act of 1965.* New Haven, CT: Yale University Press.

Gilens, M. 1999. *Why Americans hate welfare.* Chicago: University of Chicago Press.

Gitlin, T. 1980. *The whole world is watching: The mass media and the making and unmaking of the New Left.* Berkeley, CA: The University of California Press.

Goodman, W. 1990. Review/Television: Recalling Watts riots and the fires' kindling. *New York Times*, August 13.

Gottlieb, R., and I. Wolt. 1977. *Thinking big: The story of the Los Angeles Times, its publishers, and their influence on southern California.* New York: Putnam.

Governor's Commission on the Los Angeles Riots. 1965. *Violence in the city—An end or a beginning? A report, by the Governor's Commission on the Los Angeles Riots.* Los Angeles.

Gray, D. 1991. Was police investigation an empty ritual, or will it bring change? *Los Angeles Times*, July 12.

Greene, B. 1987. A hearty Yippie! for a new father. *Chicago Tribune*, September 30.

Gregory, S. W., Jr., and J. M. Lewis. 1988. Symbols of collective memory: The social process of memorializing May 4, 1970, at Kent State University. *Symbolic Interaction* 11:213–33.

Griffin, J. L. 1996. Daley lottery plan a loser with protesters. *Chicago Tribune*, 19 July.

Griffin, J. L., and A. Martin. 1996. Police spare the baton and spoil the protest; at least 500 demonstrators try hard to get arrested, but police insist on handling them with kid gloves. *Chicago Tribune*, August 28.

Haas, E. 1975. I have a suggestion. *Los Angeles Times*, March 30.

Halbwachs, M. 1980. *The collective memory.* Trans. F. J. Ditter, Jr., and V. Y. Ditter. New York: Harper Colophon Books (Originally published 1950).

Hall, S. 1982. The rediscovery of "ideology:" The return of the repressed in media studies. In *Culture, society and media*, eds. M. Gurevitch, T. Bennett, J. Curran, and J. Woollacott, 56–90. London: Methuen.

Hall, S., C. Critcher, T. Jefferson, J. Clark, and B. Roberts. 1978. *Policing the crisis: Mugging, the state and law and order.* London: The MacMillan Press Ltd.

Hallin, D. C. 1992. Soundbite news: Television coverage of elections 1968–1988. *Journal of Communication* 42 (2): 5–24.

———. 1994. *We keep America on top of the world: Television journalism and the public sphere.* London: Routledge.

Hardy, T. 1994. Not just a conventional push: City sells self to Democrats as the best place to be in '96. *Chicago Tribune*, May 18.

———. 1996. Convention had many winners, but just 1 loser. *Chicago Tribune,* September 1.

Herman, E. S., and N. Chomsky. 1988. *Manufacturing consent: The political economy of the mass media.* New York: Pantheon.

Hippies, Yippies, and Mace. 1968. *Newsweek* 72 (September 2): 25–26.

Hobsbawm, E., and T. Ranger. 1983. *The invention of tradition.* Cambridge: Cambridge University Press.

Hynds, E. C. 1980. *American newspapers in the 1980s.* New York: Hastings House.

Iyengar, S. 1991. *Is anyone responsible?: How television frames political issues.* Chicago: University of Chicago Press.

Iyengar, S., and D. R. Kinder. 1987. *News that matters.* Chicago: University of Chicago Press.

Jacobs, L., and R. Y. Shapiro. 2001. *Politicians don't pander: Political manipulation and the loss of democratic responsiveness.* Chicago: University of Chicago Press.

Johnson, A. K. 1994. Urban ghetto riots, 1965–1968: A comparison of Soviet and American press coverage. PhD diss., Univ. of Denver, 1994. Abstract in *Dissertation Abstracts International* 55 (07A): 2113.

Johnson, T. J. 1995. *The rehabilitation of Richard Nixon: The media's effect on collective memory.* New York: Garland.

Jones, J. 1975. The programs: At least somebody cared. *Los Angeles Times,* March 23.

Kammen, M. 1978. *A season of youth: The American Revolution and the historical imagination.* New York: Alfred A. Knopf.

Kass, J. 1992. Daley gives '96 convention a shot. *Chicago Tribune,* July 28.

Kass, J., and J. Heard. 1996. Daley stands tall in spotlight; glitch aside, he pushes away memories from 1968. *Chicago Tribune,* August 27.

Kaul, A. J. 1997. The case of the Chicago Seven (1969). In *The press on trial: Crimes and trials as media events,* ed. L. Chiasson, Jr., 147–57. Westport, CT: Greenwood Press.

Kendall, J. 1975. A ghetto is slow to die. *Los Angeles Times,* March 23.

Kendall, P. 1994. World Cup fans come with warning attached. *Chicago Tribune,* March 29.

Kennedy, E. 1985. The art of politics Chicago style. *New York Times,* May 5.

Key, V. O. 1961. *Public opinion and American democracy.* New York: Knopf.

Kingdon, J. W. 1995. *Agendas, alternatives, and public policies.* New York: HarperCollins Publishers.

Lang, K., and G. E. Lang. 1989. Collective memory and the news. *Communication* 11:123–9.

Lasorsa, D. L., and S. D. Reese. 1990. New source use in the crash of 1987: A study of four national media. *Journalism Quarterly* 67:60–71.

Lawrence, R. G. 2000. *The politics of force: Media and the construction of police brutality.* Berkeley, CA: University of California Press.

Lewis, B. 1975. *History—Remembered, recovered, invented.* Princeton, NJ: Princeton University Press.

Lindsey, R. 1980. A decade and a half after riots, Watts is termed "Worse hovel than it was." *New York Times*, August 10.

Locin, M. 1995. City, Democrats brace for unwelcome '68 flashbacks. *Chicago Tribune*, May 11.

The loneliest road. 1965. *Time* 86 (August 27): 9–10.

Los Angeles: The fire this time. 1965. *Newsweek* 66 (August 23): 15–17.

Los Angeles Times. 1980a. The man who started the riots can't live it down. August 31.

Los Angeles Times. 1980b. A mother battles alone to raise her son without bigotry. August 31.

Los Angeles Times. 1980c. Watts survivors: Lives torn by a bullet. August 31.

Los Angeles Times. 1992a. Understanding the riots part 1; the path to fury; chapter 2; "In L. A., you don't know where the lines are." May 11.

Los Angeles Times. 1992b. Understanding the riots part 1; the path to fury; chapter 3; the word in the streets: "Burn, baby, burn." May 11.

Love, S. S. 2001. Blood, sweat and gas: Print media and the 1968 Democratic national convention. Unpublished master's thesis, Univ. of Montana, Missoula.

Lule, J. 2001. *Daily news, eternal stories.* New York: The Guilford Press.

Madigan, C. M. 1988. Dukakis running uphill, but Bush doesn't relax. *Chicago Tribune*, October 26.

Mailer, N. 1968. *Miami and the siege of Chicago: An informal history of the Republican and Democratic national conventions of 1968.* New York: World Publishing Company.

Maines, D. R., N. M. Sugrue, and M. A. Katovich. 1983. The sociological import of G. H. Mead's theory of the past. *American Sociological Review* 48:161–173.

The man who would recapture youth. 1968. *Time* 92 (September 6): 15–21.

Mannheim, Karl. (1928) 1952. The Problem of Generations. In *Essays on the sociology of knowledge*, ed. Paul Kecskemeti, 276–320. London: Routledge.

Manoff, R. K. 1986. Writing the news (by telling the "story"). In *Reading the news*, eds. R. K. Manoff and M. Schudson, 197–229. New York: Pantheon Books.

Manoff, R. K., and M. Schudson. 1986. *Reading the news.* New York: Pantheon Books.

Margolis, J. 1988. Democrats see happy days again: Party is relaxed and confident going into convention. *Chicago Tribune*, July 17.

Martin, W. 1986. *Recent theories of narrative.* Ithaca, NY: Cornell University Press.

McCombs, M. E., and S. Ghanem 2001. The convergence of agenda-setting and framing. In *Framing public life: Perspectives on media and our understanding of the social world*, eds. S. D. Reese, O. Gandy, and A. E. Grant, 67–92. Mahwah, NJ: Lawrence Erlbaum Associates.

McRoberts, F. 1988. '68 protesters recall the past special events take a look back at convention unrest. *Chicago Tribune*, August 28.

Mead, G. H. 1929. The nature of the past. In *Essays in honor of John Dewey, on the occasion of his seventieth birthday, October 20, 1929*, 235–242. New York: H. Holt and Company.

Mitchell, J. L. 1987. Community wants more than name change. *Los Angeles Times*, July 2.

Molotch, H., and M. Lester. 1974. News as purposive behavior: On the strategic use of routine events, accidents, and scandals. *American Sociological Review* 39:101–12.

Mopping up. 1965. *Newsweek* 66 (August 30): 14–16.

Mydans, S. 1992. The police verdict: Verdict sets off a wave of shock and anger. *New York Times*, April 30.

The negro after Watts. 1965. *Time* 86 (August 27): 16–17.

Neikirk, W., and M. Tackett. 1996. The Clinton and Dole interviews; Clinton calls tax cut a threat to economy. *Chicago Tribune*, August 25.

Nelson, T. E. 2004. Policy goals, public rhetoric, and political attitudes. *Journal of Politics* 66:581–605.

Nelson, T. E., and Z. M. Oxley. 1999. Issue framing effects on belief importance and opinion. *Journal of Politics* 61:1040–68.

Neustadt, R. E., and E. R. May. 1986. *Thinking in time: The uses of history for decision makers*. New York: The Free Press.

New York Times. 1970. *New York Times index*. Vol. 57. New York: New York Times Company.

New York Times. 1986a. Abbie Hoffman plans radio show. September 2.

New York Times. 1986b. The once and future candidate. January 1.

New York Times. 1987. CBS News in search of itself. February 1.

New York Times. 1988a. The age of security. May 23.

New York Times. 1988b. Jerry Rubin is 50 (yes, 50) years old. July 16.

New York Times. 1988c. Westchester Guide. November 6.

New York Times. 1990. Verda F. Welcome, 83, a Maryland legislator. April 25.

New York Times. 1996. News summary. September 2.

Nimmo, D., and J. E. Combs. 1983. *Mediated political realities*. New York: Longman.

Noelle-Neumann, E. 1984. *The spiral of silence: Public opinion, our social skin*. Chicago: University of Chicago Press.

Nourie, A., and B. Nourie. 1990. *American mass market magazines*. New York: Greenwood Press.

Novick, P. 1999. *The Holocaust in American life*. Boston: Houghton Mifflin Company.

O'Connor, J. J. 1989. Review/television: Tributes to 8, serious and comic. *New York Times*, January 23.

Orwell, G. 1949. *Nineteen eighty-four.* New York: Harcourt, Brace & World.

Pace, E. 1994. Jerry Rubin, 1960's radical and Yippie leader, dies at 56. *New York Times,* November 29.

Page, B. I. 1996. *Who deliberates? Mass media in modern democracy.* Chicago: University of Chicago Press.

Parenti, M. 1992. *Make believe media: The politics of entertainment.* New York: St. Martin's Press.

Patterson, T. E. 1993. *Out of order.* New York: A. Knopf.

————. 2002. *The vanishing voter: Public involvement in an age of uncertainty.* New York: Alfred A. Knopf.

Peck, A. 1987. The 60s: New perspectives on a decade of hope and rage. *Chicago Tribune,* October 25.

Pennebaker, J. W., and B. L. Banasik. 1997. On the creation and maintenance of collective memories: History as social psychology. In *Collective memory of political events: Social psychological perspectives,* eds. J. W. Pennebaker, D. Paez, and B. Rime, 3–19. Mahwah, NJ: Lawrence Erlbaum Associates.

Petrocik, J. R. 1996. Issue ownership in presidential elections with a 1980 case study. *American Political Science Review* 40:825–850.

Pitt, D. E. 1988. Melee inquiry is stalled, board reports. *New York Times,* December 30.

Popular Memory Group. 1982. Popular memory: Theory, politics, method. In *Making histories: Studies in history-writing and politics,* eds. R. Johnson, G. McLennan, B. Schwarz, and D. Sutton, 205–52. Minneapolis, MN: University of Minnesota Press.

Protess, D. L., F. L. Cook, T. R. Curtin, T. Gordon, D. R. Leff, M. E. McCombs, and P. Miller. 1987. The impact of investigative reporting on public opinion and policy making: Targeting toxic waste. *Public Opinion Quarterly* 51:166–85.

Race friction—Now a crime problem? 1965. *U.S. News and World Report* 90 (August 30): 21–24.

Ramos, G. 1988. Had apparent heart attack in Zimbabwe: Dr. J. Alfred Cannon, health crusader. *Los Angeles Times,* March 11.

Reardon, P. T. 1996. Hayden courts controversy with "peace" gift to mayor. *Chicago Tribune,* August 18.

The reasons why. 1965. *Newsweek* 66 (August 30): 16–19.

Recktenwald, W. 1996a. City seems to be expecting visitors. *Chicago Tribune,* May 21.

————. 1996b. Police studying mistakes of '68: Officers assigned to August's convention are taking special classes to ensure there is no repeat of the chaotic behavior of 1968. *Chicago Tribune,* July 5.

Reinhold, R. 1992. Conversations: Tom Hayden; from inciting riots in 1968 to winning in a wealthy district. *New York Times,* August 9.

Rich, F. 1996. Journal: New Deal lite. *New York Times,* August 28.

Rimer, S. 1992. Watts organizer feels weight of riots, and history. *New York Times,* June 24.

Rivera, C. 1992. Ueberroth takes share of blame for L.A. riots. *Los Angeles Times,* July 29.

Robinson, J. P. 1970. Public reaction to political protest: Chicago 1968. *Public Opinion Quarterly* 34:1–9.

Royko, M. 1988. Fond memories of '68 convention. *Chicago Tribune,* June 24.

———. 1994. 35-cent opinions fly after each Cub loss. *Chicago Tribune, May 4.*

———. 1996. Joust for the fun of it, Democrats can make it a real party. *Chicago Tribune,* August 6.

Ryon, R. 1986. Landlords in "Jungle" making progress. *Los Angeles Times,* April 20.

Sakamoto, B. 1990. His story: "I was a teenage batboy." *Chicago Tribune,* September 28.

Salopek, P. 1996. Hayden? Daley? It doesn't seem like old times. *Chicago Tribune,* June 22.

Schattschneider, E. E. 1975. *The semi-sovreign people.* Fort Worth, TX: Harcourt, Brace, Jovanovich.

Scheutz, J., and K. H. Snedaker. 1988. *Communication and litigation: Case studies of famous trials.* Carbondale, IL: Southern Illinois University Press.

Schmidt, W. E. 1987. Chicago journal: U.S. squares off against tough gang. *New York Times,* November 5.

Schmuhl, R. 1994. Future shock: In 1996, "March madness" turns into political insanity. *Chicago Tribune, March 15.*

Schudson, M. 1978. *Discovering the news.* New York: Basic Books.

———. 1992. *Watergate in American memory: How we remember, forget, and reconstruct the past.* New York: Basic Books.

Schwartz, B. 1991. Iconography and collective memory: Lincoln's image in the American mind. *The Sociological Quarterly* 32:301–19.

Schwartz, B., Y. Zerubavel, and B. M. Barnett. 1986. The recovery of Masada: A study in collective memory. *The Sociological Quarterly* 27:147–64.

Sears, D. O., J. Sindanius, and L. Bobo. 2000. *Racialized politics: The debate about racism in America.* Chicago: University of Chicago Press.

Secter, B. 1980. The stories unfold in black and white. *Los Angeles Times,* August 27.

———. 1996. At the heart of American politics; conventions right at home here. *Chicago Tribune,* May 30.

Sheppard, N., Jr. 1980a. Chicago panel named to review police brutality cases. *New York Times,* September 24.

———. 1980b. 2 in Weather Underground are bargaining to surrender. *New York Times,* November 24.

Shiver, J., Jr., and J. L. Mitchell. 1989. Dispute over site imperils plan for Crenshaw supermarket. *Los Angeles Times,* April 23.

Sigal, L. V. 1973. *Reporters and officials: The organization and politics of newsmaking.* Lexington, MA: D. C. Heath.

Silverstein, S., and M. Lingre. 1992. Voices of business tell how to rebuild L.A. *Los Angeles Times,* May 10.

Sipchen, B. 1992. After the riots: The search for answers; angry and weary, Gates continues to parry criticism. *Los Angeles Times,* May 9.

Skelton, G. 1992. Riot aftermath: Getting back to business. *Los Angeles Times*, May 5.

Smith, B. J. 1985. *Politics and remembrance*. Princeton, NJ: Princeton University Press.

Smith, E. 1993. Transmitting race: The L.A. riot in TV news. Paper presented at the Center for Urban Affairs and Policy Research Conference on Media, Race, and Governance, Evanston, IL, February, 1994.

Sniderman, P. M., and S. M. Theriault. 2004. The structure of political argument and the logic of issue framing. In *Studies in public opinion: Attitudes, nonattitudes, measurement error, and change*, eds. W. E. Saris and P. M. Sniderman, 133–165. Princeton, NJ: Princeton University Press.

Snow, D. A., and R. D. Benford. 1992. Master frames and cycles of protest. In *Frontiers in social movement theory*, eds. A. D. Morris and C. M. Mueller, 133–155. New Haven: Yale University Press.

Spector, M., and J. I. Kitsuse. 2001. *Constructing social problems*. New Brunswick, NJ: Transaction Publishers. (Originally published 1977.)

Stalag '68. 1968. *Time* 92 (August 23): 12–13.

Stevenson, R. W. 1992. Help from many sources; repairing Los Angeles: High enthusiasm and long odds. *New York Times*, May 10.

Stewart, J. 1988. "Nonprofits" fill void to build homes in poor areas. *Los Angeles Times*, November 28.

Stone, D. A. 1989. Causal stories and the formation of policy agendas. *Political Science Quarterly* 104:281–300.

Strohm, S. 1999. The Black press and the Black community: The *Los Angeles Sentinel*'s coverage of the Watts riots. In *Framing friction: Media and social conflict*, ed. M. S. Mander, 58–88. Urbana, IL: University of Illinois Press.

Stumbo, B. 1980. Another view of Watts: Cast aside malice. *Los Angeles Times*, August 13.

Survival at the stockyards. 1968. *Time* 92 (September 6): 14–15.

Thurow, L. 1995. The rich: Why their world might crumble. *New York Times*, November 19.

Tobar, H. 1991. Dream fulfilled: Years of activism culminate in approval for Watts library. *Los Angeles Times*, November 10.

———. 1992. Like King, sculptor had a dream. *Los Angeles Times*, January 20.

Tomasson, R. E. 1984. Y.M.C.A. expands with a focus on middle class. *New York Times*, May 6.

Toner, R. 1993. Washington at work: For a bruising battle, Clinton enlists a Daley. *New York Times*, September 7.

The tough cop of L.A. 1965. *Newsweek* 66 (August 30): 17.

Tough years ahead. 1965. *Newsweek* 66 (August 30): 18–19.

Trigger of hate. 1965. *Time* 86 (August 20): 13–19.

Tuchman, G. 1972. Objectivity as strategic ritual: An examination of newsmen's notion of objectivity. *American Journal of Sociology* 77:660–79.

———. 1978. *Making news: A study in the construction of reality*. New York: Free Press.

Turner, V. 1981. Social dramas and stories about them. In *On narrative*, ed. W. J. T. Mitchell, 137–64. Chicago: University of Chicago Press.

Valentino, N. A. 1999. Crime news and the priming of racial attitudes during evaluations of the president. *Public Opinion Quarterly* 63:293–320.

Vietnam: The dissidents walk the plank. 1968. *Newsweek* 72 (September 9): 32–33.

Wagner-Pacifici, R., and B. Schwartz. 1991. The Vietnam veterans memorial: Commemorating a difficult past. *American Journal of Sociology* 97:376–420.

Wald, M. L. 1987. Hoffman: A radical in all ages. *New York Times*, February 1.

Walker, D. 1968. *Rights in conflict: The violent confrontation of demonstrators and police in the parks and streets of Chicago during the week of the Democratic National Convention of 1968*. New York: Bantam Books.

Warren, E., and S. Mills. 1994. Democrats won't spend a lot, but they'll bring gold to city. *Chicago Tribune*, July 21.

Weaver, W. 1984. Today's party conventions stand mostly on ceremony. *New York Times*, August 26.

Weber, B. 1995. May it please the court, Kunstler does comedy. *New York Times*, August 10.

Weinstein, H. 1992a. Electronics firm gives $600,000 to Rebuild L.A. *Los Angeles Times*, June 18.

———. 1992b. Ueberroth expects rebuild effort to be a long haul. *Los Angeles Times*, July 7.

Wendt, L. 1979. *Chicago Tribune: The rise of a great American newspaper*. Chicago: Rand McNally & Company.

White, H. 1981. The value of narrativity in the representation of reality. In *On narrative*, ed. W. J. T. Mitchell, 1–23. Chicago: University of Chicago Press.

———. 1987. *The content of the form: Narrative discourse and historical representation*. Baltimore, MD: The Johns Hopkins University Press.

Wicker, T. 1991. In the nation: Snakeskins and Democrats. *New York Times*, September 1.

———. 1992. Let some smoke in. *New York Times*, June 14.

The winner: How—and what—he won. 1968. *Newsweek* 72 (September 9): 30–37.

Zelizer, B. 1992. *Covering the body: The Kennedy assassination, the media, and the shaping of collective memory*. Chicago: University of Chicago Press.

———. 1995. Reading the past against the grain: The shape of memory studies. *Critical Studies in Mass Communication* 12: 214–39.

———. 1998. *Remembering to forget: Holocaust memory through the camera's eye*. Chicago: University of Chicago Press.

Zerubavel, Y. 1995. *Recovered roots: Collective memory and the making of Israeli national tradition*. Chicago: University of Chicago Press.

Index

Jill A. Edy is Assistant Professor of Communication at the University of Oklahoma.